BODY LENGTHS

BODY LENGTHS
Leisel Jones

with Felicity McLean

NERO

Published by Nero,
an imprint of Schwartz Publishing Pty Ltd
Level 1, 221 Drummond Street
Carlton VIC 3053, Australia
enquiries@blackincbooks.com
www.nerobooks.com

Copyright © Leisel Jones and Felicity McLean 2015
First published in 2015
This edition published in 2017
Leisel Jones and Felicity McLean assert their right to be known
as the authors of this work.

ALL RIGHTS RESERVED.
No part of this publication may be reproduced, stored in a retrieval system,
or transmitted in any form by any means electronic, mechanical, photocopying,
recording or otherwise without the prior consent of the publishers.

National Library of Australia Cataloguing-in-Publication entry:
Jones, Leisel, author.
Body lengths / Leisel Jones with Felicity McLean.
9781863959155 (paperback)
9781925203479 (ebook)
Jones, Leisel. Swimmers—Australia—Biography. Women swimmers—
Australia—Biography. Olympic athletes—Australia—Biography.
Women Olympic athletes—Australia—Biography.
McLean, Felicity, author.

Cover photo by Hugh Stewart
Cover design by Peter Long
Text design and typesetting by Tristan Main

Contents

~

Prologue ... 1

1. Fish out of Water ... 5

2. First Splash ... 13

3. The Big Dawgs ... 25

4. This Baby's Going to the Olympics ... 33

5. Rookie ... 45

6. Sydney 2000 ... 53

7. Training for Gold ... 69

8. Under Pressure ... 81

9. Stilnox Days ... 87

10. Olympic Lies ... 99

11. A New Start ... 113

12. Starving to Swim ... 123

13. Aussie, Aussie, Aussie! ... 129

14. Commonwealth Triumph ... 137

15. Blast from the Past ... 147

16. Matters of the Heart ... 153

17. Taking Risks ... 165

18. Crashing ... 183

19. Beijing Blues ... 191

20. Relief ... 203

21. Fallout ... 207

22. The Lonely Days ... 217

23. Opening Up ... 225

24. The Depths in the Heights ... 231

25. The Comedown ... 241

26. London Calling ... 251

27. Toxic Team ... 255

28. Breaking Point ... 263

29. My Way ... 281

30. Back on Dry Land ... 287

Acknowledgements ... 295

*This book is dedicated to all the people out there
with big hearts and even bigger dreams. Anything is possible
if you are brave enough to go out and grab life by the balls.*
– Leisel Jones

For Andy
– Felicity McLean

Prologue

In the darkness you can't see the mountains on the horizon, skulking beneath their snowy peaks. The running track with its neat lines is swallowed up by the night. And the structure we call the James Bond tower, with its strange wires and tall aerials pointing accusingly at the sky, stands in shadow.

Sierra Nevada is purple-black tonight, the colour of blood before the air gets to it. Oxygen is scarcer at this altitude, 2300 metres above sea level. Even the sky cannot breathe up here. Even the sky seems to bleed.

I leave the centre at 4 a.m. I don't say goodbye to anyone; I just walk outside to where the van is waiting for me, climb in, nod to the driver and wait for him to take me away.

We drive on and on in the dark. Morning never seems to arrive. *Am I dead? Did I do it?* I wonder. But then the airport rears up before us and I can make out the shiny lettering – 'Aeropuerto de Málaga – Costa del Sol' – so dawn must be arriving after all.

On the plane I can't figure out how I got here. Did I check in? Did someone scan my passport? (Name: Lethal Leisel; Occupation: Swimmer). I can't remember any of this. I want to call Lisa to ask how I got to this point... but there's plenty of time. I will phone her from Singapore, then again from Sydney, and from Tullamarine in Melbourne. Reporting for duty, keeping in touch, letting her know I am still alive.

Am I still alive? I have to look at my wrists to make sure. They're slick and smooth from a lifetime of chlorine and sweat. Strange to think they nearly looked so very different.

I think about my dad. *He* won't be waiting for me to call from the airport. We haven't spoken since the day he walked out on Mum and me, thirteen years ago. Up until last year, I was still pretty angry with him. A lot of people have issues with their fathers, I know. But not everyone's dad goes to the press to tell their daughter they are dying of cancer. I mean, really. I can't forgive that. What a disgusting way to give your daughter the news. It was so embarrassing – so humiliating – to have our relationship blasted all over the papers. But now I've reached something like forgiveness. It sounds wanky, but on a deep level I've gone: *Okay, you probably did the best you could as a dad.* It was a shit job, but it was the best he could do, and I've made peace with that. I'm sure his father was crap too. Whatever.

But now I find myself wondering if my father's dead. Did the cancer get him in the end? Something else, maybe? I wouldn't know. And I honestly don't care: he's dead to me already.

Lots of friends have said, 'Oh, but you'll regret it when he dies.' Regret what? He deserted us. He left us bankrupt. I'm not the one with something to regret. Why should I have to meet him? It would make me feel icky and gross. Why should I go through that?

I've always been really strong in doing what's right for me. That's one thing I'm proud of: if it doesn't feel right, I won't do it. And it feels right for me not to connect with my father. I'm not holding on to anything. I'm not angry. If I *was*, then yes, I should meet him and talk to him. But I'm not angry or bitter. I'm not anything, in fact.

PROLOGUE

Now, wondering whether he's dead, I realise it wouldn't make any difference if he was. His actual death wouldn't matter.

Does anyone's? Does anyone's death make any difference? Would mine?

I spent yesterday afternoon on the bathroom floor of my room at the Sierra Nevada high-performance sports centre, planning to kill myself. While the rest of the Aussie swimming team ate, talked, kicked a ball or watched TV, I thought about slitting my wrists. And my legs – I didn't forget my freakish, talented legs. I'd decided I would be leaving that place in a body bag.

I stare out the window at the clouds and picture myself inside the bag, as I have a thousand times already this week. I see the zipper close, the last ray of light disappearing. I am lost again in the dark, in my pain ...

~

It's yesterday, a bone-dull afternoon, and I'm back in the bathroom, staring at my wrists.

I am going to do it: I am so clear. I have saved up some sleeping tablets and I will take them all. A knife from the kitchen will do the rest: I'll slit my wrists, slash my legs, make sure I get all the big veins. I've even googled how much it would cost to send a body bag home from Spain. It's $15,000 or something like that – pretty expensive – but I've checked that there will be enough money left for Mum to pay for it.

I am determined; I know what I have to do.

I have the afternoon off training, so here I am in the bathroom preparing. I can do this. I'll take the pills first, and then I'll just cut. I'll cut them all open – my legs, my wrists – so I bleed out.

I will slice myself open and bleed purple-black like the Sierra Nevada night sky.

1

Fish out of Water

In the hospital where I am born, I am the only white baby. In 1985, in our mostly Indigenous community in Central Australia, there aren't many outsiders, let alone fair-skinned ones. In Katherine District Hospital, from the instant I take my first gasping lungfuls of oxygen, I am a fish out of water.

'Leisel?' asks the doctor.

'Leisel,' Mum says firmly. If I have to be stuck with 'Jones', Mum's not having a bar of 'Sarah' or 'Jane' or any such unremarkable name to go with it.

'You can't call her Leisel,' says the doctor, as if the question of my name is a medical one, as if his opinion is somehow warranted. 'It's not a real name.'

'It *is* a real name, and you might not know it yet, but "Leisel Jones" is a name you will remember,' Mum says prophetically.

~

Mine would have been a difficult birth, a breech birth – I try to exit the pelvis feet-first rather than head-first – but I am eventually born by caesarean. For a few moments after birth, I stop breathing and need to be resuscitated. A fish on a hook, I gulp for air.

Katherine, where I am born, is known as 'the crossroads of the outback'. It's almost 300 kilometres to the coastline in any direction, except to the formidable south, where the coast is even further away, beyond the Tanami and Simpson deserts, the two largest deserts in Australia. It's only twenty-four hours from Katherine to the geographical centre of Australia. Less than that to Uluru. There's spinifex and red dust as far as the eye can see; nearby gorges are so deep you might never find the bottom.

Life in Katherine, for the first six months of my life, is simple. Basic. My parents are travelling around Australia in a double-decker bus and my two older half-brothers are doing School of the Air. The plan is to save a bit of money, do things a bit differently. In the first months of my life I breathe in red dust and my mother bathes me in the kitchen sink.

Then one day Mum and Dad fire up the bus and hit the road again, back to New South Wales. Back 'home'. Mum's parents, my Nanna and Poppa, live on St Huberts Island, which is a couple of hours north of Sydney, on the Central Coast, so it's a homecoming of sorts. On St Huberts Island we live a more 'normal' family life: barbecues, playing in the park, visiting nearby Umina Beach with me as a toddler on the back of Mum's bike.

Except the normality doesn't last long: after two years, suddenly we're on the move again, but this time we're headed north. To Queensland. Wamuran, to be precise. A small scrap of a town, 11 kilometres west of Caboolture and an hour north of Brisbane. A scrap of a town for a scrap of a girl. We live beside 300 acres of vacant land – disused scrub. We don't own the land – could never afford to own all that – but we build a house on Alexandra Parade that backs on to the land and we pretend all 300 acres of it is ours.

So now this former 'outback' girl is a 'country' girl.

Not much water in this story so far, is there?

Well, that's not quite true. We have a creek on 'our' property in Wamuran, and a massive dam too. There's a rope swing with an old tyre, and we spend long arvos yabbying. There's even a backyard pool. But I don't do too much swimming yet. Sure, I take lessons, just like most other Aussie kids: 'learn to swim' classes to keep me safe in the water. Mum takes me once a week. Outside of lessons, however, I'm not that interested yet.

I am not a sporty kid. Active, sure; outdoorsy, yes; but not typically sporty – not in the way you see some primary school kids picking up ribbons every time they turn around. I do gymnastics, but Mum laughs about it, because I cannot, for the love of god, stay on the beam. And at netball, I'm always the last to be picked for the team. At tennis, whatever I lack in talent I make up for with talk. ('Leisel could do better if she talked less and concentrated more'; 'Leisel must try hard to stop distracting others' – just once I would like to get a report card that doesn't say these things.)

I'm not much of a runner, but when my dog, Jedda, is bitten by a red-bellied black snake, I run bloody fast.

And I do ride horses. I have a horse called Gypsy that Mum saved from the knackery. I ride him bareback, and when he kicks me off I get straight back on. He might be stubborn for a horse, but I'm a mule.

Sporting prowess doesn't run in my blood. Mine is a diverse, creative family. There are artists and inventors, as well as normal people with normal jobs, but not a lot of sports heroes kicking around. There are no amazing sporting genes for me to inherit.

But me and the two boys from down the street, we have competitions all the time, tearing down the big hill on our cheap imitation BMXs, turning at the last second to save our scrawny necks, sliding and skidding to a halt. Riding our bikes down the face of that hill on

Alexandra Parade, the boys and I are far from average. We fight it out for BMX glory. A girl in our street came off her bike on that hill once and was picking gravel out of her face for a week. That never happens to us. We're daredevils – gung-ho – the three of us.

So I guess I am sporty enough to stay on that bike.

We spend every arvo after school mucking around outside. We compete to see who can ride the fastest, who can skid the furthest and who can get the most air off a jump. We have competitions of every kind, me and the boys down the road, but strangely we never think to race each other in the pool. We don't get in it much at all, really.

~

Then one day it's all gone. The house. The 300 acres. Even the pool I haven't swum in much yet.

I am watching TV when Mum gives me the news that Dad's off. It's my favourite show: *Get Smart*, with the bumbling Maxwell Smart and the ever-patient Agent 99. I know it off by heart: the 'old phone-in-the-shoe trick', the KAOS villains. I walk around the house quoting, 'Missed it by *that* much!'

During an ad break, Mum walks in. 'Dad's leaving,' she says. 'We've run out of money.'

I say nothing. I just sit silently and wait for the ads to finish.

Dad doesn't come into the TV room to find me. He doesn't tell me himself. In fact, I never see my father again. He has gone by the time Mum tells me he is leaving.

Missed it by *that* much. What a coward.

~

Even before he took off without telling me, my dad was never a man of many words. My name, Leisel, is an anagram of his name: Leslie. Mum chose it for that reason. I was also due to be born on Dad's birthday. But because I was to be a caesarean birth, Mum was able to choose to have the surgery a day later so that Dad and I could each have our own birthday. Even so, with our almost-matching names and our almost-matching birthdays, surely we were meant to be kindred spirits. A real chip off the old block, that's what I was meant to be.

Funny, then, that it didn't turn out that way. We are both tall and strong, but Dad is quiet, whereas I'm a talker. From a young age, I'm full of life, Mum tells me, and full of words. I have so much bubbling up inside me, whereas Dad has ... what? Nothing? Absence?

It's easiest to describe my dad in terms of what he isn't. I've started racing in local swimming carnivals by this time. But Dad isn't a sports dad who rages, threatens and intimidates from the sidelines. Dad never bullies my rivals. He isn't the kind of swimming father who nearly has a heart attack on the pool deck, living each lap as if it were him in the water slogging it out, not his kid. Nor is he one of those sad, bitter fathers you see at kids' sports events, flogging his children as some sort of penance for his own childhood defeats. He isn't even one of those greedy professional sporting parents who make the headlines for syphoning money from their kid's trust account. Dad isn't any of these things – because he isn't there. He never comes to watch me swim, never once takes me to training. Dad never shows up to my swimming carnivals. He never supports me, doesn't show any interest in me. Sometimes I wonder if he cares at all.

There was one day, though, when Dad cared about something – a day when Dad was actually excited ...

I was ten when Dad bought the business that was going to set us up good. It was a plumbing business, a real money-maker. 'We're laughing now,' he told us, 'all the way to the bank.' We went down to the warehouse to admire and coo, me and Mum, with Dad leading the way. We poked around the big old barn of a warehouse. We were laughing, all of us. All the way to the bank.

Only it didn't work out like that: not like that at all. Dad never made any money, only lost it slowly.

Then all of a sudden he was losing it fast. We were bankrupt. Insolvent. And no-one was laughing. We went to the bank but no-one was chuckling. The business was gone, and Dad was off. The house was repossessed soon after.

The last time I see my father, I am twelve years old.

~

When Dad leaves, Mum and I stay on in the house together, reigning over our scrubby acreage, until the Christmas school holidays – as long as we can afford. Mum is working as a swimming teacher and somehow magics food onto our plates each night. It's breadline territory stuff: minute steak and cheap spuds, pork shoulder when it's on special, curried sausages and vegies. But it all tastes good to me. Wouldn't most kids be happy to live on curried sausages? Don't most kids have breadline tastebuds anyway? Maybe I'm not so different after all.

But I'm stranger than you might think. When I was seven, my parents drove me to Brisbane to see a paediatric surgeon, because I have a congenital abnormality, a freakish glitch. I was born with a twisted hip. It's nothing serious. There's no prolonged damage being inflicted on my body or anything like that. But I am noticeably knock-kneed, and this causes me terrible, excruciating embarrassment in the school playground.

'Please do something,' I beg my parents. 'Can't we get a doctor to fix me?'

Inside his plush surgery, the orthopaedic paediatrician smiles generously at my unsuspecting parents. 'Sure, we can correct this,' he says. 'It's just a glitch.' Then he slides a piece of paper across the wide, mahogany desk.

In 1992 in Queensland, 'correction' means surgery. It means breaking and re-setting my right hip; it meant casts and traction and all sorts of barbaric-sounding stuff. I don't care. I am desperate. I would give anything to walk across the stage at school assemblies with straight legs, to step onto a netball court without my knock-knees on display beneath my navy blue netball skirt ... I would break my legs myself for that.

Except my parents can't afford correction. One quick glance at the statement of fees the surgeon slides across the desk is enough for them to see there is no way they can pay for this. 'Um, that's a bit more than we were expecting,' Mum mumbles as she ushers me out the door.

I want to throw myself at this guy, beg him to give me straight legs, but we're out of the surgery and back on the street before I have the chance. Standing on the footpath in the blinding Queensland sunshine, my heart breaks as I stare down at my knees. They are burnished gold in the afternoon sun.

It's not until years later that we discover my knock-knees really are gold. Olympic gold. As a result of my twisted hip, I have excessive range in my hips, so that in any movement where my knees go together and then apart – a movement such as breaststroke – I am able to bend my knees wider than 99.9 per cent of the population.

Because of my physiological make-up, I can move my legs in ways almost no-one else can. I can move faster, and with more power, grabbing more water with each frog-leg kick, to give me greater propulsion through the water. It's as if I were born to do this. It's a unique gift: my special, freakish talent. And all because my parents couldn't afford to have my legs 'corrected'.

Later in my career I am dubbed 'the extreme example' whenever our swimming team works with our physiotherapists. As the physios run us through their usual tests and exercises, looking at things like shoulder extension and core stability, I am always off the chart when it comes to degree of flexibility in my legs and hips. 'Ignore her: she's a freak,' they console my teammates as I move my legs easily past the 180-degree mark out to each side. 'Don't compare yourself to Leisel, she's different,' they say.

There's that word again, I think. *Different*.

I am the white kid in the Indigenous hospital, the poor kid living on 300 acres, the swimming freak, the only child. From the moment I am born, I am like no-one else around me.

I am a fish out of water. Even in the pool.

2

First Splash

My first proper swimming lesson, age two, is a shocker. I nearly quit on the spot.

Before this, I have had a few early splashes in the pool at Woy Woy, a quiet sunny hamlet on the Central Coast of New South Wales, where I visit my maternal grandparents. For some reason, in Woy Woy in '87, they are teaching kids to swim with floaties on their upper arms. In the rest of the country this is a no-no, even in the 1980s, but apparently no-one's told Woy Woy. So at two-and-a-half, with imitation arm muscles of inflatable fluoro-orange plastic, I start making waves in the Woy Woy pool. I am a dog-paddle prodigy, a wunderkind of the water. I am super-confident and super-proud as I plough up and down the width of the pool.

But then we move to Queensland, the Sunshine State, and it is a completely different story. In my first proper swimming lesson there, I am thrown – quite literally – in the deep end. Because Mum has told her I can already swim, my teacher flings me blithely into the pool and then watches in surprise as I sink and do not swim. I sit on the bottom and stare up at the world, bare-armed, blue-lipped and about as buoyant as a brick.

'She'll come up soon. She'll surface any minute now,' the teacher mutters on the pool deck. 'Just gotta let her work it out for herself.'

Only I don't work it out and I don't surface. Eventually someone realises that without my floaties I'm useless, and they fish me from the depths of the pool. I cough and retch and then, when I catch my breath, I throw the kind of epic tantrum two-year-olds are best at. I stomp from my swimming lesson, then bolt through the front entrance gate of the pool and hole up in the backseat of the car until Mum comes to find me. I am not going back, I tell her. The water has traumatised me in less time than it takes for my chubby toddler fingers to wrinkle like prunes.

But Mum is adamant I will return. There are not many things in life that Mum will stick to her guns about. Not softly spoken, passive Mum. But learning to swim is one of them. Because we live in Queensland, where kids practically grow up in the water, and because Mum's always taking me to Bribie Island or somewhere to have picnics and muck about on the beach, she is insistent that I learn to swim. It's important to her that I am safe in the water. So much so, she becomes a swimming teacher in exchange for my swimming lessons, which she can't afford any other way.

Mum doesn't have a job at the time, so she starts working at the pool, teaching other kids to swim. It's funny – Mum only gets into it because of me, but she will teach swimming for the next twenty-seven years, long after I've perfected my dog paddle. She can't swim herself, and she hates getting her hair wet, and it's not long before she's checking with me that she's teaching correctly, but right from the very start, Mum is a pro at wrangling kids in the water.

And she needs to be. After my first terrible swimming lesson, it takes some tough negotiating on Mum's part to get me to return the following week. I don't know what she promises me (red frogs from the pool canteen? my favourite TV cartoons when I get home?), but whatever it is, it works. Back I go, and in I get, and – week by week, slowly but surely – I learn to swim on my own.

It takes some practice, though. I'm not one of those prodigies you hear about where the minute they get in the water the clouds part, a bolt of lightning hits the earth and an Olympic champion is born. I have to learn to swim just like everybody else. Kick – stroke – breathe. Kick – stroke – breathe. I even have to learn how to do breaststroke. It's not innate. Far from it. My body might be built for this strange frog-legged stroke, but my brain and limbs and muscles don't know that. I have to kick and 'bubble' and 'froggy legs' my way up and down the pool with all the other toddlers.

And yet, at two-and-a-half, I am less than ten years away from setting my first Australian record.

~

But first, long before I dip a toe in an Olympic pool, there's the Burpengary Swimming Club.

'Swimming club' is a pretty flash name for a dinky pool in someone's backyard, though, don't you think? Our local pool – a 25-metre one, half the size of an Olympic pool – is a thirty-minute drive from our house in Wamuran. It's basic: not glamorous whatsoever. It's housed in what looks like an oversized backyard shed: roller doors, corrugated-iron roof and all. In front, a house has been plonked just off the roadside – an ordinary brick blob, with its back turned on the shed out the back and the pool inside it.

Both the house and the pool belong to Colin Clifford. Col. The boss-man. He is my first real coach.

Col coaches the squad at Burpengary: a bunch of twenty or so skinny-limbed, freckle-faced kids from the local area, ranging in age from about fifteen to seventeen. To us 'learn-to-swim'-ers, squad is a big deal. It's the dream. For us younger kids, the chance to one day join Col Clifford's squad is the reason we're all here. Well, that and friends and fun and Friday night club nights, when we all race one another while our parents cheer from the pool deck and get the barbecue ready. We play 'Marco Polo' and have bombing competitions and flick each other with wet towels and do all the things over-energised, over-excited kids do. And I love it.

When I start at Burpengary, I am two-and-a-half and by far the youngest kid there. By the time I am twelve, I have been invited to join Col's 'squad' and I am training with, and racing against, kids who are four or five years older than me. It doesn't matter to Col how old you are. He wouldn't care if you were 110 and swam with one arm tied behind your back. If you can keep up, you can step up, as far as Col is concerned.

I love racing against kids who are older than me. Far out – I love racing against anyone! One of the first things I learn at Burpengary – other than how to stay off the tiles at the bottom of the pool without the aid of floaties – is that I love a challenge. I'm mad for it. You only have to think of a dare and I'm up for it. Give me a test, a task, a chance to prove myself, and I'm in. Reckon I can't go sub-two-minutes at 100-metre breaststroke? Want to see me do an underwater handstand for longer than anyone else? Dare me to set a sausage-sandwich-eating record? Watch me! I just can't help myself. And I'm sure Col uses this against me at times, manipulating my enthusiasm, my dogged determination to win, in order to make me train harder. I can see him doing it, yet I'm powerless to resist.

One day during strength training Col passes me a besser brick. Don't ask me why he has a besser brick handy. We are training in what is effectively his back shed, so maybe it is just the first thing he spots, there behind the Victa lawnmower and the old paint tins. Who knows? What I do know is this: a besser brick is bloody heavy. Like, five kilograms heavy. For anyone not familiar with the building industry or the inside of Col's shed, let's just say you wouldn't want to drop it on your toes.

This is my challenge: I have to tread water for five minutes, with no breaks, while holding a besser brick above my head. If I can do this, I will earn myself a Mars bar.

'You in?' Col asks.

I am in. I stand on the edge of the pool, clutching my brick, readying myself to jump. Col rolls his eyes and takes the brick from my hands. 'Get in first.'

I plop into the water. I probably weigh only as much as eight or nine bricks myself. Col lowers the brick down to me and taps his watch to indicate he's about to start timing. I grit my teeth and start to kick. Slow, circular, methodical kicks. *I will do this*, I think to myself, *even if my arms fall off trying*.

Two minutes pass, then – slowly – three. My legs are tiring and my arms are burning. I adjust my grip where the edge of the brick is cutting into my wet fingers … Three-and-a-half minutes. Now four … Col stares at his watch with a poker face.

'Nearly there?' I puff.

Col nods. And the thought of finishing gives me another burst of strength.

'You did it,' Col says, leaning over to take the brick. He raises one eyebrow to signal he's impressed. Then he chucks a Mars bar into the pool for me, and I grin before diving for it. Victory tastes sweet.

Treading water with a crummy old besser brick becomes a regular part of my strength-training regime. At least once a week I jump into the deeper end of Col's pool and settle into an egg-beater kick while hoisting a brick above my head. At first, I manage five minutes. Then five and a half. By the time I can get up around the six-minute mark, Col decides it is time to call it a day. I'm not sure if it's because he now deems my leg strength sufficient, or because I'm costing him a packet in Mars bars. Maybe Col never expected me to rise to the challenge in the first place. Whatever the case, we're done.

But I don't really need Col's Mars bars. I never did. I would gladly tread water with a brick for no reward. It's the sort of thing I will happily do, simply to prove I can. I don't need any incentive other than to know that I can do it.

As I get older, I train harder and harder, because I have this insatiable hunger to win. I never stop to think whether I love (or hate) swimming. That never comes into it. All I know is that I need to win, and swimming fulfils that need. I need to be a winner: swimming gives me that.

By the time I'm nearing the end of primary school, I'm training every day. Mum drives me the thirty-minute trip to the pool so I can be ready to jump in at 5 a.m. each morning. Then I train for a couple of hours, doing drills, exercises and fitness training – lap after lap after lap – until I've swum a few kilometres. Next is breakfast in the car while Mum drives me back to school in Wamuran. After school, I am back in the water by 4 p.m. and I train for another hour or two.

Homework is squeezed in either before my afternoon training session or after I get home, but I always do it, just like I always turn up at training. I want to do everything and succeed at everything. And while I am not quite as focused at school as I am at swimming, I refuse to let it slide. I can't. I'm just not that person. I want to earn more stickers from my teacher than anyone else in my class; I want to win the spelling bee despite not being the best speller in our grade. Whenever I get a 'B' on my report card, I think, *Dammit! How can I improve? How can I get better?* 'B's won't cut it. I need to be awesome at swimming *and* awesome at school. I try to be both. I try to be everything. I am never happier than when I am winning. From when I am eight or nine years old, my Type A personality is alive and kicking. Leisel the winner. Leisel the perfectionist. She shadows me in training. She shares my lane. She matches me tumble turn for tumble turn. Then she springs out of the pool after squad is over, showers and changes, and follows me to school.

~

I am in my final year at St Peter's Primary School in Caboolture, and my classmates and I are signing farewell messages on each other's school jumpers with black markers when a kid from my class approaches me.

'Are you going to swim at the next Olympics?' he asks.

I'm baffled. 'The next Olympics? You mean the ones in Sydney? In 2000?'

It's hard enough to believe that I might one day be good enough to swim at any Olympics. But that 'one day' might be in three years' time? I admire this kid's optimism, I really do. But I also let him know that he's being ridiculous.

Because it's 1997, and apart from breaking the Australian 50-metre breaststroke record at the School Sport Australia Swimming Championships in Adelaide earlier this year, in a time of 35.36, the highlight of my swimming 'career' to date is still Friday night club nights at Burpengary.

Club nights are the best part of my week. Each Friday evening I line up against the other kids from squad in a tournament of guts and glory, with a sausage sizzle on the patio outside afterwards. I am still a scrawny, runty kid – all skinny legs and knobbly knees. But that doesn't stop me swimming my heart out while Mum barracks proudly from the pool deck. All 'official' timing is done by our mums, using handheld stopwatches, and our times are recorded in chalk on an old-school blackboard (a world away from the electronic pads and scoreboards that are mandatory today). Because club night is deemed an 'official meet', these times are the ones we use to qualify for bigger comps, like regionals or states. It seems incredible, but if you have a good night at our little backyard club night on Friday, you can find yourself heading off to the Queensland State Titles.

I live for club nights, and I'm pretty good, too. But Burpengary on a Friday evening is a far cry from the Olympic Games. The Olympic Park Aquatic Centre in Sydney can hold more people than the entire population of Burpengary.

In actual fact, Burpengary on a Friday night feels like a far cry from anywhere. The town is smaller than nearby Caboolture and Redcliffe, and it's certainly nothing like the sprawling metropolis of Brisbane. There is a petrol station, a bakery and a post office. There's no local high school, and the first major shopping centre won't be built until six or seven years after I leave Col's. They do have a train station in Burpengary – only there's not much reason to catch a train there.

And so I tell that kid in my class that he's crazy. I'm just a Burpengary club swimmer and the Olympics are less than three years away. There's no way I'd be good enough by then. No way.

'And anyway,' I add, 'I'd only be fifteen.' Who's heard of a fifteen-year-old swimming at the Olympics?

He seems satisfied with this answer and probably doesn't give the conversation another thought. I certainly don't: I am too busy swimming. In addition to seven or eight training sessions and club night each week, there are also Saturday competitions now and the occasional Sunday one, too.

For every kilometre I swim in the pool, I reckon Mum racks up fifty in the car. She drives me to training, swim club, competitions, school and home. The only place Mum *doesn't* drive me is to my friends' houses to play, because there's not much time for that these days.

But I don't miss it. I've got my swimming friends and, to be honest,

I am probably closer to them than I am to any of my school friends, because we have more in common. We are all so determined. The kids in squad at Burpengary go to different schools, in different regions, but we all start and end the day together. And I love that. I love that it doesn't matter who we are or where we're from – it doesn't matter what happened during school that day or what's going on in our lives outside the pool – every morning and afternoon we're all in the pool together. We're pounding up and down in our lanes, caps and goggles on, doing our best for Col. Here, at Burpengary, I'm with the people who understand me most. The people who really get me.

The other person who gets me is Mum. She knows what makes me tick and exactly how to handle me. Mum never pushes me, because she knows I would only rebel and do the opposite of whatever she said. Instead, her attitude towards swimming is always, 'If you enjoy it, then go. But if you don't, then don't.' As soon as I learnt to swim and was safe in the water, Mum was satisfied. From that time on she never forced me to go to a training session. But she supports me, of course. (What else could you possibly call a 50-kilometre round trip, twice a day, starting at the eye-wateringly early time of 4:30 a.m.?) Supporting is different to pushing: Mum is never a pushy sports parent.

Hilariously, Mum never gets to grips with the intricacies of swimming as a sport. Sure, she understands the basic mechanics. She's a learn-to-swim teacher: she has to. But as for the nuances, even when I reach an elite level, Mum is clueless. She can't tell you the difference between a stroke rate and a lactate if her life depended on it.

But what Mum does know is that I am absolutely driven. She's very aware that if I take an afternoon off training and stay home watching TV instead of getting in the water, I'll be sulky and restless and I won't be able to shake the feeling that I'm missing out on something. If I know all my friends are at the pool having fun, there is no way I won't want to be part of that.

And then there is the winning. It's obvious to Mum just how important winning is to me. She can see the importance I place on achieving and she knows all too well how angry and upset I get with myself when I don't win. So Mum helps me to understand the sacrifices involved in achieving my goals.

'You want to win? Then you have to train. It's that simple,' she says to me. 'This is your decision to swim. You are choosing to do this. I'm not making your decisions for you. It's you who'll have to wear the consequences.'

When it comes time to compete in carnivals at the weekend, there is no point complaining to Mum if I haven't trained properly during the week and I lose. Mum makes it perfectly clear that if I want to win, I have to work hard. And because winning is so important to me, she teaches me that training should be important too. She helps me appreciate that there is a trade-off and she teaches me how to use this to motivate myself to work hard.

Mum backs my swimming, since it is what I choose to do. But beyond that, it's all me. Because I am such a driven kid, and because I like winning so very much, I don't need Mum to force me to train. I don't need anyone to wave a big stick: I am happy to wield my own stick (or besser brick, as the case may be). Even at 5 a.m. on those cool, dark winter mornings in Queensland, when the temperature sometimes dips into single figures – even then I don't need anyone else to push me. I can do it myself. If I want to win, I know what I have to do. And I want to win so damn much.

~

The other thing I want – almost as much as winning – is boys. I love boys. I love them a lot. Boys, boys, boys. And Burpengary provides them by the pool-load.

I meet my first boyfriend at the club when I am twelve. His

name is Josh Bettridge. And like so many other Queensland boys, he is cute and tanned and blond and sporty. I race against his older brother, Ben, who is fifteen, but it is Josh I like. Josh is slower than me and he can't get away. My first kiss is with Josh, down behind the pool shed on a muggy summer evening after training, when the sky screams with cicadas. It's Josh who gives me my first Valentine's Day rose. I hide it under my bed, until it starts to rot and my mum finds it and laughs – and I die of embarrassment.

It's fitting that my first boyfriend is a swimmer. And it's fitting that I have a boyfriend at twelve. I am the first of my friends with a boyfriend, the first to be kissed: I am an early achiever at everything.

~

I love being part of the Burpengary Swimming Club, with Josh and Col and the besser bricks and the blackboard with our times scrawled on it, with Friday night racing and barbecues and everyone knowing everyone else's times. We're a country club. A family. Travel ten kilometres away and no-one has heard of us, but we don't care. We're mad about swimming and we support each other and we're proud of our pool in Col's backyard. Burpengary is where I learn to swim without floaties and where I meet some of my first friends. It's where I begin my love affair with swimming.

In years to come, I will find myself thinking back to Burpengary, trying to recall what I ever liked about the sport.

3

The Big Dawgs

When I am thirteen the most terrifying thing I can think of is Sarah Bowd. Sarah swims for Redcliffe Leagues Swimming Club, which is part of the broader Sunshine Coast region in which I compete. Although she's shorter than me, Sarah is a few months older and she's curvy, confident and achingly cool. She's also a winner. Sarah wins everything. This girl only has to look at a pool to break a record. She's the best breaststroker in the state. She's the best *everything* in the state. Any distance, any stroke: you can bet your togs Sarah Bowd will win it. And because we're in the same age category, I find myself lined up on the blocks next to Sarah all the bloody time.

Redcliffe Leagues is the big brother club to our little Burpengary. It's only thirty minutes down the road from us, so it's our closest neighbour but our biggest rival. They boast some big names at Redcliffe: Geoff Huegill, Tarnee White, Rebecca Creedy and Sarah Bowd. These names are not yet synonymous with Olympic glory, but they will be, in the not-too-distant future.

Ken Wood is the coach at Redcliffe and he's one of the best swimming coaches going. He's been training Sarah since she was eight, along with her older brother, Martin. Martin Bowd is several years ahead of us and he's the ringleader among all the swimmers at Redcliffe. See? What did I tell you? Sarah Bowd is cool just by association. She's so cool it's almost funny. Almost.

At Redcliffe they all wear this red t-shirt with a picture of a bulldog on it. The bulldog is sitting on the front porch of a house, glaring menacingly at passers-by, and the caption underneath reads: 'If you can't run with the big dawgs, then stay under the porch.' I am terrified of those t-shirts, just like I am terrified of Sarah Bowd. Sarah is a big dawg, there's no doubt about that. Whereas I'm more of a chihuahua. Or a miniature poodle. I am skinny and have mousey-brown hair. I am average and shy and I come from Burpengary. I am not like funny, self-assured, strikingly pretty Sarah Bowd. The mere sight of Sarah in her 'big dawgs' t-shirt is enough to make me want to run and hide under the porch.

But one day Mum and I have a meeting with Ken Wood. Ken's watched me race, he's seen my stroke and he's identified what he thinks might be potential there. Do I want to come for a trial at Redcliffe? I glance nervously at Mum. *Redcliffe? Me?* I'm not sure I can see myself in one of those t-shirts.

But Ken is keen. 'There's no qualifying time needed or anything,' he assures us. 'I've seen you compete and I think you're good enough to join our squad. It's that simple.'

Ken has seen a spark in me. He's confident I can cut it with the big dawgs. So when I am thirteen, and after more than a decade at my old club, I leave Burpengary for the big smoke of Redcliffe Leagues SC.

It's really hard to leave my old club and my coach of eleven years. Col (with his besser brick) has been instrumental in my swimming so far. Col built me. But if I stay at Burpengary I will probably get bored eventually and quit. Col knows this, so he's understanding when I tell him I am leaving. He knows I've reached my limit in his 25-metre pool. There's only so many tumble turns a kid can do.

The pool at Redcliffe, by contrast, is a shimmering blue oasis that stretches for a full 50 metres. It's a stone's throw from the maze of canals that flow from the sparkling waters of Deception Bay, just south of Bribie Island. As the sun comes up over the water during training each morning, it looks like a tourism ad for the Sunshine State. It's a far cry from the shed and the Hills Hoist in Col's backyard.

It turns out that's not the only thing that's different from Col's.

First there is Ken Wood's long list of rules to be obeyed if you want to swim at Redcliffe. *Fine*, I think to myself. *I can do rules.* But then I learn that Rule 1 is 'No parents on the pool deck'. No parents. On the pool deck. *Gulp.* I have to leave my mum at the door. This might not sound like such a big deal, but for a shy kid from Burpengary – a shy kid whose mum has been there for every training session, whose mum never misses a Friday night club night, never skips a carnival – for that kid, Rule 1 is a very big deal. And as our car winds its way south from Caboolture to Redcliffe, circumnavigating the arse end of Deception Bay, I wonder if I'm deceiving myself. *Who am I kidding? Why did I think I might belong at Redcliffe?*

But when Mum drops me at the front entrance, I shove down the butterflies in my stomach, shoulder my swimming bag, and walk doggedly through the gate. It's time to put on my big girl pants. Out on the pool deck, Ken is already barking instructions from beneath his short, black toothbrush moustache. I walk up to him, drag my eyes from the concrete deck and, with all the courage I can muster, announce, 'I'm here to train.'

And train I do. The training at Redcliffe is a big step up for a little kid from a country club. To start with, I increase my training from seven or eight sessions per week to ten. I'm now hauling my arse out of bed for a 4.30 a.m. start every day before school, and fronting up on Saturday mornings too. And when we train, we train hard. We regularly swim between seven and ten kilometres per training session – and they're often twice a day. We do 100 × 100s (one hundred times 100 metres, or two hundred laps of an Olympic pool), which seems excessive for a thirteen-year-old 100-metre swimmer. Then, after we've swum the best part of ten kilometres, we drag ourselves out of the pool for an hour-long weights session in the gym, where I lift up to 80 kilograms on the leg press. After this we shower, change and head to school for the day, before coming back and doing it all over again in the afternoon. Seriously, there are times when I feel like I might die of exhaustion.

Some of the boys in our squad are doing things as extreme as 1500-metre butterfly with weights or in drag suits, or even sometimes with their running shoes on. That's another thing they do here at Redcliffe: swim in shoes. For weeks before I start at Redcliffe, whenever I tell people that I am switching clubs, they delight in telling me how Ken Wood makes his kids swim with their runners on. For kilometre after leg-aching, back-breaking kilometre, his squads purportedly plough up and down the pool with their running shoes laced on. Some people claim to have seen all the shoes lined up on the roof after training so they can dry out in the baking Queensland sunshine, before they are retrieved and laced on again in time for afternoon training. In the weeks leading up to my start at Redcliffe, I can't look at a pair of running shoes without my stomach doing flip-flops.

And now I know it's true: we do swim with our runners on.

Training under Ken Wood is a massive wake-up call for me. So I do the only thing I can think of: I suck it up, princess, and get on with the job. This is serious work but I want to do it. Each morning at training, after we winch the covers off the pool, I join the end of the line and jump in the pool and hope to hell that I can keep up.

The fear that I'm not going to make it, that today will be the day I get kicked out, is constant. It's unrelenting.

When I start at Ken's, I'm not as fast as the others. Nowhere near. They are terrifyingly good, these kids. They're Olympians in the making. They've all been with Ken for years, and boy does it show. They've done the hard work: they know the drills. And even though the Sydney 2000 Olympics are more than twelve months away, many of them are already household names. They're superstars: heroes. And they're ploughing up and down in the same lane as me. I pump my skinny limbs and try to keep up.

I put my head down and the improvements I see are rapid and satisfying. I enjoy the hard work, the discipline. I feel like I will get somewhere if I can just work hard enough. I am daunted, sure. I'm more terrified than I have been in my whole life. But one thing I am not afraid of is hard work, and that's what's required here. Each day I get in the water and get on with the job. Whatever Ken throws at me, whatever drill he dreams up, I do it. Even if it nearly kills me.

Then one day I reach out to take a stroke and instead I hit ... feet? I have caught up with the person in front. After all my hard work, after weeks of self-doubt, I have earned my place. Finally, I am running with the big dawgs.

~

Of course, running with the pack is not the same as being accepted. Just because I can keep up doesn't mean I fit in. I spend a lot of my time at Redcliffe trying to be cool enough to fit in. The swimming club is attached to Redcliffe Leagues Club, next door, home of many State of Origin greats. It's also attached to Southern Cross College, the local Catholic high school, where Ken is the swimming coach. Most of the swimmers at Redcliffe go to school together at Southern Cross. Others, such as Tarnee White, have recently graduated.

When I meet Tarnee, Sarah Bowd is forgotten in an instant.

Tarnee White is my new breaststroke rival. She's four years older than me and three or four seconds ahead in the pool. And in swimming, these seconds are light years. As she and I stand shivering on the pool deck together each morning, listening to Ken issuing drills, the differences between us couldn't be more obvious. Tarnee is tall, skinny and beautiful, and she has these bouncing golden curls that tumble down her back. It's like trying to compete with Goldilocks. Ken loves Tarnee. She is clearly his favourite: his golden child with her golden curls, destined to win – you guessed it – Olympic gold.

For my part, I desperately want Tarnee to like me; I'd do anything to be her friend. But for my first few months at Redcliffe I am simply too terrified to talk to her. She is so amazing and so intimidating that the thought of walking up to her and actually opening my mouth feels more impossible than any drill Ken can dream up. Instead, I remain in quiet awe. I drop my gaze reverentially whenever she walks past, and I remain a respectful distance behind her in the pool.

But after a while something strange happens: I start to beat her.

It goes like this. After I've been at Redcliffe for a few months, we decide that I should leave Tullawong High, in Caboolture, and switch to Southern Cross College. My training is going well under Ken and by moving to Southern Cross I can be part of his swimming program during school hours, too. The other bonus of Southern Cross is that it's next door to the Redcliffe pool. This means that after training each morning I only have to walk a couple of hundred metres across the asphalt and I'm at school. Mum, in particular, is a fan of this plan. She'll still have to leave the house at 4 a.m. to drive me to the pool, but instead of having to hang around waiting for me to finish and then driving me back to school, she can drop me off and go straight back home and back to bed for an hour or so before work. Other parents, like my friend Tanya McDonald's mum, sleep on the backseats of their cars while they wait for their kids to finish training. There are some mornings, trust me, when I would like to join them.

So when I am halfway through Year 9, I move to Southern Cross Catholic College and I start training with Ken during school hours, as well as before and after school. I immediately start to swim better. A lot better, apparently, because I start to beat Tarnee. Up until now, Tarnee has been far and away the best breaststroker there is. So you can imagine she's a little aggrieved when – less than twelve months out from the Sydney Olympics – this little upstart begins to beat her. An upstart trained by her own coach, no less. Fair enough, too. I'm four years younger than her – and I'd be pretty peeved if I was beaten by a nine-year-old. It's not long before I get Tarnee offside. She calls me a 'brown-noser' at training because I swim up her arse.

But if Tarnee is struggling with it, well, so am I. For months now, all I have wanted is for this girl to like me, so I wage an internal battle with myself: do I let her win and keep her (and Ken) sweet? Or do I swim my own race and not worry about being her friend? In my thirteen-year-old brain there is no way to do both, and I circle endlessly between the two options in a hopeless holding pattern: I don't want to beat Tarnee, because I want her to like me. But I can't let her win, because I'm not built that way. Plus, I worry about the fact that Tarnee is Ken's favourite. *Am I doing myself any favours by beating this girl?* I wonder.

In the end there's no choice. It kills me to beat Tarnee. But it kills me more to lose. So I swim my guts out and I savour my wins. I realise that as long as we are competing, Tarnee and I will never truly be friends – she is not that sort of person. We will be friendly rivals, but always rivals. I choose winning over our friendship.

When I started at Redcliffe I never dreamt I would keep up with these girls. With Tarnee White or Sarah Bowd. And now here I am, leading the pack. Things are really starting to happen for me under Ken. Big things, exciting things. I am running with the biggest dawgs I know.

But I never do get one of those t-shirts: they'd stopped printing them by the time I joined the club.

4

This Baby's Going to the Olympics

My stroke is all wrong. Shortly after I move to Southern Cross and start training with Ken in earnest, he points out that I'm in need of some pretty severe stroke correction. So he sets about making some changes. Big ones. Ken is fundamental in making my stroke what it will become. But one of the things he doesn't change is the way I hold my hands.

Technically, when you do breaststroke your hands are supposed to be face down so that your palms kiss the water, not the sky. By pressing downwards you lift yourself higher, just as you do when performing a push-up on land. But my hands face upwards. I push the water upwards rather than push it down, and as a result I force my body down deeper into the water. I don't know why I do this; I just always have. For me it's more natural, more fluid: as intuitive as dancing.

People are already telling me that I'm not supposed to swim like this, that I'm doing it all wrong. But Ken is more open-minded.

'Is it working for you?' he asks me poolside one morning as the sun is just beginning to streak the sky.

I nod.

'Then there's your answer.'

My hands are never discussed again.

Ken is all about embracing what comes naturally, about seizing natural advantage. If holding my palms upwards works for me, why change it? Who cares if it's 'not right' according to someone else's rules? Ken assures me it's okay by him, and at the same time he teaches me something bigger than stroke correction. I learn not to emulate other people. 'Always be a first-rate version of yourself,' Ken tells me, quoting Judy Garland, 'not a second-rate version of someone else.' Ken loves this quote. His other favourite is: 'Be kind to everyone on the way up; you'll meet the same people on the way down.' This one is William Mizner. I file it away for future reference.

The other thing about my stroke is that I sit very low in the water. A lot of breaststrokers in the 1990s are swimming really high, bobbing high and fast and furious alongside me. My stroke is much slower and much smoother and more streamlined than others' and I spend a lot of my race time underwater. 'Flowy' is often how I hear myself described. Flowy. I like that. I like to think I am somehow at one with the water.

At one.

On my own.

But that means I'm different. And different is controversial.

My slower, smoother stroke means that most of my competitors have a higher stroke rate than me. So not only are they higher in the water than me – and, therefore, much more visible – but when they are seen, they are seen to be fast. While I am swimming at a rate of forty-two strokes per minute, everyone else around me is doing forty-eight or even fifty. They're swimming high and working hard. It's energetic, powerful stuff.

Yet, despite the controversy, I'm not tempted to adapt. Like salmon heading upstream, these girls are really flogging themselves.

I like hard work but I'm not stupid. Even if it's 'wrong', I'd choose to be the 'flowy' zen master, rather than a tired old salmon, any day. Think of the energy I'm saving. Think of the oxygen. I'm doing six to eight strokes fewer than everyone else in every race. At this rate, I should be able to stop for a snooze at the 100-metre mark and still come out ahead, I tell myself.

At least, that's the idea. And it's not long before I get to test it out. Less than twelve months after I start at Redcliffe, in April 2000, I'm off to the Australian Age Swimming Championships in Perth. This is the first time I've been to Age Nationals, the national swimming competition for schoolkids under sixteen. Until now, the highest level I've ever swum at is Queensland State Titles and, to be honest, I have not really set the world on fire. I still hold the School Sport national record from back in Adelaide in 1997 but that was for the 50-metre event. It doesn't mean much for the Olympics, which only has 100-metre or 200-metre breaststroke. My times at Redcliffe are good – good enough to scrape into Age Nationals – but they're not great. They're not fast enough to give anyone at Nationals a real scare. And they're certainly not fast enough for me to start clearing my diary for Olympic trials in Sydney next month.

I am very aware that, less than a year ago, I was still puddling around in the 25-metre pool back at Burpengary, having towel-flicking and sausage-sandwich-eating competitions on Friday nights. Since I've moved to Redcliffe and started training with Ken, I've stepped things up fast. But Age Nationals fast? I'm not so sure.

Still, I've qualified to go, and Ken thinks it will be good practice for me. Personally, I'm hoping to swim fast enough to be selected for the Pan Pacific School Games next month, which are sure to be teeming with cute boys from across the whole Asia–Pacific region. But I don't say anything about my plans to anyone else. It would be too embarrassing if I failed to make the team.

So I head to Perth for Age Nationals.

But there's a spanner in the works: my period.

That's right. I'm fourteen and about to swim at Age Nationals for the first time, I'm representing my new club (a club I'm busting to impress), and on the very day I'm due to jump in the pool, I get my period.

'I have to go out there, in my tiny little togs, in front of everyone, when I have my period?' I squeak.

I am still a kid. Just a fourteen-year-old girl, and emotionally a young one at that. Mum's not with me – it's my first interstate trip without her – and getting my period is still a new (and very big) deal for me. I am so embarrassed I think I might die. Can I really go out there and swim like this?

I stand on the pool deck, biting my nails to the quick and wishing I was at home with Mum.

Our assistant coach from Redcliffe, Rhonda Smails, pulls me aside. She knows I have my period. 'Don't worry about it, sweetheart,' she says. She puts her arm around my shoulder and gives me a quick squeeze. Then she leans down and whispers so that only I can hear, 'You know it makes you swim faster, don't you?' She winks and walks off, probably not giving it another thought.

But I take her words to heart. I swallow what Rhonda says and I honestly believe I will swim faster because I have my period. *Great*, I think. *Awesome. I can do this. I'll go with that.*

And I do: I swim out of my skin that day. I win the 100-metre breaststroke in 1:08.30, which is a huge personal best (PB). It's more than two seconds faster than anything I've ever swum before.

Here I am, fourteen and swimming in a national competition for kids who are up to three years older than me, and I'm swimming faster than any of them. I'm faster than anyone else in the country. My time, 1:08.30, is by far the fastest time in Australia this year.

And this year happens to be the year of the Sydney Olympics.

Of course, it's not long before people start saying I'm the next big thing.

'How do you feel to be heading for Olympic trials next month?' the press keep asking me.

'Oh yeah, I'm excited,' I say happily. 'I've done a PB and I made qualifying time, so I may as well go along.'

'Made qualifying time?' they repeat. 'You've got the best time in Australia!'

But it still doesn't sink in. It just doesn't register that I might make the Olympic team. Not little Leisel from Burpengary. Skinny, gawky Leisel who has no money and no dad. Not me.

When I get back to Redcliffe I get back to work. Perth has been a massive high for me and somehow I am oblivious that there might be more to come, so I settle back into my everyday routine. Train, eat, sleep; train, eat, sleep. I am still riddled with self-doubt, so I always find time to be intimidated and overawed whenever I see Tarnee White or Sarah Bowd on the pool deck. I am still convinced deep down that Tarnee is faster than me, and I fall back into trying to be her friend. It never enters my head that now she might be intimidated by me!

Things are being run a little differently in 2000, the Olympic year. Usually Age Nationals (for schoolkids) are held after Open Nationals (for over sixteens), but in 2000 Opens are held second. Then, shortly after Opens there are the Olympic trials. In terms of preparation it's not great. Coming off Perth, I have to taper and recover and then immediately start heavy training again in time for trials. As I'd been secretly hoping, I've made the team for the Pan Pacific Games, but these are off the agenda now that I've qualified for Olympic trials.

'I don't want to go to trials, Ken,' I tell my coach. It's all too hard, too scary. I'd much rather be poolside at the Pan Pacs, checking out boys, than competing for a spot at the Sydney Olympics.

'No way,' says Ken. 'Pan Pacs are off. You're going to trials. That's our job now.'

I say okay, because Ken is the boss. And because honestly you could ask me to fly to the moon and I'd try it. I'm very suggestible: just look at how I reacted to that comment from Rhonda about swimming fast with my period. It was only a throwaway line, but I really believed it. I am so very young and innocent. Such a little kid. I've got no idea how the world really works.

I have always been a fish out of water. But it's more than that now. I'm a fish out of water and I'm swimming to qualify for the Olympics. I find it hard to breathe at the best of times and this is some seriously rarefied air.

~

Every man and his dog wants to make this Olympic team, our home Olympics in the millennial year. The queue for a place on the Australian swimming team stretches further than my chlorine-red eyes can see. These are the largest Olympic trials this country has ever seen.

To make the team you have to finish in first or second place in the final, and you have to swim under a specified time (known as 'A-qualifying' time). It's really strict. Only two people from Australia will be allowed to compete in each event. No arguments. It doesn't matter what you did at Age Nationals a month ago. It doesn't matter who your coach is or how long you've been training. All that counts is how fast you swim in the final. The Olympic Games really is the great equaliser: terribly fair, but also terribly brutal.

In Perth I swam 1:08.30 in the 100-metre breaststroke, and qualifying time for the Sydney Olympics is 1:10.21. So it's going to be tight. Really tight.

The trials are being held at the Sydney Olympic Park Aquatic Centre in Homebush, Australia's biggest swimming arena. The complex has only recently been completed and it can hold 17,000 spectators. And for those who can't make it to Sydney to watch, the event is being televised on prime-time TV each night. This is the real deal.

But I can't seem to grasp it:

14 years old

1:10.21 minutes

17,000 fans

and just two 100-metre breaststrokers.

I can't make sense of these numbers. They don't mean anything to me. I am oblivious to the significance of these trials, to the magnitude of the opportunity I have here.

'Cool. This will be fun,' I say to Mum. 'I'll get to meet people from all over Australia. Maybe some of my friends from Age Nationals will be there!'

The way I feel, this could be any old swimming trip. I've been taking them since I was ten. I'm hoping I'll have the chance to stay up late watching movies and maybe sneak in a Domino's meatlovers pizza or two. The usual stuff.

And if Mum is nervous or seriously thinks I might make the Olympic team, well, she never verbalises it to me. Mum's coming with me to Sydney and the only comment she makes is how great it is that she'll get to see her family while we're there. She's supportive, obviously. But if Mum's anxious, I don't know about it.

When we arrive in Sydney, I am ferried over to our team hotel in Bankstown, in Sydney's west, about 10 kilometres from the Aquatic Centre in Homebush. My roommate is my Redcliffe teammate Tanya McDonald, who is here to compete in the 200-metre and 400-metre freestyle events.

Somehow I make it through my heat of the 100-metre breaststroke, and then the semis. Before I know it, I have qualified for the final. But rather than let the pressure of swimming in an Olympic qualifier go to my head, on the day of my race I am hanging out with Tanya and we are bored. Bored, bored, bored.

Me: 'Do you want to paint our nails?'

Tanya: 'Yeah, let's paint nails.'

Me: 'I'm going to do mine red, because red Ferraris go faster and stuff.'

Tanya: 'Hey, smart! Can I use the red after you?'

Against all the best advice, Tanya and I have been to the shops. On race day, you're advised to stay in bed or at least keep your legs elevated, so they're fresh for your race in the evening. Racing starts at about seven and we all leave for the pool together at around four. So you've got five or six hours to kill from the time you get up until the time you're expected on the bus to the pool. That's five or six hours too long to expect a couple of over-hyped, under-supervised fourteen-year-old girls – on tour from another state – to sit quietly in a hotel room and do nothing. Never. Gonna. Happen.

Instead, Tanya and I take ourselves off to the oh-so-glamorous Bankstown Central Shopping Centre, in the middle of suburban Bankstown, for a spot of retail therapy. We walk several kilometres, through shops and food courts, ahead of my big race. And we buy red nail polish.

Tanya says, 'Hey, if you win tonight, you'll have to show your red nails on TV.'

'No way, I'm not doing that! How embarrassing,' I reply.

'Yeah, show them on TV. When they announce your name, while you're in the marshalling area. Just hold up your hands so I can see your nails on TV.'

'Uh, I think I'll have more to worry about tonight than my nails!'

~

That evening, I line up in the marshalling area with seven of the eight fastest female Australian breaststrokers of all time. In lane one is the queen of Australian breaststroke – and my personal hero – fellow Queenslander Samantha Riley. Sam is the current world record-holder (with a time of 1:07.69). She's also a former World Champion and is here to qualify for her third Olympics. In lane two is Rebecca Brown, former world-record holder in the 200-metre breaststroke and ranked fifteenth all-time best in the world in this event. Rebecca is back on track after a short slump in form and she has something to prove in this race tonight. In lane three is Brooke Hanson, who swam a PB in the heats earlier in the week.

And then there is me.

As the television cameras pan to me, standing sheepishly behind lane four, I raise my left hand in a reverse high-five, showing my red fingernails for the world to see. I am about to swim the biggest race of my life so far – an Olympic qualifying event – and here I am making good on a bet with my friend. It's almost inconceivable. And so the first time the world sees Leisel Jones, fastest qualifier in lane four, I am doing something dumb.

'Nice touch,' says commentator Ray 'Rabbits' Warren on the Nine Network. 'Hey, look, Mum! I painted my fingernails just for you.'

Next to me, in lane five is Caroline Hildreth. Caroline looks about five years older and ten years wiser than me. She swam a PB in the first semi yesterday and now, standing here looking ominous in her black 'Fastskin', she looks like she might do it again.

These new Speedo Fastskins have just been invented and are the bee's knees of swimsuit technology. The suits are made from spandex and nylon and increase glide through the water, just like the skins of dolphins or seals. They are supposed to reduce drag by up to four per cent. But I opt for my skimpy little Aquablade togs, straight from the 1980s, with their high-cut legs and their low-tech fabric. I will not be seen dead in togs that reach down to my knees.

On the other side of Caroline is Tarnee White, sporting her red and white Redcliffe swimming cap, just like me. Tarnee was just off her best time in the semis yesterday and yet, as the TV commentator points out, 'She's capable of anything, Tarnee White.'

Next to Tarnee is veteran Helen Denman, who won silver at the '98 World Swimming Titles. And in the final lane is Nadine Neumann, Olympic finalist in the 200-metre event in 1996.

All in all, it's quite a field. These girls have years of experience between them. Olympic experience. World Championship experience. They're all capable of swimming sub-1:09s and they've all trained for the past four years for this moment. There will be nothing in it. Microseconds. Nanoseconds.

But I don't really appreciate any of this. I'm too busy thinking about Josh Krough.

Josh is from my squad back home. He's the older brother of my good friend and teammate Jayne. He's also unimaginably cute.

Before my race, Josh and I had been mucking around in the marshalling area together, when he'd said to me, 'I dare you to make a peace sign for the camera if you win.'

Now, if you're a fourteen-year-old girl and a cute boy dares you to make a peace sign if you win, then I bet my last buck that's what you'll do. Especially if you're the kind of kid who can't pass up a dare.

'A peace sign?' I say to Josh. 'Sure, whatever.' And so while the rest of the field is focused on Olympic glory, I am distracted by Josh and the thought of making peace for him.

But forget where my mind is: my body is here. My shoulders, my biceps, my wrong-way-round hands. My legs, my feet, my abnormal hips. Everything is pumping, working in synch.

When the starter's gun fires I am a bit slow to start. I finish the first twenty behind, but this is my style; I am comfortable here. Tarnee takes it out hard, but when I touch the wall at the 50-metre mark I've made up some ground. I'm right behind Tarnee, outside the world-record split by 1.39 seconds. Tarnee leads into the second 50 metres, with me in second place.

Finally, with only 30 metres to go, I pull out in front. At last I'm hitting my pace. With 10 metres to go, I take a comfortable lead and bring it home fast.

I hit the wall first.

'Leisel Jones wins!' shouts Rabbits Warren to everyone watching at home. 'At fourteen years of age! In 1:08.71!'

I stare at the scoreboard in disbelief. I've swum a personal best and qualified for my first Olympic Games. Tarnee's come second in 1:09.05. Caroline Hildreth also swam a 1:09 (1:09.22) but she's missed out on Olympic selection.

'What a moment!' Rabbits says. 'Leisel Jones – this *baby* – is going to the Olympics!'

I give a goofy grin, my tongue wedged between my front teeth. And what's the first thing I do when I win – on prime-time television, for the entire world to see? You guessed it: I raise my hand in the internationally recognised symbol for peace.

~

Well, at least that's what I thought I was doing. But it was probably naive of me to think my two raised fingers would be interpreted as peace. Who makes peace in elite-level sport?

Instead, my gesture is branded as the 'V' for victory. I am the victor, the winner. What else could I possibly have meant? After all, I was the young underdog and I won, so wouldn't I want to lord it over everyone else?

Wrong. It couldn't be further from the truth.

When my photo appears on the front page of the paper the next day, with the caption '"V" for Victory', I am mortified.

'I sound so stuck up!' I say to Mum on the phone. 'It makes it look like I was rubbing it in my competitors' faces, and it wasn't that at all!' How ironic that my symbol of harmony was mistaken for a sign of aggression. At the very least it should have just been read as a symbol of my crush on Josh.

My peace sign, the red-fingernail dare: these are just silly jokes with my friends. They're signs, if nothing else, of what a little kid I am still. I'm not ready for this. I'm only fourteen – a very young, very sheltered fourteen at that.

But the media wants a victor, not a dumb kid, and from the instant my palm touches the wall at 1:08.71, my life changes.

When I entered the water, I was a schoolkid in Year 9 at Southern Cross College; when I leave the pool, I am an Olympic qualifier. I am an Australian representative. Swimming is no longer what I do; it's who I am. With one single swim, I have forged my identity. I am Leisel Jones, the swimmer.

This one minute and eight seconds when I'm fourteen years old will define my identity for the next fifteen years. Perhaps the rest of my life.

Of course, I have no time to let this all sink in. I float at the end of my lane in a daze. This baby is going to the Olympics.

5

Rookie

When I spring out of the pool after my race, I am overwhelmed. Where do I go? What do I do now? This is a new club I've entered – an Olympic club – and I don't know the rules, don't have a clue. I stand dripping awkwardly on the pool deck until Ken motions to me from over near the marshalling area. I head over to him, relieved. It's as if I'm five years old again, lost in the supermarket and I've just spotted my mum.

'Ken!' I call.

Then Tarnee appears beside us and bursts into tears. She's overcome with the emotion of it all. I give her a hug and for a moment the two of us could be back on the pool deck at Redcliffe. Training partners, teammates and nearly – but not quite – friends, even in this instant. It feels just like any old day at training – until Nicole Livingstone starts to interview us for the Nine Network broadcast. I've never met Nicole, only watched in awe as she swam at the 1988, 1992 and 1996 Olympic Games. Now she's talking to me on live TV.

'Teammates at Redcliffe Leagues Club and now teammates on the Australian Olympic Team – wow!' Nicole says. 'Leisel, what did you think when you touched the wall and had a look at the scoreboard?'

'I'm absolutely amazed,' I say, and when my voice comes back at me through the microphone it's tiny and squeaky and straight from the school playground. I sound like a kid. I sound like I'm sucking on helium. 'My first Olympic team at fourteen? Uh, I never imagined it ... I was just hoping to do well!' I couldn't have been any greener if I'd tried.

Tarnee, meanwhile, is in floods of tears. She tells the camera that, with Ken, she's been working towards this moment for fifteen years, and when she tries to thank him more tears flow. 'This has been a goal of mine for so long and I just can't believe it's happened!' she says, and when she talks you can't help but be moved, because it's so obviously genuine and so very heartfelt. It's exactly what Nicole wants to hear.

~

In the next few weeks, I learn a lot about what the media wants to hear. The Olympic trials go for eight days and after that it's straight back to school for me. But things have changed since I left a fortnight ago. Media helicopters arrive, ferrying news crews to my playground. Channel Seven rocks up to my maths class to interview me and my classmates. *A Current Affair* cordons off half the library to film a story about me carrying out a 'normal' day at school, which is hilarious, because 'normal' doesn't usually involve a TV camera crew. When I left to go to trials, I told my teachers I was 'just popping off for another swim meet'. 'What homework can I take with me?' I asked them. Now I've come back with my homework half-finished and a TV crew in tow.

Because Ken Wood (with his uber-squad) is the swimming coach at Southern Cross, there are other Olympians on campus here. Tarnee White, for one. And Geoff Huegill. But it's the fourteen-year-old freak who's the really big news. I have journalists following me between classes and trailing me to training in the afternoon. Everyone wants a quote; everyone wants a cute story. As a gawky teenage girl who doesn't want to stick out, I find the whole thing weird. Bizarre. It's off-putting, intimidating and embarrassing, to be frank.

Not that you'd know it from my happy-go-lucky interview patter. I have received no media training from anyone yet – no constructive advice, not even from Mum, whose guidance on my newfound fame, on everything in my life, runs to 'Just do your best' – but I know enough to be all Queensland sunshine for the camera. I'm all blonde hair and toothy grin. I am the kid next door, the up-and-comer. The Australian Tourism Board could bottle this stuff.

But for all my apparent sunniness, my smile is as manufactured as the ones the journalists flash back at me. I learnt a hard lesson at trials when my red fingernails and alleged 'V'-for-victory sign made me front-page news. Kids stop in the playground and flash me the two-fingered 'V'. Everyone saw what I did. Everyone knows and they think I was lording it over my rivals.

So I am a little wary of the media now. I've seen how they can twist things. So I decide I won't give the press much wriggle room. I will be squeaky clean. I will make sure there is absolutely no way the media can misconstrue what I say or do. In the days and weeks after I return to Redcliffe, as I begin to build my new training regime, I begin to build a new self too.

From now on, there will be no mucking around in front of the media. No more jokes, dares or silly stuff. I think about all the times I've enjoying casting myself as the butt of the joke, all the times I've gone after the cheap laughs. Those days are over. I pack them away like that Valentine's rose from Josh Bettridge back in Burpengary, shoved under the bed to be forgotten. I am a professional now – an Olympic representative. I will no longer be my dumb, daggy self.

I become self-conscious and serious and I filter what I say. I am always polite and obliging, but I talk in clichés and 'sports-speak'. I self-censor. I'm bland and predictable. I am whiter-than-white. In short, I have become a marketer's dream.

~

The Olympics are in September, but before that is orientation camp. This is the final camp before competition and it's always held in the same region as the Olympic host country so we have a chance to acclimatise and get over jetlag, but never so close that we're in our competitors' pockets. This August we're heading south.

'Melbourne!' I yell to Mum as we chug down the M1 on our way to Brisbane airport. 'Do you think there'll be time for shopping?' Olympics be buggered, I am still a teenage girl.

'Using whose money?' Mum yells back, laughing. We're both shouting so we can be heard over the noise of our old, beat-up, green VL Commodore station wagon as it bangs and shudders its way down the highway. It whinges and complains and carries on.

Until suddenly it doesn't. Suddenly, we've stopped.

'Oh my God,' whispers Mum in alarm. 'Oh my God, we've broken down!'

I stare at the itinerary in my lap. I am horrified. I'm about to travel to my first Olympic orientation camp and I can't even make it safely to the airport?

'Don't move!' Mum orders. Then she leaps from the car and starts running down the freeway to find an emergency telephone.

When she gets back several minutes later, she is red and sweaty and teary. Her shirt clings to her back.

'They're on their way!' she says. We sit in the car in nervous silence as we wait for the RACQ (Royal Automobile Club of Queensland) to come and rescue us.

'Reckon you could do with a trade-in,' the RACQ guy says jovially, when he arrives thirty minutes later. He takes one look under the bonnet and shakes his head. Still he gives it a go, dipping sticks and checking tubes, until – amazingly – he thinks we might be good to go.

'Take it easy,' he tells us. 'No hooning, you hear me? She might not take it.' He taps the bonnet to indicate he's talking about the car. But one look at Mum and he could just as easily be talking about her.

We get to the airport in the nick of time. When we set out from Redcliffe that morning I'd laughed at Mum and her urge to always be embarrassingly early. 'Who takes two hours to do a half-hour drive?' I had teased her. Turns out *we* do.

As we pull into the drop-off bay, I turn to face her. She's teary again. Her baby is going away.

I shrug and grin. 'Thanks, Mum,' I say sheepishly. For getting us going early. For getting us here in one piece. For everything you've ever done throughout my entire life to get me to this moment.

I give her a hug and clamber out of the car. I think about everyone else on the team cruising to the airport in their Range Rovers, Volvos or flashy Mercedes Benz people-movers. No-one else seems to have the money problems we do. Here are Mum and I, povo Redcliffe bums, in our terrible green Commodore that almost didn't make it. But looking at Mum – at her literal sweat and tears – I know I wouldn't swap with anyone else.

'Have fun, kiddo,' she says through her open window. I wait for it. 'Just do your best,' she says, predictably. Then she's off and I am alone. I wander inside the airport to find my new Olympic family.

~

We have a great time at camp. This is a good bunch of people. There are a lot of big personalities, but everyone works together. We are a team: the Aussie team. We are here to get to know one another, and I like what I find. Because it is my first orientation camp, I am a 'rookie' and therefore required to embarrass myself by performing a skit at 'Rookie Night'. I don't need a second invitation. A few of us get together and organise a send-up of *Perfect Match*, the 1980s TV dating show. I dress as a boy and Ray Hass, the backstroker, as a girl: the two of us are the perfect match at the end. Everyone thinks we're hilarious. We bring the house down.

Sometime during camp, word gets out about my car breaking down on the way to the airport. Typical me, I lead the charge, joking about it among my new teammates. '"Leisel the bum", that's me,' I tell them. 'Anyone got any spare Olympic medals I can take to Cash Converters? I thought I'd buy myself a pushbike...'

We laugh and I pretend it's not half true.

~

You can imagine my astonishment when someone actually takes me seriously. Someone like Ford. When I get back home after the Sydney Olympics, there is a brand spanking new Ford Laser in the driveway.

'Uh, who's visiting?' I ask Mum, as we pull up alongside it in our clapped-out green machine.

'No-one,' she says. 'It's yours. The Ford sponsorship guys dropped it off for you while you were away.'

'Bullshit.' I've never been inside a new car, let alone owned one.

'Leisel! Language!' I might have just scored us a sponsorship car from Ford but I am still a fourteen-year-old kid. 'Don't swear,' Mum admonishes me.

But when we take the new car for a spin around the block, we're both as juvenile as each other. We go for a cruise by the beach at Redcliffe, windows down, radio pumping, hoping the neighbours will see us. We giggle like sisters as we run our hands over the showroom-fresh upholstery and across the shiny new dashboard.

'I can get used to this. This is me,' I say to Mum, even though I have never – neither of us has ever – owned anything as expensive as a new car in our lives.

Never mind that I am still two years too young to drive it.

Mum rolls her eyes. 'C'mon, it's time for dinner. Then homework, miss.' And we head home to eat more two-minute steaks.

~

When I make the Olympic team, I join the Swimming Australia payroll. Well, sort of. I don't get a regular salary, and I'm certainly not considered a medal contender, so I don't receive any of the medal incentive money from the Olympic Committee that's sloshing around. But I do get a one-off payment of $5000. It is deposited directly into my bank account on a Thursday afternoon, and a fortnight later it's still there. I'm too scared to touch it.

'They're paying me to swim?' I am gobsmacked.

I'm told I can only ever expect to receive sporadic lump sums for being an Australian representative swimmer. Say, one payment per Olympics, and perhaps quarterly payments during non-Olympic years, all around the $5000 mark. That adds up to about $20,000, maybe $25,000, in an Olympic year, as my full-time earnings. It's not nearly enough to live off, but I think it's Christmas. I'm too conservative with my money to spend it frivolously, and because we have no money at home my earnings are quickly used up paying for groceries or school stuff or household bills or going towards the rent. But I don't mind: I'd rather help pay for the electricity than sit in the dark.

Mum never puts any pressure on me to earn money. Not once. But she also doesn't have the luxury of saying 'no thanks' when the money comes in. We need it: it's that simple. After I started swimming with Redcliffe Leagues, Southern Cross College offered to waive half my school fees if I went there. They knew the only way they could get me to swim for the school was for them to drop the price. Without discounted fees there's no way Mum could have afforded it. And if I had to accept a scholarship so I could go to school there, so be it. I could deal with that.

I view my swimming earnings in much the same way. If swimming can help us financially, why wouldn't I let it? You think I'm so proud I'm going to send that car in the driveway back to the showroom? That'd be crazy.

In the past I never took much notice of the fact I was one of the poor kids at school. But now that things have changed, I'm aware of a difference. All of a sudden, I'm bringing in more than any of my friends could ever dream of earning at Macca's or KFC or wherever they're flipping burgers at weekends. I'm earning so much money, I'm supporting my mum! I cannot wipe the smile from my face.

But while I'm busy counting my dollars (and my lucky stars), I fail to see the greater cost. Because in that one race at trials – in that one minute and eight seconds, when my life changed irrevocably – my relationship with swimming changed too. I became a swimmer, but swimming became a job.

Swimming has always put food on our table and saved us from being homeless. The money Mum makes as a swimming instructor has been our only source of income for years. But for the first time, I am the main breadwinner.

And that's a heavy responsibility for a fourteen-year-old.

6

Sydney 2000

I am off to swim at the Olympics. But first, let me tell you about the time Kieren Perkins rejected my request for an autograph. That's right. Kieren Perkins, OAM. Olympic gold medallist and one of the best long-distance swimmers on the planet. Swimming's Mr Nice Guy. Rejected my request for an autograph.

It goes like this. I am competing alongside Kieren at the Queensland State Championships in Chandler, Brisbane. It's my first State Titles, whereas Kieren is an old hand. He is the VIP of the VIPs here, and that's saying something when you cast your eye across the pool deck. Hayley Lewis, Susie O'Neill, Glen Housman, Grant Hackett, Sam Riley – they're all here. But Kieren's star shines brighter than them all. He's already picked up gold in the 1500-metres at both the Barcelona and Atlanta Olympics and he's well on his way to repeating the trick again in Sydney. I am in awe.

Over the next two days, I watch Kieren from afar. I am hoping for an autograph, so I carry my club cap and a black marker with me everywhere I go (even when I go to the ladies' toilets). But the Queensland State Championships are massive. They're by far the biggest state swimming meet in Australia, with thousands of kids competing. So whenever I see Kieren, he is surrounded by a crowd of adoring fans. The only time he is alone is when he is in the pool. And sure, I want an autograph, but not enough to scuba-dive into his lane to get it.

But late on the second afternoon of competition, I see Kieren standing alone on the pool deck. He's just finished his race and is heading for his swim down. I realise it is now or never. I am painfully shy and incredibly nervous, but I force myself to walk up to my idol and hold out my cap and pen.

'E–excuse me,' I stammer in a tiny voice, skinny and awkward in my Redcliffe club uniform. Kieren stares at me. 'Mr Perkins? Please can I get your autograph?' Asking Kieren Perkins for an autograph is more nerve-wracking than competing in any of my races this week.

For a moment, I can see he's confused. *Now?* I can see his brain trying to process it. *Is she really asking me now?* He is red-faced and dripping wet: he looks exactly as you would expect someone who has just swum one and a half kilometres at full pelt to look.

'Not now! I'm about to swim down!' he barks. 'It's not the right time!' And he walks off past me and heads for the warm-down pool.

I slink away, burning with shame.

In retrospect, it was a terrible time to ask him. After his race, the poor guy probably wanted to lie down for a week. I would have after a 1500-metre event! And there I was bugging him to sign my cap.

I do everything I can to bury that memory.

Now, less than two years later, I am staring at Kieren Perkins again. He's much drier this time. And happier too. Elated even. Also, he hasn't just swum 1500 metres. No, this time he's walking, quite leisurely, around the Sydney Olympic stadium at Homebush while 3.6 billion people – including me – look on. It's the Opening Ceremony of the Sydney Olympics, and Kieren is marching as part of the Aussie contingent. I watch him smile and wave to the crowd.

I'm not marching, because today is Friday and my first heat is on Sunday morning, so I've been advised to skip the ceremony, as it means a lot of standing around getting hot and tired. A bunch of us from the swimming team are watching the ceremony on TV together, inside the athletes' village. I watch Kieren and the others stroll proudly across the screen in their green and gold. I look down at my uniform, then back at the screen. It seems impossible I'm in the same uniform, on the same team, as the great Kieren Perkins. Two years ago I was asking him to sign my club cap and now here we are, on the same team. It sounds so corny, but I feel like a winner just being at the Sydney Olympics. Just taking part, just getting a t-shirt. (I actually got one this time – unlike back at Redcliffe!) I feel like my life is complete.

My friends at school are going to be so jealous! I think gleefully. I stare at the screen, soaking it all up. Everything is so big, so overwhelming and so terribly exciting. The theme from *The Man from Snowy River* is belting out while dancers perform elaborate simulations with Victa lawnmowers. It's mad. It's spectacular. The whole thing is surreal.

I can't take it all in. I can't believe my eyes. As ever, I'm gasping for air – but this time I love it.

One morning during competition, I sit beside Kieren. We're high in the stands above the pool, with a bunch of other people from our team. Kieren chats politely, taking an interest; he couldn't be nicer. I don't mention the autograph. We watch the athletes on the pool deck below warm up, bouncing on the balls of their feet and swinging their arms wildly across their chests as if trying to grab onto this incredible experience. Sitting here with Kieren, watching all this, I feel on top of the world.

I am probably really annoying to my teammates sitting around me. To these people – who have dedicated the past four years to training, not to mention the entirety of their lives to their Olympic dream – I am a little kid who can't keep still, can't settle down.

But I can't help it. I can't shake the feeling that I've snuck into a party. A party at Disneyland. After dark. Without any teachers. I am underage and overawed. I am having an absolute ball.

I room with Sybilla Goode. Sybilla is a great girl who, unfortunately, will not get the chance to swim at Sydney. We are put together because we are the youngest on the team. But I don't know how seventeen-year-old Sybilla feels about sharing with a kid who only just turned fifteen.

The Olympic experience is amazing no matter how old you are, though. It really is. I am leaving the pool complex one day when I am swept up in a crowd of people – picked up as if by a wave. Everyone is cheering and smiling and having a great time as we move en masse along the boulevard outside the pool, a giant human crocodile, grinning our toothy smile from collective ear to ear. It's incredible, this crowd – confronting too, because I'm not good with crowds – but mostly just incredible. *You won't see anything like this ever again*, I tell myself as I let myself be carried happily along.

Living in the Olympic village is like being in a gated community. It's a little like how I imagine retirement-living to be. At least, it would be if retirement-living came with 10,651 residents, from 199 different countries, all in the very best physical condition of their lives. On second thoughts, maybe a retirement village isn't the best comparison.

The village in Sydney blows my mind. There are 2000 houses. In the swimming alone, there are nearly 1000 people competing, from 150 nations. That's a lot of boys to check out! The village dining hall is the size of three football fields. There's a games hall, a cinema, doctors and dentists, hairdressers, a laundry, nail parlours and souvenir shops. The village even has its own post office. And inside the village everything is free. You can eat what you like, have your hair done for nothing, get a manicure or get your shirts dry-cleaned. You can go and get your teeth filled for nix. Even the vending machines that seem to be on every corner are operated by a single Olympic coin that we are all issued on qualification. You buy your drink, then your coin is spat out again. If you wanted to, you could drink endless Cokes all day long.

Then there's the food. Every cuisine is available here, every food you could imagine. In the food hall there are Italian, Spanish, Chinese, Mexican, Thai, Greek and modern Australian sections: the works. In the centre of the room, there are rows and rows of salad bars, and mountains of fruit, plus cutlery piled high. There are trays of free Snickers, free Mars bars, free Macca's; there are endless fridges full of every soft drink ever invented. And as you head for the door, there are freezers to one side stacked high with free Magnum ice-creams.

I look at it all longingly. *I will be back here*, I vow. *In my second week, after I've finished racing, I will have fun in this room.*

During our stay in the village we are all required to abide by the rules of our sport's governing body. For us, that's Swimming Australia. But the rules, as far as I can work out, are pretty relaxed. Support your teammates and cheer loudly. Attend team meetings. Do your job, swim hard, and fulfil your Olympic contract (that is, don't bring your sport into disrepute). That seems to be the extent of it. Beyond this, we are free to govern ourselves. And in the second week, after all the swimming events are finished, it seems to me that it becomes a free-for-all. Do what you want. Knock yourself out. And if you don't come home, that's not Swimming Australia's problem. If you make yourself sick bingeing on McNuggets in the food hall, don't call us: that's the philosophy. *Fine by me*, I think to myself.

But for all my awe, all my kid-in-a-lolly-shop amazement about the Olympics, I am seriously unfazed when it comes to the pool. I'm not daunted by racing, not even particularly nervous.

My heat for the 100-metre breaststroke is tomorrow morning, so tonight, which is a Saturday night, and the first night of swimming racing, I am heading home early from the pool to get some rest. A bunch of us who are racing tomorrow take the bus back to the village. But the remainder of the team is at the pool, gearing up for a big night.

The boys are racing tonight – our 100-metre freestyle relay team. And while the Americans have not once been beaten in this event since it was first introduced back in 1964, there is a buzz building tonight about our Aussie team. Michael Klim, Chris Fydler, Ashley Callus and Ian Thorpe: these boys are the best hope we've had in years. And ever since the Aussies almost beat the USA at the last Games, in Atlanta, the rivalry between the two nations has been fierce.

'Smash them like guitars!' was the brash instruction from American sprinter Garry Hall Jnr to the rest of his team. The trash talk leading up to the event has only added to the hype, and I don't think there's a single person in Australia who isn't watching the race tonight.

Including us. Instead of going to bed, we head straight for the dining hall to watch the race on the big-screen TVs in there. Us Aussies take up one big, long white table all to ourselves, while the Americans claim another just two tables down from us. There's some mucking around and a bit of name-calling while we all get settled in for the race.

We chew on our nails for a bit when Ian Thorpe, the anchor leg, who is still puffed from winning gold in the 400-metre freestyle half an hour ago, splits his suit on the pool deck. People rush to him, unzip him and take ten minutes or so to pour him into a spare suit.

Then suddenly they're ready to go. Michael Klim is up on the blocks. He gets away fast – bloody fast, in fact – breaking the 100-metre freestyle world record with a time of 48.18 seconds.

We are cheering ourselves hoarse; now we are up on the table!

No-one is getting any rest here tonight. 'Aussie, Aussie, Aussie! Oi, Oi, Oi!' we shout obnoxiously as Chris Fydler hits the water in front of the US.

Two tables down, the Americans are going nuts; they are up on the table too, stomping and cheering just like us.

The windows are rattling and there is food going everywhere, but we don't notice, don't care – Ashley Callus is still in front!

We are so loud I can't believe they can't hear us at the stadium. We are screaming and jumping on the table as Thorpie hits the pool. He starts hard and in front, but Gary Hall is too much, and by the turn the Americans are out in front.

'Go Aussies!' we scream.

And then Thorpie picks it up a gear and pulls out in front.

'Go Thorpie! Go Aussies!' We are shouting so loud. We jump and scream, glued to the screen.

And we *win*! Our boys win. They bring the house down.

Euphoric with victory, they play air guitar, for the whole world to see, and we strum along from atop the table in the dining hall. The Americans applaud graciously and climb down from their table.

We are so pumped I could go out and swim my race right now.

~

But by the time I step out onto the pool deck for my final the next night, my nerves have finally kicked in. So far, everything at this meet has been straightforward. Forget that it's the Olympics: I've just been doing my own thing. *Oh, it's the heats? Guess I'll go out and swim fast. Oh, I made the semis? Cool. I'll go out and swim fast again then.* I've had nothing to lose and nothing to prove; I've just focused on what a thrill it is to be take part.

Now, though, I have found some butterflies for my stomach. *I shouldn't be here*, I think. *This is an Olympic final. A final at the Olympics!*

I keep waiting for an official to tell me I'm in the wrong place, to guide me kindly back to the marshalling area. But no-one comes. No-one even blinks. I guess I'll just have to play along.

I take my place among a formidable line-up. Penny Heyns from South Africa is in lane two. She holds the world record (1:06.52) and the Olympic record (1:07.02) and my money is on her to take out the gold, although her compatriot in lane four, Sarah Poewe, is the fastest qualifier tonight. Next to her in lane five is Megan Quann from the USA. None of us know much about her. In fact, I've barely heard of her before this week. Quann's not considered a name; she's not a threat. But if you've made it to an Olympic final, you must be able to swim.

I'm next to Quann in lucky lane six – at least it's always been lucky for me. And I'm doing everything to feel lucky tonight, let me tell you. I'm calling on the power of the green and gold. The Southern Cross is plastered across my team togs and I'm wearing my Aussie cap proudly. Earlier in the week, a bunch of us stuck temporary Australian flag tattoos on our arms, and now I flash my right bicep to the crowd to indicate I'm swimming for them. They go mad. Next to me in lane seven, Tarnee White grins at me nervously when she sees the home crowd erupt.

Then we're up on the blocks and the crowd falls silent. I stare at the unbroken water in front of me.

Well, this is new, I think. I give a nervous grin. *I guess while I'm here I may as well give it a crack.*

Then we're off.

I get away okay and relax into my stroke.

Susie O'Neill once told me: 'Pretend there are black curtains on either side of your lane so you don't see anyone else's race.' I use her advice now. I put my head down and swim my own race. I will do this my way. I will do it myself.

If I had glanced up, I would have seen that, off to my right, Penny Heyns gets a flying start and immediately takes the lead. Next to me Megan Quann pulls ahead. This girl is not mucking around. She is doing her bit. But this is still the Penny Heyns show, and by the 25-metre mark the South African is ahead of the pack by a healthy metre. Quann and Poewe are battling it out for second.

Penny turns first, hitting the wall in 31.10. She's 0.6 seconds off world-record time. Unaware of what the others are doing, I'm a little off the pace now. I turn in fifth place, but my curtains are up and I don't know and don't care. As we head into the second fifty, Penny still leads the charge, with Quann and Agnes Kovacs from Hungary both picking up the pace. But I am digging deep – working hard – I am giving this thing my very best shot.

It's all down to Penny Heyns and Megan Quann – until suddenly I'm the one picking up pace. I'm coming from nowhere. I'm hitting my stride. There's ten metres to go and I'm taking no prisoners. I mow down Kovacs and Poewe and – was that Penny Heyns? Suddenly there's a chance I might win this thing.

I am oblivious to everyone else in the pool. Megan Quann is now half a body length in front, but I don't see her. I focus on my own race. I'm coming up fast. I'm giving it my all. *Harder! C'mon, LJ! You've got this!* I will myself on. My legs are burning, my lungs are on fire. My forearms feel like they've been hit with a mallet. *This is what all your training is for! This is your time!* I don't know it yet, but Megan Quann, the unknown from the USA, is the only thing now between me and Olympic gold. *I can do this! I'm doing this! I am!* I push myself onwards but the wall gets in the way.

I pull up fast and hard, gasping for air. My lungs and muscles are on fire. I'm all red cheeks and yellow cap as I turn and squint at the scoreboard. I drag my goggles up onto my forehead as I wait for the numbers to appear – to make sense of what just happened.

5 – 1; 6 – 2.

I squint at the digits.

Wait, *what?* Did I just get second? Did I just come second at the *Olympic Games?* Somewhere, in another universe to mine, a television camera is zooming in on my confused face. I squint some more. Megan Quann has touched first and won the gold. And she's done it in 1:07.05, only 0:00.03 seconds outside the Olympic record. I have come second in a time of 1:07.49. It is a personal best for me. I am absolutely stunned. Shell-shocked. I never, ever dreamt this might happen. I am ecstatic, of course, but mostly just dazed. *Is this really happening? Is this real?* I wonder.

Beside me, Megan Quann is screaming, jumping and waving her arms in the air. She's as surprised by her performance as the rest of us are. I manage a half smile as I wave to the crowd. They're chanting my name like I'm some sort of rock star, some sort of god. I am bewildered.

I lean on the lane rope and call out, 'Megan?' But she's too busy going crazy to hear my small voice. Eventually, she leans over and hugs Sarah Poewe, the South African in lane four. Further along in lane two, our queen, Penny Heyns, has got bronze. Megan Quann and I are just kids, teenagers. Megan is sixteen and I turned fifteen last month. We're almost a decade younger than Penny Heyns, and yet here we are, taking out the top two positions. My time of 1:07.49 has smashed Samantha Riley's Australian and Commonwealth records. I wouldn't believe it if I couldn't see the board. Over in lane seven, Tarnee White, my Redcliffe rival, came seventh. I wave, but she can't see me through the madness.

The crowd is chanting 'Leisel! Leisel!' so I get out of the pool and wave to them.

Then I pause. *What do I do now? Do I congratulate other people? Is there an official I need to see?* I need someone to tell me what to do.

But before I know it, Linley Frame, a former Olympic breaststroker herself, is by my side with a microphone in her hand. I shift gears and compose myself, think about what I should say.

'Leisel Jones, congratulations!' Linley says. 'You're fifteen. Your life's changed so much in the last few months. Did you imagine this, though?'

That's an easy one. 'No!' I say honestly. 'Never a silver medal at the Olympics. Oh my God!' I put my hand to my mouth to indicate my shock – and there are my racing-red nails for the world to see.

Linley asks if I took it out a bit faster in the first fifty than in my earlier heats.

'I think I did take it out a bit hard,' I agree, 'but Ken was always saying that if I come out of the first fifty, if I'm first, well I've got a great home leg, so I could have got first.'

Wait. Did I just say on national television that I could have got first? I blink blindly at the light on the side of the camera. My face flushes. Around me, a thousand bulbs are flashing in my face. I panic. I can't come across as ungracious, not even for a moment. I am thrilled with second. I am over the moon. But how to convey this? How do I let people know?

'But I'm very happy with it!' I add quickly, meaning my second-place swim. My place on the team. My place in the universe.

Even if it's not genuine – which in this case it is – this is what you have to do when you win. Nobody likes a sore loser. For years and years, each day in training you tell yourself, *I have to get first, I have to get first.* Nothing else will do. Nothing else matters. Then, in those first moments after you've swum your race, in the blink of an eye, while you're still working out what just went on, what actually happened, and with 20,000 screaming fans bellowing your name, you must flick the switch, turn up your smile, look at the camera and say, 'Oh, I'm so happy with second. Second is just peachy!' You work so hard for first, but must immediately be seen to be thrilled with second, even while the adrenaline is still pumping so hard you're not sure *what's* happened.

I turn to Linley. 'Can I say one more thing?'

She nods and I grin and face the camera. '"Hi" to all my friends at swimming! I know you wanted me to say "hi"! So there you go!' And just for good measure I flash my red nails again.

I might only be young, but old habits die hard.

~

After my race, everything is new. There is the experience of the medal ceremony (new). Of standing on the dais with the Australian flag being raised behind me (new). And of the weight of a real Olympic medal in my hand (very new). It's about the size of a large watch face and feels as heavy as a couple of king-sized Mars bars. I think back to Col and his Mars bars at Burpengary. That was only a year or two ago, but it feels like decades.

Standing on the dais I try to look professional. But how? Do I smile? Or should I try for something more reverential? I wish I'd had time to get a blow dry. *Focus, LJ!* I chide myself. *Now, more than ever, you don't want to miss a thing!* But if I think too hard about it, I start to freak out. *Holy crap, I just got a silver medal at the freakin' Olympics?* My mind spins and I start to shake. I am better, I decide, when I think about my hair.

I am on cloud nine after my race, but I can't go out and celebrate. I am too young to get into any bars and even if I wasn't, I wouldn't be allowed to go out partying: I still have races to swim. But it doesn't matter: I host my own private celebration party, alone in my room, and I eat three boxes of McDonald's cookies. I picked them up from the dining hall after my medal ceremony and now, when I put that first biscuit in my mouth it tastes of sweet, sweet success. It's been so many years since I've been allowed to eat a Macca's cookie that this tastes pretty damn like celebration to me. So tasty! So crunchy! This is victory in a biscuit.

Later in the week I swim in the final of the women's 4 × 100-metre medley relay. I didn't take part in the heats (Tarnee looked after the breaststroke leg), but because of my individual racing times this week I step into the team for the final race. I can imagine what Tarnee thinks about that. I know how I would feel. Still, that's the way it works.

Our team for the final is amazing: Dyana Calub, Petria Thomas, Susie O'Neill. And me. I want to laugh when I see them standing together in their Kermit-green robes in the marshalling area – these swimming legends, these idols of mine. I want to laugh, want to cry. *What am I doing here?* I wonder for the millionth time in my life.

Dyana gets us off to a great start with the backstroke leg, and as she powers back to the wall for her second fifty, she's hot on the heels of the formidable USA, our rivals. But today Dyana is giving them hell. There's less than a second in it as she approaches the wall. I should feel elated but I can only find terror. *What if I stuff this up? What if we lose and it's my fault?* I swallow hard and I can taste my fear. I set my mouth grimly and get ready to dive.

Slap – blink – splash. Dyana is home and I'm in the pool. I put my head down and I swim for all I'm worth. I've swum in relays before, plenty of them, at club and state level. But never in an Olympic final and never with legends like this. I try to forget that Susie O'Neill is standing at the end of my lane, sweating on my every stroke.

Slap – swish – push. I hit the 50-metre mark and turn hard. My turn is fast and I don't waste a second looking to see where the Americans are. I don't want to know. I just keep my head down and power on. I hit the wall in 1:08.08. It's a good time, more than a second faster than Tarnee's time in the heats, yet I'm still worried.

I watch Petria butterfly like a demon. Then Susie, our anchor leg, brings it home hard. In the end, we finish second. Another Olympic silver medal!

We cheer and high-five each other; we hug with joy.

The USA have won in 3:58.30 – a new world record. And we set an Oceania record. Japan came in third and they're ecstatic with that. The Japanese girls bounce around the pool deck, grinning.

But I can't shake the feeling that I have let my team down. *Was I too inexperienced? Too slow on my changeovers maybe?* My teammates are full of praise but I am quick to criticise myself.

The day after the medal ceremony, I take out my telephone card, the one issued to every member of the Australian team, and I use a payphone to call Mum.

'Hey, it's me.'

'Leisel?' Mum sounds surprised to hear from me.

She's staying with her sister, Morny, and her brother-in-law, Jeff, in the north-west Sydney suburb of Ryde. She's seen me at the pool complex a few times, and we spent some time together after my 100-metre final, but we haven't really been in touch much during the Games. Mum will stay with Morny and Jeff until the Games are over, but given how little we've been able to see each other, she may as well be back in Queensland already really.

'Yeah. It's me. How are you going Mum?'

'Good. Morny and I have just been watching the women's basketball on TV. Leisel, are you alright?'

I could say: *Am I alright? Mum, I've just won two Olympic silver medals! Of course I'm alright. I'm on top of the world!* But Mum knows me better than that.

'Um, yeah. It's just, I was thinking... I might kinda be ready to go home.'

There's a pause while Mum considers this. 'Home?'

'Yeah. Like, um, now I've finished racing maybe I could come and stay with you and Morny? Or maybe we could just head back home? Not much point hanging around...' I trail off.

'Leisel, has something happened?'

'What? No, no, nothing like that. It's just, you know. I dunno. It's a bit lonely here, I guess. And I just wondered what my friends at school are up to...'

Because amid all this newness, amid all these foreign and exciting things – or perhaps because of them – another feeling has emerged. I am homesick. I miss Mum and my friends. I am lonely in the village. I don't know many people and there's no-one my age here. Everyone is so busy, so focused on their jobs, and I am lost, awkward and shy, and I want to go home.

Mum and I talk for a bit and she's patient with me. She's softly-spoken and considered, but she's also very firm. 'Leisel, don't you think you might regret it if you leave now you've finished racing?'

Maybe, I concede.

'I know it's hard and that you don't have your friends around you, but this is an amazing thing you're experiencing. An Olympic Games here in Australia. This won't come around again. This is once-in-a-lifetime, Leisel.'

She is right, of course. As far as first major meets go, swimming at an Olympic Games, in your own country, at the turn of a millennium, is the pinnacle. Most people begin their careers with a Pan Pacs or, if they're lucky, a World Champs. But an Olympics? The size, the scope, the pure festival madness of it all... The Olympic Games are a whole new level of crazy. They're bigger and louder than anything else on earth. To be exposed to this so early in my career is such an advantage for me. It should mean that everything that comes afterwards will feel like a cakewalk.

Or maybe an anti-climax.

And I didn't expect the feeling to hit me quite so soon.

The Sydney Olympics have been incredible. My medals are amazing. It will take months, maybe years, for me to fully comprehend the last couple of weeks. But right now? I am ready to pack up and head home.

'Stay,' Mum urges me. 'Stay and soak it up and try to enjoy yourself. Oh and Leisel, promise me one thing?'

'Sure,' I say uncertainly.

'Go to the Closing Ceremony, will you? No matter what happens during the next few days, going to the Ceremony will give you closure.'

'Uh, sure thing, Mum.'

Closure? I just want a buddy, someone to hang out with. But Mum thinks I need closure?

Nonetheless, I promise Mum I will get some closure. And I promise her I will hang around for the final week of competition and try to have some fun.

One of the main problems is that at fifteen I can't go out drinking with the rest of the team, and that seems to be the main way they let their hair down. I could sneak out, of course. Use a fake ID. But that's hard to do when the whole country knows your face. When you're 'that famous kid from the Olympics, the one who's just fifteen'. No bouncer is ever going to fall for it.

But I bunker down to try to have some fun. I go and watch some of the other sports events, tagging along with some of the older kids on my team. And I march in the Closing Ceremony, although I'm not sure if it really brings closure.

It will be years before I get much of that in my life.

7

Training for Gold

Here's the worst-kept secret in swimming: everyone wees in the pool. The boys are the worst, turning the pool orange with their vitamin-infused pee, or swimming out to tread water at the 5-metre mark for no reason other than it's 4.45 a.m., it's cold and dark and they can't be bothered getting out of the pool to wee. A bloom of orange trails them back to the wall like an algae bloom. Some people sit on the grate at the side of the pool to do it. It's a little less antisocial than doing it right in the pool, but gross all the same.

Personally, I prefer to make the trek to the toilets. Aside from anything else, it's a good way to waste some time and miss a few sets.

There's trouble when the new 'super suits' are introduced. Ever tried weeing when you're cling-wrapped in rubber? There's nowhere for it to go. It's like taking a bath in a hot pool of wee. These things are not designed with weeing in mind.

Pool peeing etiquette. Cold mornings. Early starts . . .

Life returns to normal after the Sydney Olympics. I slip straight back into my old routine. It's nice to be home. The Olympics were amazing but I'm more of an everyday life kind of person. I like the rhythm of hard work, the routine of training. I'm more comfortable in Redcliffe than on the world stage, any day. And while winning two silver medals at the Olympics was incredible, it's only made me more determined to win gold.

I'm still training with Ken, and it's still as intense as ever. I am up each morning at 4.10 a.m. and standing outside the roller doors of the pool twenty minutes later. But before we can get wet, the covers have to be pulled off the pool. This is a job for the youngest of the team, with no exceptions. Being an Olympian doesn't grant you any special favours at squad. As the runt, every morning my freezing hands drag on the wet metal wheel and the rollers inch the covers off the pool. I haul and scrape and slip and ache. I get a workout before I get in the water.

We drag down our trackies and shiver and whinge. Then Ken appears on deck, handing out A4-sized whiteboards and issuing us with chinagraph pencils. We take our pencils and begin to write down today's drill:

Tues. AM.

4 × 250 free/back

8 × 50 drill

3 × 400 individual medley on 6 min 30 sec

5 × 500 freestyle

4 × 200 paddles and fins

10 × 50 kick/drag

So we're doing a one-kilometre warm-up today, alternating between freestyle and backstroke. Then a 400-metre drill. Our main set includes individual medley (all strokes), plus 2.5 kilometres of freestyle. This is followed by a swim-down using paddles and fins for 800 metres, and then finally 500 metres of kicking, wearing a drag suit. That's almost 6.5 kilometres all up.

Faces drop. Lips pout. But there is no such thing as an easy session.

We scribble down our sessions from Ken's main board, then stick our pencils to the board with a blob of Blu Tack stuck on the end. We will use the Blu Tack again at the end of the week to rub off our sessions after they've been recorded in our logbooks.

Right now, though, we kick off our thongs and slap on our goggles. We are in the water at 4.45 a.m., running and diving and breaking the glass-like surface. Maximum impact. Minimum cold. We do anything to get out of this cold morning air.

There are tears this morning, just as there are most days. Stinging eyes, goggles full. 'It's the chlorine!' we say if anyone notices us sniffling through each set or sobbing at the turns. *Why am I doing this? I want to go home.* Will this be my mantra forever? *I want to go home.*

One hour gone. Then slowly, another. And then at last the session is over. *I survived! I made it!* And suddenly things don't seem so bad. A hot shower. A bowl of cereal. Now we're all laughing and joking and mucking around. 'Nice goggle marks!' 'Who nicked my deodorant?' And then: 'See you again this arvo!' Because remember? We're doing this all over again this afternoon after school.

Training never changes. It never will.

The other thing that doesn't change – will never change – is Ken. It's like he prides himself on it. He is consistently tough, consistently consistent. This man will be poolside for the rest of his life.

So when event camp rolls around, we know what to expect from Ken. Event camps are held each year and bring together the top fifteen swimmers at that time in a particular stroke. This year, the breaststrokers are off to Cairns. All the top coaches are invited along. The idea is that we'll all bond a little and have a break from our usual training routine, while getting some valuable racing experience.

But Ken sees event camp as an opportunity for one thing and one thing only: showing off. With all the best coaches in Australia assembled in one place, and the cream of the competition there, just asking to be psyched out, Ken is in his element. He's at his gruelling, merciless best. *Look what I make my swimmers do!* his walk says. He strides poolside, his pants hoisted high. *You call that a set? This is a set!* His mouth twitches under his ever-present black toothbrush moustache.

Ken isn't satisfied unless he has worn down the best swimmers that the rest of the country has to offer.

We start our day with 5 × [4 × 50 brst – 45 on 3:30]: four lots of 50-metre breaststroke (that is, 200 metres of breaststroke in total), and each lap on a 45-second time cycle. I do the lap in about 36 seconds, which means I have 9 seconds to rest before it's time to go again. This whole set is on 3:30 minutes, which leaves me with about 30 seconds of rest between each round. And there are five rounds, or 1 kilometre, of this to endure.

Or then there's 20 × 100-metre breaststroke, with each 100 metres to be completed in 1:30 minutes. That's about 30 minutes of solid swimming, on a freestyle time cycle. I know professional swimmers who couldn't do two laps that quickly in freestyle, let alone breaststroke! I touch the wall at 1:24 and have six seconds to catch my breath before I have to go again. And we are supposed to keep this up for 30 minutes?

Or the worst one: 20 × 100-metre breaststroke/freestyle combinations on 1:30, with a dive. That means one lap of breaststroke, then one lap of freestyle, quickly jump out of the pool and then dive in again. And this whole rigmarole is to happen in under 90 seconds. And be repeated for half an hour.

It is insanity. People cry. People throw up at the side of the pool. People drop out, one by one, until I am the only person left in the pool. Which is exactly what Ken wanted. *Look at me!* his demeanour shouts. He strides along the pool deck, trying not to grin. *Look at me and my fifteen-year-old prodigy with the Olympic-sized heart!* He keeps pace with me, walking along the edge of the pool and willing me on.

There's no-one else in the whole of Australia who can keep up with me right now. There's no-one in Australia who's dumb enough to try. Ken's sets are gruelling. They're ridiculous. But because he is my coach, because the gauntlet has been thrown down, I plough on. I will make this happen. I will cry and quiver and burn till it is done.

When it is done, I am inwardly proud. But I am also fuming. I am raging about how Ken went about it. I hate showing off. I hate being watched. If I'd completed those sets at home, in private, unnoticed by anyone else, I would be happy. But to do it here in front of everyone else? That's not my style.

I am still fuming later that day when we all go out on a boat trip to the Great Barrier Reef. We're bonding, us breaststrokers, us fish people, at the Reef. Bonding by spending an afternoon out of the water: on top of it instead of in it for a change. Tarnee White is here, and all the boys from our team, including Regan Harrison, Ryan Mitchell and Brenton Rickard. Regan is my mate, but Ryan intimidates me. He's so suave, so confident. Confident people scare me. But we're all here today, all in it together.

Once we're out at the reef, we get the chance to jump in the water again. People plop over the side to scuba-dive.

I'm on my way to get kitted out when Ken approaches and stops me. 'You're not going in.'

'Huh?'

'You're not allowed to swim. I don't want you swimming.'

I don't want you swimming. Coming from Ken, these words sound comical: ridiculous.

'What do you mean? That's what I do. I swim.'

I don't add: *And you're not my dad. You can't tell me what to do.* But I'd dearly love to.

'You're not swimming here,' he says. 'Not in the ocean. You'll get an ear infection.'

Then he wanders off and joins the rest of the coaching staff.

If I was riled before, now I am seriously mad. *Who does he think he is? He can't tell me what to do!*

But he can and he does. He is my coach and is not to be argued with. Because of my age, my relationship with Ken is very much a parent–child one. I am the kid he never had. I am by far the youngest swimmer in his charge, so he takes his responsibilities with me very seriously. I am allowed no opportunity to make mistakes (or to learn any consequences from making them).

To be fair, Ken is more of a father than my real father ever was. He is also much stricter than Mum: Mum is a firm believer in skinning a knee rather than being wrapped in cottonwool. She's a have-a-go Mum, a be-it-on-your-own-head Mum. She's fail-and-learn, not stay-safe-at-home.

When Dad left, Mum said things were up to me now as far as staying in touch with him went. 'It is completely your choice,' she said, 'whether you stay in contact with your father or not. If you choose to still see him, if that makes you happy, then go for it. But I will not have an opinion. It has to come from you.' We were in the car on the way to training when she said that. Given what she was going through at the time – the separation, adjusting to being a single parent – I was impressed with her strength. She was not in touch with my father at all, but she was happy to support me if I stayed in contact. She was adamant: 'I am not going to persuade you either way. This is your choice. It is your decision. I can't make it for you.'

Ken, on the other hand, is more than happy to make my choices for me, more than happy to stop me from diving on the Great Barrier Reef in the pristine ocean waters that are probably ten times cleaner than some of the pools I swim in every day.

I'm sure he didn't tell Geoff Huegill not to go in the water. Geoff would have said, 'Screw you!' And rightly so.

But I cannot say that. I am little Leisel. So, after all my back-breaking hard work in the pool that morning, I miss out on scuba-diving in the afternoon. According to Ken, I am too young and too precious to risk getting hurt. I am his little protégé. Everyone else is allowed to go swimming but my little ear canals are too sensitive. Yeah, right! I am old enough to train in the water all morning long, but by mid-afternoon I am too young to go swimming? Ridiculous. I've swum with a broken toe before! That didn't stop me training. But now he's worried about my ear canals? I scowl. I sit with crossed arms. He makes me feel like a racehorse, not a teenage girl, like my body is a machine to be maintained, not to be enjoyed. I have no control, no independence.

My relationship with Ken is reaching its limits.

There's no time to dwell on this now though; I've got other things to worry about. Shiny things. Gleaming things. We are off to the World Championships in July and this time I want gold.

~

The 2001 World Aquatic Championships are to be held in Fukuoka, Japan. They will be two weeks of top-notch competition; every major swimming nation in the world (more than twenty countries) will be represented. In terms of prestige and significance, the Worlds are a big deal. But while Fukuoka will be impressive – the Marine Messe indoor pool, for instance, will seat 10,000 spectators and cost US$4 million for the two-week period – it won't be the same as Sydney last year.

And that's a good thing! I think to myself. In Sydney I won silver, and this time it will be gold.

Gold, gold, gold.

I was a wildcard in Sydney. No-one, least of all me, seriously thought I would make the final. No-one dreamt I'd win silver. But now in Fukuoka, the pressure is slowly beginning to mount. It's mostly coming from me, but there is talk from other quarters too. There's a bit of buzz, a little bit of hype. After Sydney, people are more used to seeing me on the podium in the green and gold. They've come to view it as normal. But they are also aware that I am still two months' shy of my sixteenth birthday, and so no-one dares to hope for too much yet.

I, on the other hand, expect the world. World Championship gold. Gold, gold, gold.

~

At the team hotel in Fukuoka one morning, our manager gathers us together for the birthday of one of our teammates. When we're assembled, a cake is produced. A real cake! Chocolate frosting and everything! We are hushed with reverence. A cake is good. A cake is a big deal. Our team dietician is in charge of birthday food around here, and normally we're only allowed a cupcake or a mini-mud cake – something tiny and portion-controlled, often in a serving for one, which means the birthday boy or girl gets to eat while the rest of us stand around salivating. But this time the dietician has gone all out. She's been to the beautiful cake store out the front of the hotel and found us a cake in the shape of a fish.

'I couldn't resist it,' she tells us. 'I know it's big, but a fish just seemed so appropriate for swimmers.'

The cake could be in the shape of a donkey for all we care. It's cake, it's covered in chocolate and it's big enough to share: that's all we care about.

We dutifully sing 'Happy Birthday'.

Then the birthday girl blows out the candles while we all stand around wishing she'd hurry up and cut the cake.

'Is it good? I bet it's good!' We're all jostling and shoving and fighting over the forks.

Then the birthday girl lifts that first sweet, sweet piece of cake to her mouth, she takes a bite, and she – spits it out? We watch aghast as this beautiful object, this thing of joy, falls from her mouth and spills apart on the carpet.

'Oh my God! Is that salmon?'

The birthday girl spits and coughs and we laugh. We have to hold one another up we laugh so hard. Because underneath the chocolate frosting, buried among the sponge cake, are bold pink flakes of tinned salmon.

The fish cake is fish. It's really salmon.

That's it! The dietician is banned from all future birthdays!

~

I'm competing in both the 100-metres and the 200-metres at this meet. I've been playing around with the 200-metres for a while now at training, but Fukuoka marks my international debut in this distance.

While my racing schedule might have expanded, my training routine remains 100 per cent the same. Under Ken, my race warm-up for any race, regardless of distance, looks like this: first, I swim 400 metres of alternate freestyle and backstroke (that is, 50 metres of freestyle, then 50 metres of backstroke, alternating until I reach 400 metres). Then it's 5 × 100 metres of freestyle and backstroke, only this time I 'descend one to five' (that is, I get faster with every 100-metre set). Next is six laps of 50-metre 'open'. 'Open' means 'explode out of the blocks', or swim breaststroke as fast as you bloody well can. This is followed by 35 metres of freestyle, and this continues for six laps. But for those first 15 metres of each lap, you should be going flat out. Sometimes these laps are 'open and closed', which means swimming flat out for the last 15 metres too (so, flooring it for the first *and* last 15 metres of each 50). Finally, I do dive sprints to finish. This means diving in, swimming 50 metres 'descending' again (so building my speed), then jumping out at the end, turning around, diving in and doing it again.

Then there are the drills. One 'pull' of your arms to every two kicks. Or 'submarine' breaststroke, which is breaststroke underwater. Or breaststroke 'pull' but with a butterfly kick; this one we do using flippers or 'fins' too.

After this is the medley work, where I swim a variety of strokes to get all my muscles moving, and by this time I'm feeling pretty warm. To stay warm, I go and have a long, hot shower, then I dry off, put my suit on and have about 40 minutes before my race to get myself mentally revved-up too.

All in all, I swim a minimum of 1500 metres to warm up for a 100-metre race. For the 200-metre event, I swim two kilometres, which is a lot of swimming for a pretty short race. My warm-ups never change. And while I like the routine – I find the familiarity of it comforting – I do wonder if it's really necessary.

∼

My meet in Fukuoka is a strange mix of triumph and defeat, highs and lows. A combo as weird as salmon and sponge. Despite all my plans for gold and glory, and despite two very promising swims in the heats and the semis of the 100 metres, I go on to lose in the final. I come second to China's Luo Xuejuan. It's a race I was supposed to win and I am devastated. I get silver when I really should have got gold. I seem to be developing a bad habit of that.

My race plan for the final was the same as ever: go out and swim hard. This is all I know. There's no planning, no tactics. I swim sans strategy. It's more than that, though: I have not yet learnt how to win, how to put a race together. I need to learn how to compete. I need to learn how to have control. In terms of mental composure, I am all over the shop, and my racing technique is haphazard at best.

I am carrying my 100-metre defeat with me when I swim the 200 metres later that week. It is weighing heavily on me. And yet I should be pleased to be swimming in the 200-metre event at all. Just to be competing in this distance is a milestone. I qualify for the final but miss out on a medal, coming fourth with a time of 2:25.46. It's respectable for my first attempt, but somehow I still feel disappointed. Fourth is so close, yet so far. Almost, but just not enough.

After my individual finals, I feel low – but then things turn around with the medley relay. I swim with Dyana Calub again, but this time we also swim with Petria Thomas and Sarah Ryan. And incredibly – unbelievably – the four of us win. We beat the Americans. The Americans! They whipped us at Sydney last year, but now we return the favour. We win gold in a heart-stopping time of 4:01.50 to their 4:01.81; it is the first time the USA have been beaten at world or Olympic level in this event. Ever.

What's more, Australia beats the Yanks in the overall gold medal count as well, meaning we assume the global number one ranking in swimming for the first time since the 1956 Melbourne Olympic Games.

We're number one! We are ecstatic. We sing bye-bye to that American pie all the way back to Oz.

8

Under Pressure

I come home from Fukuoka to face a drug test. It's nothing to do with me or my results; it's just a regular part of the job. Drug testing is the worst thing about swimming. As soon as you become a professional swimmer, you must register with ASADA (Australian Sports Anti-Doping Authority), WADA (World Anti-Doping Agency) and FINA (Fédération Internationale de Natation) – a whole alphabet soup of organisations – to prove you are not taking drugs. Every three months, you have to go online and fill out a three-page questionnaire for FINA and ASADA, called your 'Whereabouts', specifying where you will be for one hour per day, every day, for the next three months. You have to tell them where you will be, when you will be there, what you will be doing and where you were the night before. There are bail conditions more lenient than this. Then, whenever ASADA or WADA or another organisation is in the neighbourhood, they pop by for a visit and you have to pee in a cup with the toilet door open, to show you are clean.

Let me be clear: I am not against drug testing per se. Not at all. In fact, I think these organisations do an admirable job keeping our sport clean. And it's not like I've got anything to hide.

My problem is with the process. Pee in a cup? With the toilet door open? Really? There's got to be a better way.

But if there is, ASADA hasn't heard about it. They are here again at training this morning. They come once a month, picking people at random for testing. In my registration log, I told them I'd be here at the Redcliffe pool, from 4.30 a.m. onwards, six days a week, ready and able to pee (just not overly willing). Thank God I'm not sick, or stuck in traffic. Because if you say you'll be somewhere and you're not there when they arrive, you get a strike against your name. Three strikes, and you're banned from the sport, which, in theory, makes it possible to get a life ban for being tardy. Or being bad with online logbooks. This is a staggering thought. So I am glad I'm here this morning, even if it does mean being tested. I only wish I hadn't just had a wee ...

Drug testing is all part of the job for me: the job of swimming, which is now my day job. My all-day, every day, no-holiday-pay job. At the end of Year 10, after I get back from the Fukuoka World Champs, I quit school.

I leave school, I have turned sixteen, and life is sweet.

Like everything else, leaving school was my choice: my decision, on my terms. Mum said it was up to me. But it didn't feel like there was much of a choice. In 2001, at Southern Cross Catholic College, there is not much support for someone who is underwater for more than thirty hours per week. The Queensland school curriculum doesn't allow for my training, doesn't accommodate my absences. I can do Years 11 and 12 over three years instead of two, but in reality that won't be enough. Getting a free period here or there is nice, but it's hardly enough time for me to complete the mountain of missed work that's fast piling up. There's no way I can swim 100-plus kilometres each week, travel to international competitions and complete Years 11 and 12 – and there is no other option. We don't have enough money for a tutor; we barely have enough for school, even with a sports scholarship. So I leave.

'I can always finish my QCE later,' I say to Mum. *Yeah, right, like I'm going to do that.* I shove my uniform to the back of my wardrobe.

But what I think of at the time as liberation turns out to be something else altogether. After training each morning, I bypass the school gates and head blithely home to – what? Several hours of uninterrupted stewing? A long stretch of worrying, stressing and overthinking? With the distraction of school gone, I spend my days planning, dwelling and generally obsessing. There is no point in my day when I am not thinking about swimming. And at the end of a slow day spent entirely in my own company, I am back at the pool for training again, swimming up and down in my own silent world.

It's not that I'm bored: far from it. I'm too industrious for that. I divide my time methodically between exercises, strength training, eating and sleeping. I am a swimming machine, an aquatic android. But while quitting school removes the stress of study from my life, I seem to double my worries with my increased focus on sport.

It all puts a lot of pressure on my swimming. I no longer have an escape route, a Plan B. *If I don't have swimming, I don't have anything*, I say to myself. This is not helpful in any way, but it's something I bring to every race. *If I'm not good at this, what am I good at?*

Socially, I miss out too. Because I leave school early, I never go to a school formal, never go to a dance. I don't go to the movies at the weekend; my only friends are swimming friends and we're all too busy swimming. I don't go to parties (not that I am really a party person). I miss out on all that normal teenage stuff – the bad music, the messy drinking and the long-haired boys.

I do have a boyfriend though. His name is Trevor Whitehead and I meet him – where else? – at a swimming carnival. Trevor is a surfie who lives on the Gold Coast. He swims for the Palm Beach

Currumbin Swimming Club, and each weekend, after Saturday morning training, I shower and wash my hair, then drive thirty minutes down the coast to Trevor's house. We spend the weekend hanging at the beach: he on his board, me on the sand. In my time off I really appreciate staying dry. I stay at his place on Saturday night and then drive home again on Sunday. Trevor is tanned and ripped in that surfing way. And I'm pretty sure that Mum hates him. You could say Trevor is my nod towards normality, a slice of the life I left behind when I left school.

During that first summer after I leave Southern Cross, many things change: my routine, my focus, my friendships. But the newest and strangest thing of all is that, for the first time in my life, I have money. I have sponsorships that earn me an income. At first they are low-key, a bit of fun. But soon I am offered bigger and more lucrative deals. Innoxa and Thalgo and Speedo sign on. So too do Ford and Uncle Tobys. The fine print varies between each arrangement, but mostly I am required to make several public appearances per year, wear or use their products and swim fast. Really, really fast. *I can do that!* I think. *Choose me! Trust me!*

I am sixteen when I buy my first house. With a mortgage, of course. I am mortgaged up to my goggle marks. But it's a home and it's ours and – unlike my dad – our house can't up and walk away one day. Mum and I live in my house in Redcliffe together, Mum teaching swimming part-time and me swimming to pay for the rest of the mortgage. It doesn't occur to me that it's not normal for a sixteen-year-old to be the breadwinner of the household or that not everyone my age is buying houses.

What does occur to me, though, is that I have responsibilities. I have a full-time job and a mortgage and household bills to pay. My swimming pays for just about everything. Mum is still earning the minimum wage, and Dad left us in an enormous financial hole.

So even with all of my sponsorship deals, we're not yet back in the black. I might have been to the Olympics and broken world records, but we're heavily in debt.

'If you leave swimming, what will you do?' Mum asks whenever I am fed up or tired or feeling despondent. I know that in her own funny way – her pragmatic Mum kind of way – she's trying to be encouraging. But I feel the pressure to support her all the more.

If I leave swimming, what will I do? Swimming is no longer fun. It is simply a job now. I'm working so hard to pay off the house and support me and Mum. The pool is a workplace; swimming is my profession. Because I didn't finish school, I can't go to uni anytime soon. So if I'm not swimming laps then I'll be a bum, won't I? How can I hope to pay the mortgage? At least, that's how it feels to me. And if I screw up, it'll all be my fault. I've got nothing to fall back on. If I screw up I can't go home to Mum's with my tail between my legs and ask her to help me out. *Ding dong! Hi Mum, what's for dinner? Mind if I move back in for a while?* I can't do that, because my mum lives with *me*.

So now every race, every swim meet, every international competition feels like a risk. *Don't screw up. Don't blow this. You can't afford to lose!* This is what I tell myself every time I'm on the blocks.

It is what I am thinking when I put on the green and gold and head to the Manchester Commonwealth Games.

~

The Commonwealth Games are more relaxed than the Olympics and much more low-key, given that many of the big swimming nations, such as the USA, aren't included. When we arrive, the Manchester pool feels dark and dingy somehow, although that might just be because of the weather outside. Since swimming is a summer sport, we get used to perpetual sunshine as we travel the world to compete, so the grey skies of Manchester are something of a shock. So too are our dorms. That's right: we're sleeping in dorms in the athletes' village in Manchester, complete with bunk beds and everything. Our accommodation is never glamorous, but these bunk beds are something else. It's like being back on school camp. It's like the Girl Guides I never joined.

Bunk beds aside, Manchester is a great meet for me. I win the 100-metre and 200-metre breaststroke events. These are my very first titles on the international stage, and my heart swells when I stand on the podium and hear our national anthem playing for me. Mum isn't here to watch me at these Games, because she couldn't afford to come, but I can imagine her at home, cheering and crying with joy in front of the TV. I can't summon tears myself though: I'm too busy feeling relieved.

I did it! I made it! I've survived another day.

I might have just won my first international title, but I am still just sixteen years old, and I'm all on my own.

Except when I'm peeing: the ASADA guys like to be there for that.

9

Stilnox Days

It's 2003, and I'm in Barcelona. We are here for the World Championships, and it's an important meet, because next year is an Olympic year. The Worlds serve as something of a practice run for the Olympics.

I am queuing in the hotel dining room with the rest of the Australian team. It's lunchtime and we're hungry. Hungry in the way that swimming kilometres makes you hungry. Achingly hungry. Delirious, desperate and dreaming of carbs. The line for food snakes around the dining hall. It looks orderly enough, but peer a little closer and you'll see it's first in, first served. Youngest to the back! Respect your elders! Stacks on! Over here! The boys push and laugh.

I pick up my plate, knife and fork, and take my place near the end of the queue. In front of me, two guys are talking and gesturing, but I can't make out what they're saying.

Then all of a sudden the younger one, the one with a shock of sandy hair, turns to me and points his fork at me. I blink and back away in surprise. He stares at me. Without any hint of humour, he says, 'I wouldn't waste my time.' He turns his back to me again.

He wouldn't waste his time on what? I'm stunned. I put down my plate and cutlery, and hurry away. *What did he mean? Is it some kind of joke? Is he saying I'm insignificant? What have I ever done to him?*

I know this boy. He started on the team only a year or so before me and we share the same management team. We could be friends; I'd like to be friends. But from what I've seen, he has trouble letting people in. I've watched him chatting with other people on the team, having a great time, getting along famously – and then, out of nowhere, he'll cut them down. 'That was really dumb,' he'll say and walk off leaving them speechless. Even now, after this incident, I wouldn't say he's malicious, or even particularly mean. Just warped. He has a warped sense of humour.

He's a big deal at these World Champs, though. He's having a good meet. With three gold, one silver and one bronze at this meet alone, this kid is a household name. You might remember him from the Sydney Olympics? His name is Ian Thorpe.

~

There are a few new names in the Australian swimming team at Barcelona. A few new ones, and some old ones missing. Kieren Perkins retired after Sydney 2000. So did Susie O'Neill. We may be heading into the meet with the world number one ranking, but this new-look Australian team has something to prove.

Another big name who is missing is South African Penny Heyns. For the longest time – five years at least – she has been the biggest name in women's breaststroke. Penny was born during the era of racial segregation and was South Africa's first post-apartheid Olympic gold medallist, in Atlanta in 1996. She has held a staggering fourteen individual world records during her career; she is one of the best female breaststrokers in history. A Penny Heyns record is a formidable thing. An awe-inspiring, fear-inducing thing. Now, however, Penny has hung up her togs. She bowed out graciously with a bronze at Sydney in 2000. And all the top breaststrokers are jostling to take her position.

I'm jostling too. But I've got a bit of a handicap, because there's one more new name in the Australian camp in Barcelona in 2003: Stilnox.

Stilnox is a sleeping tablet, an allegedly harmless drug. It is known for its fast absorption (peak absorption kicks in just thirty minutes after taking it) and also for its addictive nature. The side effects of Stilnox are many: they include, but are not limited to, dizziness, headaches, fatigue, nightmares, nausea, vomiting and muscle weakness. Then there's worsened insomnia, hallucinations, agitation and unexpected changes in behaviour such as rage or confusion. Oh, and don't forget sleepwalking, sleep-driving, sleep-eating and sleep-sexting. By the end of the decade, coroners will have found that Stilnox contributed to the deaths of several people who met violent and unexpected ends. For instance, there's the tragic story of Mairead Costigan, a philosophy graduate who died after falling from the Sydney Harbour Bridge during what was believed to be Stilnox-induced sleepwalking. After the *Sydney Morning Herald* reported the story, highlighting the dangerous effects of Stilnox, the paper received dozens of emails and phone calls. People knew this drug; they were frightened of it. And by 2012, the Australian Olympic Committee chiefs will have banned athletes from using it, after former Olympian Grant Hackett called Stilnox 'evil' and was admitted to rehab for his addiction to it.

But in 2003 Stilnox is still the go-to drug for Australian swimmers. Having trouble sleeping? Have a Stilnox! Bit wired? Bit tired? Got a headache? Try Stilnox! In Barcelona the team medics will provide us with a generous supply, with practically no questions asked.

Personally, I rarely have trouble sleeping. Jetlag isn't a problem for me, and I find I'm usually so buggered after training that not even the pressure-cooker environment of international competition can keep me awake. I could sleep on a barbed-wire fence. In fact, I often find myself yawning involuntarily in the marshalling area before I race. (I later learn that this is to do with thermoregulation: that it's the brain's way of increasing heart rate and blood flow to the head and cooling the brain. Once I learn this, I stop worrying about yawning and start using it to my advantage. *Sorry to yawn! But this is just so easy. I'll see you at the finish line, folks!*)

But sometimes I do suffer from the 'taper sillies'. This is a common complaint among swimmers when we 'taper off' our training so that we conserve energy ahead of a big race. As you scale down your training schedule and simultaneously scale up the excitement and nervous energy, it's much harder to sleep. Here in Barcelona, after sitting around resting all day in a hotel room, literally putting my feet up, I am wired and silly. I am bouncing off the walls.

I am rooming with medley-freestyler Jessica Abbott (Jabbott), who is only one month older than me and who seems to have just as much excess energy. We're like puppies. We can't sit still. We've made banners for our room and sung stupid songs. We've painted our nails (an oldie but a goodie) and we've watched so many movies we've exhausted the hotel's selection. We've had a lot of fun – it's been one of the best lead-ups to an international event I've ever had – but now, though, we cannot sleep.

'Should we go and see the doctor?' Jabbott asks.

'Sure. We'll get some medication,' I say.

Of course, in our team, medication equals Stilnox, and Stilnox equals crazy.

In less than an hour we are back in our room, lying on our twin beds, each with ten milligrams of the non-benzodiazepine coursing through our veins.

'Jabbott?' I ask tentatively. 'Is it just me, or is the room spinning?'

'My room's spinning too!' she shrieks.

I could reach out and touch her, our beds are so close, so the ridiculousness of what she's just said – of her having a separate room – sets us off. We're giggling and spinning. We are completely off our heads.

'This is like Alice in Wonderland!' she says.

'Like we've fallen down the rabbit hole, Jabbott. Hey, get it? Rabbit. Jabbott.'

This sets us off again. As seventeen-year-old kids (seventeen-year-olds who have never touched alcohol, let alone psychoactive z-drugs), Jabbott and I have no idea what has just been prescribed to us. I can see little creatures dancing on the end of my bed. Leprechauns and rainbows. I am rolling and spinning. We are falling on the floor.

Is this like being drunk? Like being high? I don't have any life experience to know what to compare it to. I'm guessing it's a bit like being on acid. Whatever it is, it's unlocked some part of our brains reserved for the ridiculous. Jabbott and I are hysterical.

'Electrical!'

'Chemical!'

We're having way too much fun. And as we finally drift off to sleep several hours later (probably several hours later than we would have done naturally), I think, *No wonder the rest of the team are in on this.*

That's right: pretty much everyone's doing it. Within the Australian swimming team, Stilnox is freely available at any time. It's simply a matter of presenting to the team doctors and asking for it. In fact, as Jabbott and I found out, you don't even have to request the drug by name. Just telling one of our doctors we're having trouble sleeping is enough to elicit Stilnox tablets. It's the first choice of our medics.

Admittedly, at this time everyone believed the drug to be harmless. What is staggering, however, is that once Stilnox is prescribed to us, nobody monitors our intake or our reaction to the drug. We are free to choose how much we take and how often, as we all dose ourselves. No-one warns us to be careful how much we take. It's staggering. Quite aside from the fact that many of us are still kids, all of us are elite athletes whose bodies are their livelihoods. That we are given prescription drugs so freely and with so little supervision is quite shocking.

Jabbott and I are some of the last people on the team to catch on to the Stilnox craze. While we're just starting out, some of the others have got it down to a fine art. The older swimmers teach us that for the best results you need to pop a pill then fight against sleep for the next half an hour or so. If you can get past these first thirty minutes, you get to the next stage – the fun stage – the 'high' that Jabbott and I experienced accidentally on the first night we took it.

On the international flights to and from meets, everyone on the team has competitions with one another to see who can last the longest without falling asleep. On the flight home from Barcelona, I compete against one of my teammates in the seat behind me. We both take Stilnox at the same time and then battle it out to see who can stay awake the longest. I have no recollection of what happened next, but I wake up several hours later with blisters around my lips and gums.

'Did any food come out in the last few hours?' I ask the poor guy seated next to me. He is not part of our team – just a random passenger.

'Uh, yeah,' he says tentatively. 'And it was blazing hot, but you scoffed it really fast.'

I have burnt my lips and the inside of my mouth. I have bleeding gums and a swollen tongue. Behind me, my mate had fallen asleep before his food arrived, so his mouth is spared.

'You fell asleep first!' I crow. 'I won!'

On the same flight, Travis Nederpelt, a champion butterflier from Western Australia, is hallucinating from Stilnox. He is sleepwalking up and down the aisle of the plane. He is wearing headphones and trying to plug the cord of them into mid-air. At the same time, he believes he has broken his leg and is dragging it behind him, while shouting to the flight attendants to come and administer first aid. Of course, there's nothing wrong with his leg. Watching Travis limp up the aisle is the most hysterical thing I have ever seen. He's a hilarious guy anyway, but right now I think I might die from laughing.

~

Between the pill-popping, we also do a little swimming in Barcelona. On the morning of my 100-metre heat, I wake up slowly, drugged. I have had a couple of Stilnox the night before (strictly to get me off to sleep this time, not for recreational purposes, but the hangover the next morning doesn't know the difference).

I'll be fine, I tell myself. *It won't seriously affect me.* I am young and invincible; I'm still one month away from my eighteenth birthday.

And in my heat I *am* invincible. I win easily in a time of 1:07.75. I am the fastest qualifier going into the semi, the fastest out of the top sixty-five female breaststrokers in the world. I am ready, I am pumped.

This gold is mine.

I return again that evening to swim in the semi-final. And as I line up for my race, I am thinking about Marilyn Manson. Yes, the shock rocker with the white eyes and bleeding make-up. The biggest goth of them all. In the winter of 2003, I am going through a heavy-metal/goth-rock/shock-rock phase. A 'music your mum hates' phase. Whatever Mum doesn't approve of, I love. And right now that's Marilyn Manson. 'The Dope Show', 'The Beautiful People': I know all of his songs by heart. But the tune running through my head on the night of the 100-metre breaststroke semi-final is 'Sweet Dreams (Are Made of This)', Manson's cover of the Eurythmics classic from 1983 (a song written before I was born.)

I bounce around the marshalling area on the balls of my feet, swinging my arms and mouthing the words. I am picturing Manson, with his creepy knives and strange tattoos, as I jump around on the pool deck – thinking about Marilyn Manson in the middle of this family-friendly venue.

And as I line up on the blocks, I am super relaxed. I am having fun singing my song. I'm psyched, I'm ready; I can do this thing.

Then I am in. I am wet. I am pounding up the lane, blood pumping, heart racing. My stroke is smooth and rhythmic. I feel good: fast. But I can't get this song out of my head. The chorus is stuck on repeat.

At training, I often sing in my head to stop myself from getting bored, to stop the tedium of the black line from swallowing me up. I sing or I study. During exam time, I ploughed up and down, hour after hour, trying to memorise the symbols on the periodic table or the formula for the quadratic equation. I came up with cute acronyms and linked them to whatever set I was swimming, so that when I got to my exam I only had to regurgitate that mnemonic from the third 50-metres ... But today it's choir time.

Stop singing! I yell at myself. *Concentrate! This is a semi-final at the World Championships for God's sake!*

But Marilyn Manson is a determined bugger, and tonight it seems he's going nowhere. I can imagine the press asking me about my game plan after this race. 'Oh yeah,' I'll say, 'I just sang a little goth-rock, you know: the kind that comes with censorship warnings for parents on the CD covers. And I found that really helped me find my focus ...'

When Ken and I chatted about my race earlier in the week, we decided my strategy should be 'swim hard'. That's all. It's that simple. I am in the first of two semis for this race so I don't have the luxury of seeing the other race times before I swim. 'If you want a spot in that final,' Ken warns, 'then just swim bloody hard.'

And I am swimming hard. But I'm still singing too. My stroke, my breathing: I'm marching to Marilyn Manson's beat. I hit the wall and turn and peer at the scoreboard. Then I scream.

Oh my God! Did I just break the world record?

I cannot believe it. 1:06.37. It's my first world record. I've shaved 0.15 of a second off the existing one and I've swum a personal best. Sweet dreams sure are made of this.

I scream and cry and jump around in my lane, slapping the wall and grinning my head off. On the pool deck, Ken is wildly giving the thumbs-up sign. *A world record! You've made the finals and you've swum a world record! We're on top of the world!* his thumbs are saying. In the pool, I still can't believe it. I'm staggered. I knew I'd swum hard, but not that hard. I had no idea I was even in WR contention.

Then I remember. This was no ordinary record: this was a Penny Heyns record. This record was set by one of the best breaststrokers to ever walk the planet. By the woman who never wore goggles, even when racing, so superhuman were her powers. I have broken a Penny Heyns world record. I have never been so damned proud.

At this single moment in time, no-one in history has ever been faster than me.

That is the coolest thing in the world.

~

After my amazing swim in the semis, however, it all comes crashing down for me in the final. I do the unthinkable. I lose. Having broken the world record just yesterday, I bomb in the final and finish third.

Luo Xuejuan of China wins the gold, followed by Amanda Beard in second who is 0.05 seconds ahead of me.

I am shattered.

Later in the week, I come in behind Amanda Beard again, this time in the 200-metre event. Amanda wins in a time of 2:22.90: a new world record. Only, *she* had the sense to get a medal for hers.

I also collect another bronze, this time for the medley relay, which I swim with Giaan Rooney, Jessicah Schipper and Jodie Henry.

Barcelona has been a roller-coaster of a meet for me. My first world record. Then a devastating loss. And no gold medal in any of my events. I've had a lot of fun at this meet, but a lot of heartbreak too. And I am now convinced that Stilnox is not for me. With such small margins, and with so much at stake, I'm nervous about anything that mucks with my training.

I find that whenever I take the drug I wake up feeling groggy and hungover the next morning. Foggy. Even after a light swim, I can't shake the sensation the air's turned to soup. Of course, if the air is soup, then the water feels like mud. Thick, gloopy, gelatinous mud. Stilnox has got to be detrimental to our performances, I decide. Not only is it taking us about half a day to wake up, but when we finally do shake off our hangovers, we're still tired and lethargic and well below par. And the crazy thing is we really don't need it. I'm sure that for most of us basic relaxation techniques like meditation could be used instead of drugs. Plus, the more we take it, the more we find we need it, and the higher doses we need to take. I start off needing two tablets to get to sleep and then sometimes three. By the end of the meet, I cannot sleep without it. But the thing is, I also can't swim my best *with* it.

Sure, I may have got a world record, but I then bombed in my final, and I'm positive Stilnox is a big part of the reason why. And I'm sure it's the case for others on the Australian team, too.

But nothing will be said about our Stilnox use yet. Not for another decade or so.

~

Late in my trip to Barcelona, I get to meet Penny Heyns. She's been sitting in the stands each day for the past week or so, enjoying herself, just taking it all in, probably relieved she doesn't have to get wet. She must have been there when I broke her record: the thought fills me with pride and horror in equal amounts.

I've never met Penny before now. She is so amazing and so much older than me that I've always found her impossibly intimidating. She's got a stocky build, strong and powerful, and is quite beautiful in her strength. And there's also something about her that says 'calm'. She's not scary in the way that someone like Amanda Beard is scary. Amanda is off-putting precisely because that's how she wants you to feel: put off. But Penny is something else. She is awe-inspiring. And as a result I am both awed and inspired when I meet her.

'Congratulations!' she says warmly. 'That was some swim you put together in the semi.' I am sitting in the stands with her, several days after my race. She has called me over, has requested to speak with me, so that she can congratulate me herself. 'So you've broken my record?' she asks.

I nod, dumbstruck. I am sitting on the stadium steps, just below Penny's seat. I have chosen a step at her feet. I am here to pay my respects: to worship.

'You know, that's what it was there for,' she says kindly. 'To be broken.'

I nod again.

When I leave her a few minutes later, I am glad we have met. I am better for the experience. In this sport, it's not every day you meet someone as nice as Penny Heyns – and the fact she is like that after such a long and hard career is even more impressive. I vow to remember that.

That, and to leave the drugs alone.

10

Olympic Lies

It's 2004. The Olympic year.

The first thing I see inside the international terminal, en route to Athens, is Laurie Lawrence queuing at check-in with a roll of artificial turf under one arm. Once an Olympic coaching legend, Laurie doesn't coach anymore, but he's still a big part of the Aussie entourage, travelling with us to motivate, inspire and unite the team.

Right now, we're united. United in disbelief.

'Grass?' We tease Laurie. 'We have to bring our own grass?'

We've all heard the rumours about the Olympic village in Athens. That it's a little rough around the edges. That it makes the Acropolis look five-star. But BYO buffalo is ridiculous, even if it is plastic.

Laurie, however, is insistent.

'This is homegrown Aussie pride!' he shouts at us, though this grass has not been grown – or rather, produced – anywhere other than a plastic factory. Laurie doesn't care. And Laurie never speaks; he only ever shouts. He shouts like it's the last 25 metres of the final and in the lane next to you Amanda Beard's togs have just fallen off. He waves his roll of shiny green plastic spikes at us: 'I've got the green, now you bring the gold!' Then he's off giving a rendition of 'Aussie, Aussie, Aussie! Oi, oi, oi!' that echoes round the terminal and makes the windows shudder.

Later, on board our flight, I ask Laurie about the grass. He tells me it's for the patch of dirt outside our Aussie compound in the Olympic village. The village will be our base for almost a month, so Laurie wants it to feel like home. Plus, you get the sense he's marking our territory, protecting our turf, building us a barricade of inflatable boxing kangaroos.

'And where else would we put the Hills Hoist?' Laurie deadpans. And I've known him long enough that I'm worried he might just be serious.

Turns out, however, that the grass was a good idea. Athens is diabolically unfinished. It's comical how dodgy things are. There are dirt mounds and construction sites all over the place. The plumbing is shoddy and we are banned from putting any toilet paper down the toilets. Instead, we have to dispose of it in rubbish bins in the bathrooms. One of our swimmers, Giaan Rooney, nearly floods her entire apartment when she forgets and tries to flush toilet paper down her loo. There are six-inch nails lying around, so we can't walk anywhere, even the pool deck, without shoes on. And the pool itself is an outdoor affair, so when we're not battling it out with our competitors, our inner demons or the stopwatch, we're fighting against the elements. Every second day or so, the wind picks up, coating the surface of the water with a thick, sludgy layer of dirt.

Laurie should have brought more grass, I think.

Then, the day before my first final, I score myself a black eye. One of the things you have to get used to as an Aussie swimmer is the fact that everyone else in the world swims in the opposite direction. Just as we drive on the left side of the road, in training we swim on the left of the lane, whereas everyone else (apart from the New

Zealanders) swims on the right. This makes it hard to warm up. You either have to get a lane strictly for Aussies and Kiwis, or you have to reverse how you swim. Having trained every day for years and years going clockwise (even your tumble turns are done with a clockwise approach), you suddenly have to reverse it in the lead-up to your Olympic race.

Today, during the swim-down after my semi, we have an Aussie lane going our way, but one of the European guys jumps into it and begins swimming the other way. He hits me smack in the face at full speed, and my goggles, which have no foam, cut me under my eye. Way to put a girl off before her race.

However, us Aussies have brought a secret weapon from home. There, perched proudly on our plastic grass are our POOS (Parents of Olympic Swimmers, or – in non-Olympic years – Parents of Our Swimmers). For most of our POOS, this is their one big trip for the year, the big overseas adventure to watch their kids swim. My mum saves up all year for a trip like this. They all wear matching caps and t-shirts and who knows what else, all printed with 'POOS', and they think they are just hilarious. There they are, lined up next to the American parents, who always look so slick, so cool, as if they've just stepped out of a Tommy Hilfiger ad. There are our POOS. The dags!

For me, Athens is a farce even before racing has begun. Walking around the pool deck in my togs and runners so I don't impale myself on a rusty nail. Training in reverse. Remembering not to flush the toilet paper ... But it's not the hastily constructed buildings or the unflushable toilets that are the fakest part about Athens. It's not even Laurie's plastic grass. No, the falsest thing about my 2004 Olympic campaign is what my coach tells me.

According to him, I'm in unbeatable form.

~

As I hit the wall and look up, Ken shakes his head in disbelief. '1:08.19!' he exclaims. 'You're unbeatable! Unbeatable! No-one in the world is doing these times!'

And so it goes. Every day: a better time. Every set: a greater accolade. I'm astonishing, incredible. I am by far the best women's breaststroker on the planet. I don't get out of bed for anything less than a 1:10. In the months and weeks leading up to the Athens Games, I am training harder than I have ever trained before. I'm training harder and harder, and my coach is talking more and more bullshit.

'There is absolutely no way you can be beaten,' Ken tells me. 'You're the best there is.' 'You're unstoppable.' 'You're a machine.'

The only problem is: it isn't true.

Like most athletes, swimmers are much slower in training. When we train, we're swimming kilometre after kilometre, and often with fins or drag suits or our slow togs on. (Yes, your saggy old togs do make you swim slower.) We get tired, we get bored and, as a result, in training we can be up to 12 seconds slower over 100 metres than we are in races.

And yet, according to Ken's stopwatch, I am doing sub-1:10s every time I get wet. These are speeds I might produce in a race. There were swimmers who would be slower in the semis at Athens.

Ken has always had a quick trigger-finger on the stopwatch. But can he really be that quick? *The man is an Olympic-level coach*, I tell myself. *His timing can't be too far off the mark.*

And so I buy into the dream. I pay up in full. If Ken says I am number one, I'll believe his maths. If he tells me I am the world's best, well, I must be. And when Ken tells me I am doing 1:08s in training, then my only thought – the only possible thought – is: *Imagine what I'll do when I race?*

Ken has me believing I am the best in the world. And when he isn't yelling out my mind-blowing times, Ken is busy convincing me I am better than Brooke. 'Do you think Brooke is doing these times?' 'You think Brooke's doing a 1:08 in training?'

Brooke Hanson is my rival, my main competitor. She is also my friend. Brooke swims for Nunawading Swimming Club in Melbourne and is the only person in the world in the last twelve months to have put a scratch on me. At the Nationals in March, Brooke won the 100-metre breaststroke; it was the first time I had lost a National Championship since I started swimming in them. Now, though, Ken is convinced of my superiority and is reminding me of it at every tumble turn. 'This is seconds ahead of Brooke!' 'You're gonna smash Brooke!'

Oh, for God's sake, shut up! I want to yell. *I don't care about Brooke!*

I am not, by this stage in my career, interested in comparing myself to others. It might sound strange for a professional athlete, but I've been learning to focus on my own results lately. I just don't think it's any of my business what other people are doing, even my competitors. Also, who's to say Brooke won't pull something out of the bag on the day? I might be destroying every one of her training times, but what's stopping Brooke – or anyone else for that matter – pulling out a 1:07 in the final?

I am only ever interested in competing with myself, so Ken comparing me to Brooke every day is doing my head in. But because he is my coach and therefore to be respected – and because I am only a kid, so what do I know? – I don't say a thing. I just swim harder and hurt more. As if this will guarantee me gold in Athens. *I will earn this medal. I will deserve it more than anyone else*, I tell myself.

In the month before we take off for Athens, I set a new world record in the 200 metres at a meet in Brisbane. 2:22.96. I am ready.

Then, several days before we leave for the Games, my local Ford dealership invites me down to their showroom. I am sponsored by Ford and ever since I won silver at Sydney in 2000, I have been zipping around Redcliffe in a snazzy red Laser. Now, however, there is talk of an upgrade.

'See that?' the manager says, pointing along a row of gleaming, metallic beasts. Their duco is so shiny I feel I should break the surface and start swimming laps in them.

I follow his finger. 'That one?'

There, in all its majestic lime-green glory, is the most lurid, most garish, most hands-down showy car I have ever seen. It is love at first sight.

'That?' I say again excitedly. 'That green one on the end?'

'That's the one,' he says. 'You win gold in Athens and that XR6 is yours.'

And that's it: I'm a goner. I want it, and I want it bad. Just ten minutes in the Torque Ford showroom and I realise I've been colour-blind. For the last four long years, I've been focused on gold, when the whole time I should have been dreaming of lime-green. I tell the manager I will be back for my car. I swear I will. I will come straight here from the airport after Athens and I'll bring my gold medals with me. I'll wear them into his showroom right here. He shakes my hand and pats my back and tells me he doesn't doubt me.

Now I've got lime-green pressure to go with my regular Olympic-flavoured pressure. Olympic-sized pressure to win Olympic gold.

Because I won two silver medals in Sydney, I tell myself that the only option in Athens is to win gold. Gold is the natural progression. It's the inevitable result. And of course this time I want three: 100 metres, 200 metres and the medley relay. Three gold. An Athenian trio. A rolled-gold trifecta. Three gold to hang from the lime-green rear-vision mirror of my new XR6. Nothing else will do.

Looking back, it wasn't even that I particularly wanted a green XR6. If Ford had never earmarked it for me, I would never have known I needed it. Mostly it was the fact that it was a free car (a free car!) that sucked me in, because I still hadn't shaken the 'poor kid' mentality. I'd eaten too many minute steaks and cheap spuds for that. I am still fighting hard to dig me and Mum out of the financial hole Dad left us in. Every time I line up on the blocks to race, I am thinking about mortgage repayments and grocery bills and how a good performance now could pay our electricity bill for the next twelve months. When I see 'AUS' on the board beside my name. I have an urge to draw a line through the 'S' to turn it into a dollar sign. Yes, I am swimming for my country, and I couldn't be prouder. But I am also forced to swim for money.

Money and a car. I imagine myself pulling out of the showroom in this lime-green monster and laugh when I remember how our battered old rust-bucket broke down on the highway en route to my first Olympic trials back in 2000. That memory will never truly leave me. Nor will my insatiable hunger to win. I want this car. I will win this car. Deep down, I am still that twelve-year-old kid treading water with a besser brick above her head just to win a Mars bar.

So when I arrive in Athens in August 2008, I am here for gold. I have been convinced that I cannot lose, that I cannot be beaten.

But that's not right. Anyone can be beaten.

~

My first race is the 100-metre breaststroke, and I go into the event as the firm favourite. I am the fastest qualifier, having set an Olympic record of 1:06.78 in the semis the day before. This is more than a second clear of Brooke Hanson and almost two seconds faster than the USA's Amanda Beard.

I cannot lose. I will not lose.

But in the final I am nervous, unsettled. I am strangely quiet in the marshalling area; I am not my chatty, silly self. I stand on the blocks thinking, *This is it. This is do or die.* As if I will be taken out the back and shot if I don't win this race.

My dive is average, my stroke rate the same. My tumble turn (usually one of the best in the world) lets me down, and I struggle to bring it home in the last 25 metres, and finish third. Chinese swimmer Luo Xuejuan takes out the gold, and I squint at the board to see who is second.

Brooke.

Brooke Hanson has beaten me in the Olympic final. So much for Ken's confidence. I have lost to Brooke by one hundredth of a second.

I am shocked.

~

People often tell me what an honour it is to be an Olympian. 'It's such an achievement just to be there,' they say.

Let me tell you this: I don't get up at 4 a.m. every morning and swim twelve kilometres a day 'just to be there'. I don't do three-hour gym sessions just to be there. I don't do weights until I want to cry, I don't eat like a robot, and I didn't give up school and my friends and being a normal kid just to be there. I do it to win. And when I don't win? When I come third in an Olympic final that I am the fastest qualifier for? When that happens, it hurts so much I want to die.

I go to bed that night and cry. I feel like I have let my coach and my team down; I feel like I've disappointed the whole of Australia. I think about Mum and all the hours she has spent driving me to training, all the weekends she has given up to watch me swim. The thought of her and all the other goofy POOS, who were so excited and nervous before my race, makes me sob even harder. Going into the event, I was still brainwashed enough to believe that I was unbeatable, that Brooke's win at Nationals was a mistake. A blip. I had all of these people to impress – my coach, my team, my country, my mum – and I never thought I could lose.

The next day I have a day off. A day to stew, ahead of my 200-metre event the following day. Inside the Olympic village we have very limited access to the outside world. There are no newspapers and there is no news from home, so we know nothing of the outside world. In 2004, there isn't easy internet access everywhere like there is now, and we certainly don't have the internet on our phones. You have to go to a PC if you want to look anything up. But you don't. You have a job to do and you focus on that – and it never occurs to you to google yourself. So when our swimming team manager bails me up in a corridor that morning and begins ranting at me, my first reaction is simply confusion. I have no idea what she's on about.

'Your attitude is going down very badly back home,' she says. 'The Aussie fans are deeply unimpressed and you're being crucified in the press.'

I am baffled.

'You might want to work on that attitude of yours, Leisel.' Without any further explanation, she stalks off down the corridor.

My attitude? I've just swum the most disappointing race of my life and people want to complain about my *attitude*? Fair enough if it's about my stroke rate or my tumble turn or my performance in the last 25 metres. I have a few complaints of my own to register about these things. But my attitude?

And that's not the worst part. The worst part is that I have to get up and do it all over again tomorrow. I still have the 200 metres and possibly the 100-metre medley relay to go.

I can't help feeling that this conversation should never have happened. For a start, the swimming team manager should never have spoken to me (that's a job for our media manager who, on this trip, happens to be Brooke Hanson's dad.) Moreover, nothing should have been said by anyone until after I'd finished racing. But as mad as I am that this conversation took place, I have to put it out of my mind and focus. Somehow, I have to get my head together and get back in that pool.

But first I want to know who's been saying what about me.

The 'who' bit is easy. It doesn't take me long to learn it was former Olympic swimmer Dawn Fraser. Dawn, who has been here and done this, and who should know better than anyone the kind of pressure I am under.

The 'what' part is harder to swallow. Dawn has told the papers that I am 'suffering from having a swollen head' and that I haven't been 'the most popular person in the team' because of the way I 'turn my back on my rivals'. (Here, she is referring to Ken's technique of separating me from my rivals. Even in training he makes sure Brooke and I are in separate lanes, or in separate training groups. 'This is stupid,' I complain. 'We're friends!' And we are. We had fun together at our orientation camp in Stuttgart, ahead of Athens. We will room together in 2006. But Ken will not be moved.)

Dawn is out of line in commenting on something she knows nothing about: namely, me, who she's never met. But it's not just that. Nor is it just that her comments seem to be made in response to a photograph of me on the podium, a photograph that, taken in a split second, appears to show me scowling. (In fact, I am scanning the crowd for Mum's face. I am devastated with my performance. I am bitterly disappointed. And I am looking for my mum for some reassurance.) No, it's more that I feel like Dawn should be on my side, in my corner. *I'm swimming for the same country as you did!* I want to shout at her. *We're on the same team, Dawn, remember?*

But then I read the thing that will get to me most about Dawn's tirade – the thing that reaches into my guts and twists them hard. Dawn calls me 'a spoiled brat'.

A spoiled brat.

When does Dawn think I was a spoiled brat exactly? When Dad walked out on me when I was twelve years old and our house was repossessed? When I was sixteen and we used the money I earned from swimming to pay the mortgage and put food on the table? Is that when Dawn thinks I was the most spoiled?

She clearly has no idea of the pressure I am under to win.

And so I seethe for the next twenty-four hours.

I am seething when I lose the 200 metres to Amanda Beard by 0.23 of a second. And I am still seething when we win the 4 × 100-metre medley relay in a world-record time of 3:57.32. But I don't dare look like I am seething. From now on, I will only go out and front the media with a great, big, stupid grin plastered across my face. *I will never again be myself in the public eye*, I vow.

In fact, the only time I am not seething is when I see Brooke near the pool deck and I walk slowly and deliberately towards her.

'Brooke?'

She looks up. At the best of times, Brooke has a reason not to like me. We're rivals, after all. I understand this. In the previous twenty-four hours I have taken her place in the gold-medal-winning medley relay team, and that alone is reason enough to resent me. Brooke beat me in the 100-metre breaststroke final and so automatically earned a place in the medley relay final. But our relay coaches were aware that my best time was around a second and half faster than Brooke's time in the individual final. I also had some Olympic experience under my belt and they knew they could rely on me to step up and perform under pressure. And so they chose me to swim. It was an unusual decision, a controversial one, and one that would have done my reputation back home no favours. Because, technically, Brooke had earned a start. I knew I could do a good job, but even so, all I could think as I stood on the blocks was: *I'm already public enemy number one and you've gone and put me in the final? What will the ramifications be?*

The truth was I never put any pressure whatsoever on the coaches to pick me. And I want to let Brooke know. There has been talk in the Australian media in Athens of a rift between us and I want to make sure Brooke knows there's no animosity on my part.

'People are saying we're fighting,' I say to her. 'Just so you know, that's not how I feel. I have no hard feelings towards you. Never have.'

I explain to her about Ken's tactic of isolating me, how he is constantly pitting me against her. Perhaps this is the reason for rumours of a catfight between us, I suggest. 'I'm really sorry if you've been offended throughout any of this, or if you think I don't like you. It's just not the case,' I say.

Then we give each other a hug. It's simple and private. And so much better than making cruel and bitter comments in the national press, don't you think, Dawn? When Brooke and I leave Athens, it's on good terms. Screw Ken and his rules. Screw Dawn and her fucked-up opinions.

~

After Athens, our team heads to the Greek Islands to celebrate. Mykonos: one of the most stunningly beautiful places on the planet. But I can't even raise a smile. I am convinced my teammates don't like me, and I spend days by myself, lying in bed.

I have failed; I am a failure. There will be no new car, no sponsorship deals, no money to help us pay the rent again next month.

I am, above everything else, devastatingly disappointed in myself. I want to go home, but I am fearful I am going back to face an angry Australian public. I want to crawl into bed and never leave it again. I have lost; I am a loser. I am alone and scared, and exposed on the world stage. The way the media is reporting things makes me feel as if I have shot someone, when all I did was try my best.

I turned nineteen the morning after the Closing Ceremony. I'm now well and truly an adult, according to the law. But if this is what it feels like to be an adult, I want my money back.

After my final press conference in Greece, one of the journalists asks me for an autograph. I sign it, of course. But as I do, I say to them, 'I'll sign this if you can please write the truth about me. Please write that I'm not really like they are saying I am.' I don't know if they ever do.

I go to the markets in Mykonos, where Jodie Henry buys herself a giant yellow diamond ring to celebrate her performance at the Games. Jodie is the golden girl of Athens, with her three gold medals and three world records, and I am so happy for her. I really am. Jodie is a genuinely nice person, not like some athletes who are just in it for the fame. She hates all that stuff and I really like her because of it. But while I am pleased for Jodie, I can't help but think, *What happened to me?*

In Athens, every time I jumped in the pool I felt the pressure building and building, getting worse and worse, until I was begging Ken not to make me race.

'Can't I pull out? Can't I pull out of this race?' I asked Ken at one point. It was the Olympic final of the 200-metre breaststroke. My pet event. 'I don't want to swim. I don't want to go out there,' I tell him.

I have never had the luxury of a sports psychologist, because Ken won't allow them. They are for weak people. For losers, not winners. But that's what I need. I need help; I need support. What I do not need is the likes of Dawn Fraser beating up on me, because I am now more than capable of doing it myself.

And so begins my long battle with depression. A battle that nearly ends everything.

A New Start

I return home to Brisbane and try to forget Athens, forget I ever went to that crumbling ruin of a city. This would be easier, however, if my first job off the plane wasn't a welcome-home parade. It's hard to forget you've been away when there's a 10,000-deep crowd in the street to welcome you back.

I am riding down Queen Street Mall, perched high on the back of a convertible, and there is an ocean of people in all directions: toddlers and grandparents and just about everyone in between. There are men and women in business suits who have given up their lunchbreaks so they can see us; kids in school uniforms, their safari hats pulled down low to keep the scorching midday sun out of their eyes. *How do I thank these people?* I wonder. *How can a quick smile and a wave convey just how much they mean to me?*

Then a woman leans forward from the crowd and for one moment I think she might be about to throw something. A tomato? A rock? 'You've got to work on your attitude, girl!' is what she eventually hurls at me.

I'm shocked. Is that what everyone thinks? Are all these people pretending to cheer and smile at me, but really they're thinking I'm a bad loser? A poor sport? I choke back tears. I try to look grateful and gracious; I try to look happy. But this woman gets to me. She really does. *What did the media say about me while I was in Athens?* I wonder. *What is it that these people think they know about me?* It's my fault, I suppose. Me and my stupid blank face. People think I'm angry or disappointed if I'm not grinning my head off when I'm standing on the medal dais. I don't mean to look ungrateful. I don't mean to look anything at all.

And the truth is, sometimes I don't feel like grinning. Sometimes I feel like crying or screaming or punching a wall. After all that training, all that effort, sometimes second place just isn't good enough. Sometimes it just won't do.

I wish I was better at faking it, I think. Also, *I wish she had chucked a tomato.*

~

After the parade, Geoff Huegill comes up and punches my arm. As well as being on the Olympic squad with me, Geoff, who we call 'Skippy', is my teammate from Redcliffe. 'Hey, aren't you going to get a tattoo?' he says. 'Wanna do it now?'

Skippy's right; I am planning to get a tattoo. At the Sydney Olympics, when I was only fifteen, I said that if I made it to a second Games I would get a tattoo. Now, at nineteen, I am legally old enough to get ink. Fresh off the plane from Athens, today's as good a time as any.

'Sure,' I say to Skippy. 'Why not?' It's turning out to be a good day for letting strangers stick pins in me.

Skippy takes me to a tattoo artist in The Valley (Fortitude Valley, in Brisbane). The guy is a mate of his and Skippy rates his work. I ask for a tattoo of the Olympic rings that will sit just below the line of my togs on my lower back. Working painstakingly, the guy stencils the image onto me then tells me to look in the mirror.

I take a quick glance.

'No worries?' he says.

'No worries,' I say. 'Looks fine to me.'

I walk back over to where he is armed with the needle and I brace myself for the pain.

'Stop! You can't tattoo that!' Skippy says. The tattoo guy and I look up alarmed.

'It's upside down!' Skippy says.

He's right. The Olympic rings icon – the internationally famous symbol for sporting aptitude and (presumably) an ability to know up from down – is sitting upside down on my lower back: two rings on the top, three on the bottom.

'It's three rings on top! Three on top!' Skippy and I say, while falling all over each other laughing. 'Take it off!'

The tattoo guy does as we instruct.

'Can you imagine if you hadn't pick up on it?' I say to Skippy. 'I would have looked like the biggest idiot! Oh, my Olympic rings? Yeah, I'm from Down Under. We like to stand things on their heads here...'

Skippy and I double- and triple-check the colours of the rings before we give the final nod. Then I bend over a stool and white-knuckle it for the next forty-five minutes or so while I get inked. *Mum would totally disapprove of this if she knew*, I think with teenage satisfaction. I don't care. Not too many people have an excuse to get the Olympic rings tattooed on them. I grit my teeth and squeeze my eyes shut as I lean over the stool, my hair flopping towards the floor.

Citius, Altius, Fortius. The Olympic motto: Faster, Higher, Stronger. That's what I'll be. That is my future.

Faster, higher, stronger. I'll win gold next time. I'll beat them all.

~

Just about everything else in my life is turned on its head in the weeks and months after I get back from Athens. The first thing I do is call a press conference to announce that I am switching coaches. I need a new start, a new approach. After five years and two Olympics, after all Ken's smother-love parenting, I have decided I need a new coach. At the conference I field a barrage of questions.

'What made you choose Stephan Widmer?'

'What do you think you can achieve with Stephan?'

'What about Ken? He got you to your first two Olympics. Don't you owe it to him to stick around?'

'Have you told Ken? How did he take the news?'

'Are you and Ken still on speaking terms?'

'Why change now?'

'Why not change later?'

'Why didn't you change earlier?'

But my favourite question – and hands-down the funniest thing I have ever been asked by a journalist – is, 'So, Leisel, tell me: are you a Buddhist now?' The reason for the question is the book I am reading: *The Art of Happiness* by the Dalai Lama. One of our team managers on the Australian team lent me a copy after she saw how angry and frustrated I was after Athens.

'A Buddhist?' I repeat. 'Am I a Buddhist now?' I don't know what a Buddhist is supposed to look like (I haven't got to that chapter yet). But standing there wearing my Team Australia tracksuit, with my racing-red fingernails and my chlorine-bleached hair, somehow I don't think I quite fit the bill.

Anyway, Stephan is my Buddha. He's my maharishi now. My guru. With his sensible sandals and his all-seeing blue eyes, Stephan fast becomes my Swiss saviour in the Valley pool. Stephan gives me a whole new approach to swimming, a whole new direction.

He even gives me my very own mantra: 'This is my job. I know what to do.' Stephan has me repeat this 20,000 times on a race day to remind me of all the training I've done. 'This is my office. I come here to work.' My job. My office. I can do this.

Stephan teaches me to approach my swimming calmly and rationally. 'You have a job to do, that's all,' he tells me. It's not scary or intimidating. Swimming is simply what I do, day in, day out. Rain, hail or shine. Over and over and over again. And so when the time comes to race – no matter how big the event, no matter how high the stakes – there's no need to choke. I am just carrying out my job.

Stephan also teaches me to be methodical and precise and to focus on my technique. He is Swiss and his brain works just like the intricate, beautiful watches his country is so famous for. He is a joy to observe. His analysis, his strategising: it's all new and amazing compared to my training with Ken. Everything we do is done for a reason. I no longer have the sense that I'm swimming kilometre after empty kilometre just because that's what's always been done. Stephan likes details and methodology. He likes there to be a reason for everything. And for the first time in my life, my training sessions are mentally exhausting. I love all the thinking, rationalising, planning and correcting. Unlike Ken, whose focus was on distance, Stephan will stop me after 100 metres if my stroke is not right. If I'm fatiguing, he will point it out; he won't let me get sloppy. He is very technically advanced, and he is not afraid to try new ideas. Stephan has one house rule: no mobile phones at the pool. Each arvo at 3:30 p.m., my phone goes in my bag and I'm not allowed to touch it again until after I'm dry. I like this: I like his thinking. We are here to work; we are here to focus on swimming.

This is my job. I know what to do.

As soon as I switch to Stephan, he wants to start from scratch. 'Let's change your stroke, let's be more efficient here, more streamlined here . . .' He is going to rebuild me, re-mould me. He will make me his own. Where Ken was all about embracing who I was, Stephan can see who I am going to be.

I watch videos with Stephan: hours and hours of footage of myself. Stroke after stroke, lap after lap. Stephan is not interested in having me campaign against anyone else. There's no talk of Brooke or Tarnee or Amanda or whoever. It is all about me. About who I can be.

About me, and also about 'efficiency'. He repeats the word all day long: hardly efficient, but he gets it through our thick heads. Stephan's accent is heavy; he carries Switzerland with him here in The Valley. And when he's not talking 'efficiency', his other favourite is 'undulation'. He says it deeply, with meaning and with passion. He sounds like Schwarzenegger, telling us to 'undulate'. *Un-du-laaa-shon*. The word undulates itself as it echoes off the tiles. It is a joke in our squad for a long time.

But he does get us undulating. We are smooth and rhythmic; we are moving with the water. Up and down, up and down: we are dolphins, we are seals. Stephan is instrumental in changing my stroke. The changes he makes will set me apart from everyone else for the rest of my career. He takes me from good to great. He creates my stroke.

Then, when he's fixed my stroke, he starts on my head. 'Are you enjoying your swimming? Do you like coming to training?' he asks. No-one has ever asked me this before. 'Do you know why you're doing this exercise? Can you see the point of that?' He strengthens my brain while he tones up my body. Stephan teaches me how to compete, how to behave. He turns my attitude around. Stephan shows me that, come race time, the only real competitor is the one in my head. He teaches me to recognise what I can control. 'These things,' he tells me, tapping his head, 'are the only ones to worry about.' He makes us leave our issues behind when we train: we physically touch the door frame as we enter the pool deck to show we have left our problems at the door. It is mental, he teaches us, this swimming game. This job. He wants the best from us, the best *for* us. And he knows the way to achieving this is not by physical punishment.

By early 2005, within six months of starting with Stephan, it is working: I am winning. I have never swum faster than I have with him. When I race now, it's structured: planned. It feels right. I have a completely different racing warm-up now, one that's much shorter and that includes lots of explosive work at the start to wake me up and get me going. Like 'dive 25 metres descending' (that is, getting faster and faster), which warms me right up and perfects my technique.

My gym program is also new. I have started at the Queensland Academy of Sport (QAS) and I have a proper gym coach and a proper regime for the first time ever in my career. No longer just some guy running the local leagues club (as I've always had in the past), my coach is a professional and it shows from day one. Anthony Giorgi is the head coach at QAS and he has me working on my technique, doing some proper lifting. Back at Ken's, I lifted adult weights as a thirteen-year-old. But 100-kilogram leg presses and pec machines have nothing to do with swimming. It was all about how much we could lift, how hard we could go. There was no strategy, no planning. Looking back, it was probably dangerous. Now, however, my gym training is structured and safe. I do lots of leg work and strength work. I hold the girls' chin-up record, for doing a chin-up with 36.5 kilograms strapped around my middle. (We use a 20-kilogram plate, a 10-kilogram plate, a 5-kilogram plate and one 1.5-kilogram plate. I look like the Michelin man, but made from steel.) I love the work. I love using weights. And I am leaner and fitter than I've ever been before.

But it's not just my physical fitness that Stephan is concerned with. One day he stops me on the way to do my warm-down.

'What are you doing outside swimming?' he asks. 'What do you do when you leave the pool?'

The list is short. Eat, recover, dream about swimming.

With Stephan's encouragement, I enrol at the Australian Institute of Applied Science (AIAS) at Stones Corner in Brisbane. I am going to do a diploma of beauty therapy. Mum saw the ad; she cut it out of the local paper for me. It's not something I ever thought about doing until now, but as soon as Mum suggests it I like the idea. Beauty therapy. Why not? I'm interested in beauty and healthcare. I like making people feel pampered and special.

It's somewhat ironic that I choose beauty therapy as a hobby: as a swimmer, my body is treated like a machine. Swimming doesn't allow time for pampering, doesn't care how you're feeling. Swimming is about performance, not appearance (although, you'd be forgiven for forgetting that on weigh-in days, when we stand around in our togs and await judgement on our bodies from our coaches, dieticians, gym coaches and the rest).

Just as my school did, the college gives me a scholarship so I can afford to attend. The course is great. We learn how to do facials and waxing, and learn all about various skin products. It's not rocket science, we're not saving lives, but it's fun and interesting, and most of all: it's not swimming.

The college is very flexible about accommodating my swimming schedule and I attend classes maybe twice a week, for a three-hour session each time. Some weeks I only manage to go once, sometimes not at all. But the teachers are always very understanding and I stick it out for two years all up. It's such a good distraction; it's just what I need. And at times the course content is actually really useful. Learning about the structure of our skin and the best ways to look after it helps me protect my skin, given all the chlorine exposure it gets. I have acid burns in several places on my body from swimming in chlorine for so many hours. I can never do enough to soothe my raw skin. But now at least I know a few things that might help.

I don't have loads in common with the other people on my course, but I find I enjoy chatting to people about something – anything – other than swimming. Many of them don't have a clue who I am or what I do, and these people are my favourites to talk to. Sometimes when I introduce myself to people I meet, they respond with, 'I know who you are! Why do you bother to introduce yourself?' But at college most people don't know who I am and I certainly don't tell them. I love that they haven't heard of me. I can think of nothing worse than meeting someone for the first time and assuming they know me. *Don't you know who I am?!* Yuck. How horrible. Sam Riley once told me that her dream job was to wear a wig and work as a checkout chick at a Coles. The anonymity! Being inconspicuous! She could think of nothing better, and I totally get it. Quite often when I fill out forms and I'm asked my occupation I will write 'unemployed brain surgeon' or 'out-of-work circus clown'. It's not that I'm ashamed of being a swimmer – it's just that I don't want to stand out. I don't need other people to know who I am. I am quite often featured in the local *Redcliffe & Bayside Herald*, so when I go to the corner shop to pick up milk, people recognise me and stare and whisper and point. I have taken to wearing hoodies and dark glasses, even at night, so that I don't get noticed. I don't want to be seen.

For someone studying beauty, I am terribly uncomfortable in my own skin.

12

Starving to Swim

I am always on a diet, always counting calories, obsessing over food, and always, always hungry. I am insatiable. I cannot eat enough. I am still a teenager, with a break-neck teenage metabolism, and after swimming and training for hours each day, I can never seem to fill myself up. And yet I still try to diet.

Last year was 'My Year Without Chocolate', in which I didn't eat a single square of chocolate. Not one piece. It was all my own idea and it nearly killed me – very nearly broke my spirit – but I'm sure it went some way towards keeping the kilos off. I don't drink and I don't eat cheese. I skip ice-cream, hot chips, burgers and pies. The sight of a piece of mud cake can reduce me to tears, worse if it has chocolate icing. Christmas is the hardest, because it's peak training season. Nationals are in March, so I have to be extra strict at Christmas. And all of this has to come from me. I am the one who has to stick to the regime. Beyond the beady eye of my coach, it is up to me. When I'm at home, when I'm out with friends, I have to be good. I need the willpower of a saint. But I am strong and determined.

Also, I am convinced I am fat.

Whenever I have to stand on the pool deck in my togs, listening to my body being discussed like it's an engine and not the arms, legs, thighs and stomach of a teenage girl, I am self-conscious and miserable. I think I am just too fat.

Part of the reason for this is that there is nothing strategic about my diet, nor about the diet of anyone I know. Despite the ad hoc appearance of dieticians in our lives (such as at the Fukuoka World Championships, where they popped up with that salmon cake), we receive no sustained scientific dietary advice. The only dieticians in my life are affiliated with the QAS, and they're seen as extraneous: outside help you can seek if you really need to shed some kilos or put on some bulk. They are not part of our 'team', not in the way our coach or gym trainer is. And seeing a dietician is on par with seeing a sports psychologist: not encouraged. Back when I swam with Ken, he never wanted us to deal with outsiders – coaches knew best – and his strategy when it came to diet was to put most of the girls in our squad on meal-replacement shakes at some time or another. *Diet shakes, yeah, that's a good idea for a teenage athlete!* We were always getting weighed in, always being judged. We were actively encouraged to skip meals to lose weight. It is irresponsible and terribly damaging. And it's a quick way to screw up a teenage girl's metabolism, to say nothing about the state of her head.

Even now at the QAS we are all weighed three times a week. Weigh-ins take place on the pool deck in our togs, and we are weighed in front of our squad (girls and guys together), plus a team of coaching staff. There are men there as old as our dads, all watching our embarrassment as we are publicly weighed.

Weighed, weighed and weighed again.

Some of the coaches at the QAS gym have a thing going called '6:1.20'. This is their code, their secret talk. They think we don't understand when they call a girl – it's always a girl – a '6:1:20'. But when she's crying in the showers later, it's because she knows that

'6' stands for the sixth letter of the alphabet, '1' the first, and '20' the twentieth. F. A. T. Doesn't take a genius to bust that one open.

There is one girl who is really struggling with an eating disorder. Only months ago, she was one of the stringiest girls in the gym, but in the past few months her weight has gone up, so now she gets the 6:1:20 nickname among the coaches. We would never use it among ourselves. It's disgusting. Someone should stop them. But that's what the culture is like here. If my weight goes up even 0.2 kilograms, I know about it – *everyone* knows about it – and I panic and think: *Am I going to cop it? Are there going to be questions asked?*

Two hundred grams. That's nothing. That could be your period. That could be a big glass of water. Still, around here 0.2 is 0.2, and there will be questions to answer.

The other thing we do – the thing that's worse than weigh-ins – is skinfold testing, every four to six weeks or so. I have been doing skinfold or pinch tests since I was fourteen, but they are not getting easier. If anything, as I get older, I hate the experience more and more. It's humiliating. Just like at weigh-ins, for skinfold tests we line up poolside in our togs. Then some guy from the QAS uses callipers to pinch the fat on our stomachs, the top of our thighs, our calves and those awful bits on the back of your upper arms. Once it's done, you have to stand there while your results are entered into the computer and then spat back out at us as a single, scary digit: your skinfold measure.

It doesn't matter that the test is unreliable, that accuracy relies on the same person making consistent measurements at fixed spots on your body with a fixed amount of pressure each time, every time – not measurements made several weeks apart, possibly by different people. And it doesn't matter that the test ignores each individual's unique body fat distribution, or that it only measures one type of fat (subcutaneous adipose tissue, or fat immediately under the skin). No, none of this matters. Nor does your embarrassment, your anxiety or even the fact that it is creepy it's so often a man doing the testing. What matters is whether your skinfolds have gone up or down.

I am always big around the middle. My skinfolds on my stomach constantly let me down. This means my overall results are never low. I am not a lean swimmer. For me to get a skinfold result under 70 is pretty difficult, whereas most people, especially the freestylers, are down around 50 to 60. So I hate skinfolds day.

We try every trick in the book. We starve and dehydrate ourselves, which leaves us listless for the rest of the day's training. We do anything to get that dreaded number lower. 'What were you today?' we ask. 'Did you go down?' We stand on the side of the pool, everyone comparing their results. I train with Libby Lenton: she's a sprinter, so she always has low skinfolds. She is always in that happy 50–60 band, while I wobble up around 70.

So many questions are asked of us when we don't get a result the coaches are happy with. 'Why are you not lower?' 'Why haven't your skinfolds dropped today?' 'What are you doing?' 'What are you eating?' We have to justify and explain.

A bad skinfolds result leaves me devastated for the whole day.

And all this without any proper nutritional advice. Mum makes sure my diet is 'healthy' by keeping the fridge stocked with fruit and vegies. There's always fresh ham and salad sandwiches for lunch. Lots of carbs. Steak and salad. Pasta. It's pretty balanced, pretty lean, but Mum is no dietician. She's no sports nutritionist. So why is my only healthy eating advice coming from her?

From everyone else – swim coaches, gym coaches, physios and the rest – the message is clear: starve, starve, starve. Not that they explicitly say this. They just say you need to get your skinfolds down somehow, and let you draw your own conclusions: swimming six hours a day is not doing the trick. Oh, and they say you're only allowed half a protein bar, because 'There're too many calories in a full one.' 'What else did you say you ate today?' 'Have you thought about meal-replacement shakes?'

Any advice we receive from the dieticians at the QAS is generic, the same info doled out regardless of whether you're male or female, a sprinter or a distance swimmer. It's one-size-fits-all, though there are no two sizes the same here.

One evening I am walking down the main street of Cairns with my good friend Jessica Abbott. We are at a training camp – or supposed to be – but Jess and I have snuck out for a contraband ice-cream. Here we are, walking through downtown Cairns, gobbling down our Bubble O'Bills, when Jess spies her coach, Alan Thomson. Without a word, she shoves her ice-cream into my chest – just rams it there, smearing ice-cream down my t-shirt. Thommo is Jess's coach, she is his athlete, so he controls what she puts in her mouth.

They're mine! Of course both ice-creams are mine! This is what my grin says as Thommo wanders past.

Jess and I laugh about it now, but she wasn't laughing at the time. A girl could get in serious trouble for eating an ice-cream.

Some girls I know get in trouble for eating more than 50 grams of carbohydrates a day. That's a small packet of sultanas. It's insane, this world, this weird mindset where we have to hide what we eat.

I am forever trying to diet. I am swimming more but trying to eat less.

I am a healthy teenage girl but I'm convinced I am fat.

But most of all? I am hungry.

The whole thing is sick.

Top: Relaxing poolside, Northern Territory, 1985.

Sand in hair, don't care! St Huberts Island, age two.

Below: With Ken Wood.

Top: Winning the coveted towel, as age champion, Sunshine Coast District Swimming Association, beside Josh Bettridge (right).

Right: My first Age Nationals, in 1996.

Below: Opening a new pool in the Tiwi Islands when I am about fifteen.

On the dais at Chandler in 1997. Look at those flippers!

My family cheering me on during Sydney 2000.

Flashing the peace sign at swimming trials in 2000.

Our gold medal-winning medley relay team at Athens 2004: Petria Thomas, Jodie Henry, Giaan Rooney and me.

With Anna Poleska and Amanda Beard after the 200-metre medal ceremony in Athens.

Training at the Valley with Stephan, 2005.

International competition, 2005.

In the Valley pool, 2005.

Taking out the gold in Montreal, 2005.

Smiling for Mum, after winning that elusive individual gold in Beijing, 2008.

All dressed up for a shoot for the *Age*'s *Sport & Style* magazine.

Trying to find my smile in Sierra Nevada, 2009.

'This is my office. I know what to do.' Focusing during the 2010 Delhi Commonwealth Games.

With Blair Evans and Meagen Nay in Shanghai, 2011.

In Shanghai in 2011 with Kelly Stubbins.

It's all about balance: hitting the gym in Brisbane in the lead-up to the London Olympics.

With backstroker Sophie Eddington at training camp in Hawaii, 2010.

The other athletes head off to the Opening Ceremony as we watch from our balcony in the London Olympic village.

Watching the London Opening Ceremony from at home in the village.

Old habits die hard: my painted nails at London 2012, bearing the initials of our relay team (Emily Seebohm, Alicia Coutts, Mel Schlanger).

Never leave your hair extensions lying around – helping myself to a mullet in the village at London 2012.

Getting some closure at the London Closing Ceremony with Meagen Nay.

At the London Closing Ceremony.

Mum and Nanna in early 2013, just months before Nanna died.

Biting my nails before going on stage for TedX Kurlipa, where I talked about success in 2015.

13

Aussie, Aussie, Aussie!

We're off to Canada. The 2005 World Aquatics Championships are in Montreal, so we are headed for the land of moose, Mounties and maple syrup (though, of course, there will be no maple syrup for us).

On the flight over, I have been reading my Buddhism book again, and this stuff is making sense. It's hitting the spot. After my 'apocalypse at the Acropolis' last year (as I've come to think of the Athens Olympics), I am determined that things will get better. So I make a conscious decision to enjoy every moment of our meet in Montreal, to soak it all in, to lap it up. And not just the good bits, either: I will savour both the highs and the lows, this trip. I'll take the rough with the smooth.

I have even decided to take some photos. This is something I stopped doing way back when the novelty of international competition wore off, when I couldn't focus on anything that existed outside my lane in the pool, regardless of which country I was in. But now all that is going to change. Now I will take everything in. And where better to get snap-happy – where better to make time to stop and take in the view – than in a place with some of the most spectacular scenery in the world? When I get off the plane at Aéroport International Montréal – Pierre Elliott Trudeau, I am armed with a shiny new camera to go with my shiny new attitude.

And my attitude works.

Nothing worries me this trip, nothing at all. Not our uniforms (which are actual ski pants with thick woollen lining, because someone forgot to tell the Aussie designers that it's summer here in the northern hemisphere). Not the occasional tantrum from my roommate, freestyle-queen Libby Lenton. (Everyone on the team knows Lib can throw a tantrum like it's nobody's business, but on this trip there's hardly any of that. We're too busy having fun. We are having a blast. In Montreal, Lib's such a good person to have around.) Not even the comments to the media from my longtime rival, Brooke Hanson, that she's in the best condition of her life going into this meet. 'I had my skinfolds done and they're the lowest they've ever been,' Brooke tells the *Age*. *Skinfolds, shmimfolds*, I think.

In fact, not even the icy atmosphere in the marshalling area bothers me here. Normally at a big meet like this, the marshalling area is full of silence, fear and quiet intimidation. That, and clear-skinned Americans in their hoodies and headphones, doing their best to look fearsome. But not today. I have cruised through the heats and the semis of the 100-metre event. And so today, the day of the 100-metre final, the marshalling area is full of my noise as I bounce and stretch and jog and talk.

Oh boy, do I talk. Where I would normally curl up with my headphones and pretend to be like everyone else, today I am wholly and unapologetically myself. I laugh and tease. I trash-talk Tara Kirk from the USA, who is one of my closest rivals and one of my closest friends on the international scene. I muck around with Jessica Hardy, another American and a girl with a really good sense of humour. Jess broke my 100-metre world record in the semis last night, so I tell her I am here to nick it back. She laughs. 'Bring it on,' she says. She knows I'm not seriously trying to unsettle her. That I'm incapable of ever psyching anyone out. That I'm just being myself, and that means being silly and chatty and friendly and dumb. Maybe it's just the woollen ski pants, but today the marshalling area is feeling decidedly thawed.

Then suddenly it's time to de-robe for our race. I snap my goggles on my face and tug my cap on over them. I always have my goggles super-tight (so tight that I have a bone growth on my eye socket from the pressure), but today I loosen them a fraction. They're loose; I'm loose. I'm ready to have some fun.

I go to the edge of the pool, kneel and splash water on myself. I don't like to be dry when I go into a race. The water feels cold. It is a shock when it hits my face, even though I know it can't be (FINA mandates it must be between 25 to 28 degrees). In a few moments when the race starts, I won't feel it at all.

I run through my mantra as I splash myself. Slosh! *This is my job, I know how to do this.* Splash! *This is my office. It's 50 metres long, 2 metres wide and filled with water. When I rock up to work, I know what to do.* Splish! *This is my job, I know how to do this.*

I walk back to my seat feeling calm, confident and in control. No-one is asking me to speak Japanese or perform on trapeze. This is my job. I do this every day.

This is what I do. I can do this. I stand behind the blocks, repeating it again and again.

For the first seven years of my career, I only ever thought about the end result. I focused on the time I wanted to get or a record I wanted to beat. Later, it was the medal I had to win, a bill that had to be paid. But Stephan changed all this. Now I think about the process instead. I don't fixate on the wall, but on how I'm going to get there.

The whistle blows and we're ready to start. Stephan's voice is in my ear: 'Let's control the start. We can't control the last 25 metres, because we're not there yet. Let's control the start and get the best one we can.' *This is my office. Let's control the start.* I am shaking and bouncing and blowing out air.

The second whistle blows. I step onto the blocks. I always do a two-footed start. Everyone else does a track start, one foot forward, one foot back. But I stick with my slower two-footed version because it's all that I know. This is my office. This is how we do things here.

Then it's whistle number three and away we go!

I break the water and head straight into streamline. Hands on top. *Think slick, think slick.* I am streamlined. The water gushes past. I press my hands down and slide into my pull-out, breaking the water smoothly at the 10-metre mark. I must control the first 25 metres. For me, this means getting into a 42-stroke rate, or 42 strokes per minute. I know when I am there. In training, we wear clickers inside our caps that beep when we take a stroke, like a metronome or a ticking bomb. So I know what a 42-stroke rate sounds like and what it feels like. If you go out too fast, you just rip the water; you don't hold a thing, you rip it to shreds. My body is so finely tuned, so in synch with the beat, that if I'm even one stroke too fast I can tell: I can feel it. I have that much connection to my stroke and to the water. I don't need a clicker in my ear.

But today I am fine. In fact, I'm bang on. I am feeling the water, holding it. I am smooth and sleek – and quicksilver fast. After three or four long strokes we're 25 metres in. Now is the time I begin to build. I shift up a gear: 42 to 43. I am slippery smooth, almost marine.

It takes 18 cool strokes to get to the 50-metre mark. I don't count them but I'd know if I took too many. I hit the wall fast and in total control. I am one of the best turners in the world by this point in my career. I have worked so hard on this, turned so many times, I can twist and flip almost easier than I can swim straight. Hands to feet, hands to feet. Get on, get off, get on, get off. Flick, swish.

Then it's straight back into streamline before I pull out again. Breathe, stroke, rise, fall. My first two strokes off the wall are so sleek, so smooth, I almost want to stay in them forever. But then I'm building, building, building again. Stephan always says to swim like a Ferrari. Don't crunch through the gears: instead, build, build, build.

I burst into the final 25 metres. I am starting to burn. My lungs are on fire, my forearms are in agony. I can't move my fingers; lactic acid has them now. My legs feel as though they're not moving at all.

I am burning alive, but I'm steaming home. Build, build, build. Never rip. Never break. I am burning and rasping, but still I don't rip the water. I just build, and build again, and then I build some more. I am smooth and flat and I'm coming home fast. *All you've got to do is be first on the wall. All you've got to do is be first on the wall.*

I am burning and steaming. I am dying out here. *All you've got to do is be first on the wall. All you've got to do is be—*

First? On the wall? I pull up fast, pant and stare. My palm presses the tiles and I suck in cool air. I am screwed, but I know I've swum a good race.

In fact, I have blitzed it. I have won gold. After Sydney, after Fukuoka, after Barcelona and then Athens, finally – *finally* – I have got what I wanted: my first individual gold medal at the world level. My time of 1:06.25 is a Commonwealth record and relegates the Americans to second and third place. Jessica Hardy came in second in a time of 1:06.62, while Tara Kirk is in third with 1:07.43. I have missed Jessica's new world record by 0.05 of a second. But who cares? At last the national anthem will be playing for me! I look to the sky. The grey blanket overhead is heavy with rain. I squint at the clouds, at the evening sky. 'Thank you, thank you,' I say. Because there, pushing through the clouds, are my lucky stars.

I spring from the pool and meet the media head on. Finally, a gold! And I'm the second-fastest 100-metre breaststroker of all time. I won't have to fake my smile for the camera today.

But as I stand on the side of the Jean-Drapeau pool, something happens to me that has never happened before: I am lost for words. I grin apologetically. 'I'm a bit overwhelmed,' I confess to the camera. 'I'm a little bit shocked.' I shuffle awkwardly. I stare at my feet. And then, like the sky, I well up with tears.

I do a victory lap after the ceremony to spread some of my joy. I seek out Stephan in the crowd and throw him my bouquet. Then I see Mum and I run to the edge of the crowd. I stretch up to reach her and I hug her hard. I owe her everything.

~

Later in the week, having already proven something to myself, I go out and win the 200-metre event too. I smash it, in fact. I demolish the world record and leave my competitors more than six metres in my wake. I am body lengths in front. There is no-one else in the finishing shot. I have swum a new record of 2:21.72.

Technically, this makes sense. My stroke is more suited to the longer event: I should be better at the 200 metres than the 100 metres. My stroke is flatter and smoother than a conventional stroke, so I conserve more energy than just about anyone else in the pool. But I'm still bloody shocked. The 200-metre breaststroke is similar to the 200-metre butterfly: they use most of the same muscles and both are hideously painful. By the final lap of the 200-metre final, I am burning. I want to stop and ask the crowd for a fire extinguisher. But I don't stop. I don't quit. I just build, build, build. And somehow, through all the pain, I'm the first to touch the wall.

For me to win gold in this event – and almost a second under world-record time – is really something else. I am stunned. Thrilled!

And it shows. For the second time this week, salty tears of happiness pour down my cheeks.

This new attitude, this contentment thing: I decide I might just like it. In fact, with two gold medals clinking around in my bag now, I'm beginning to think that just maybe it suits me. The press certainly thinks so. 'Leisel comes of age in Montreal,' they say. 'New coach and new attitude seem to have done the trick,' they say. I'm not used to this happy relationship with the press. But, just like everything else in my life right now, I decide to go with it. To sit back and roll with it. If the media wants to forget all the things they've said about me in the past, who am I to bring them up again?

But even though the press show signs of warming to me, I don't dare hope that the Aussie public might begin to do so too. It will take more than one good meet to change their opinion of me. I know that.

But things are helped later in the week when we win the medley relay. Our team of Sophie Edington, me, Jessicah Schipper and Libby Lenton manage to hold off the Americans in a time of 3:57.47. When we win, we jump, scream, hug and sing. We shake Parc Jean-Drapeau, Aussie-style.

Our relay gold caps off an impressive fortnight for the Telstra Dolphins. It's our best medal haul in eleven World Championship campaigns. We take home twenty-two medals in total, including thirteen gold. In fact, we win a gold medal on every night of competition in Montreal. And we are second only to the USA.

Much of this can be put down to our new head coach, Alan Thomson. Thommo became Australian head coach at the beginning of the year when Leigh Nugent stepped down, and Montreal is his first World Championship as the boss. Under Thommo, things on the team are sweet. He fosters a great culture, a real team spirit; he knows how to bring people together. The first thing he introduces are compulsory team meetings. Each afternoon at about 4 p.m., before we head to the pool to swim in our finals, Thommo gets the whole team together to watch the TV highlights from the night before. There's music and cheering. We all high-five and slap each other on the back as we watch each other's races. There's Jodie Henry winning gold! There's Hackett in the 400 metres! It really fires us up, watching each other's inspirational swims. *I can do that too!* I feel like shouting.

It's a totally positive vibe. There's no blame, no disappointment. No-one is ever made to feel like they've done a poor job, and everyone is genuinely happy for their teammates' victories.

In later years, the culture of the Aussie swimming team will come under fire, and when it does, I'll be ready to tell anyone who listens that we need to think back to Thommo and his compulsory meetings that fostered team spirit.

But right now, in Montreal, during the reign of Thommo, Australian swimming is leading the world. We are so strong, in so many events. Libby is dominating in the freestyle; I have the breaststroke. We have the best women's medley relay this country has ever seen. We are world-beaters and record-breakers. We Aussie women are just unbeatable and it gives me goosebumps every time I think about it. These are our golden days; it's our time to shine. And so much of it is due to our amazing team spirit.

I cap off my year by winning *Swimming World* magazine's World Female Swimmer of the Year, 2005. I'm honoured to receive it, especially as a breaststroker. We don't have the same glamour or glory as the freestylers, who swim faster than anyone else in the sport.

I'm excited about being Swimmer of the Year, but I'm more excited about how well our team is doing right now. The Aussie team generally, and our women's medley team specifically. We're doing amazing things together. Awesome things. Together.

That's what I find really inspiring.

14

Commonwealth Triumph

At the Commonwealth Games in Melbourne in March 2006, I will be sharing a room with my arch rival, Brooke Hanson. My nemesis. Or so the media would have you believe. In actual fact, Brooke and I have no hard feelings towards one another, and whenever we see each other in the marshalling area we always get on fine. Sure, we wouldn't have been each other's first choice as a roommate, but having learnt that's how it's going to be, Brooke and I will be grown-up about it. Just because we're competitors (we'll be swimming in the 50-metre and 100-metre events against each other), doesn't mean we can't get along, right? Who knows? We might even enjoy it.

I am swimming in the 50-metre breaststroke event in Melbourne, which I don't normally do. I'm terrible at it because I'm only just hitting my stride by the time the race has been won – usually by somebody else. Plus, the 50 metres is not an Olympic event, so I don't normally bother with it. However, I've qualified for Melbourne, so I will swim, even though I know I won't win with Jade in the pool.

Jade Edmistone trains with me at Commercial. She's had a good year so far, starting with the Commonwealth Games trials in February, when she swam a PB in the 100-metre breaststroke to become the second-fastest Australian of all-time (just shades behind my record). She also improved on her own world record in the 50-metre event, setting the first world record at this new Melbourne pool. She's in shape, she's swimming fast and, what's more, she likes this pool. Jade's got this in the bag.

The 50 metres is my first event in Melbourne. As I sit in the marshalling area, my fingers and toes are gradually turning blue. This Melbourne pool is cold and windy. One side of the complex is perpetually open to the elements, so by this time of the evening, when the wind whips around and the cold, dark night floods in, it is freezing. *Remind me again why I signed up for this crap?* I think. I have been stomping around the pool complex all day saying this. Eventually Stephan told me to keep my attitude in check, but this has only made me madder than ever. *I should channel this*, I think. *I should use my anger. That, or go and take a hot shower and climb into bed in my warm PJs* ...

I am wearing my light-blue Speedo Fastskins tonight. Light-blue is my colour; pink is Libby's. And no-one else is allowed to wear our colours. Fastskins have still only been on the market a short while. This is the second incarnation of the design, but things don't seem to have improved much. The suit is as uncomfortable as all hell, riding straight up the clacker. You've got to make sure you're wearing it right or you might flash the spectators your camel toe. You're alright, I've learnt, as long as you keep your legs together, but this is difficult if you plan on swimming breaststroke.

As I sit, shiver and try to pick out my camel toe without anyone noticing, I start to get mad. Really mad. And stubborn too. *Who wouldn't be feeling grumpy?* I think. *Who wouldn't be stroppy about swimming in this stupid iceberg of a pool?* Just because I have a job to do here doesn't mean I have to be happy about it.

I'll show you, Stephan! I think as I stand behind the blocks. *How dare you tell me to keep my attitude in check!*

And I'll show you too, Jade! I think as the whistle blows. *How dare you be so good at the 50 metres!*

I am petulant when I swim and – my God! – I win gold? I swim out of my skin and somehow I win. I beat Jade, I beat my own record and I take out the gold in a time of 0:30.55. I'm shocked. It would seem I swim quite well when I'm cranky.

Maybe I'm not so bad at the 50 metres? I think. And maybe, just maybe, this meet won't be so bad after all. It hadn't occurred to me before now, but it's possible I could win three gold in one Games here in Melbourne: the 50-metre, the 100-metre and the 200-metre.

I have a new goal, a fresh challenge. The besser-brick balancer inside me is back.

~

My Nanna, my mum's mum, has come down from St Huberts Island to watch me swim in Melbourne. It's a really special trip for her. She is eighty-eight and in a wheelchair, but she has been determined to watch me swim at an international meet for so long, and now finally she has her chance.

My auntie and uncle (Mum's brother) are also here. They have travelled down in a campervan and are staying at the local caravan park, and the two of them take Nanna out for lunch one day.

As my uncle tells it, they are waiting to catch the tram to lunch when my uncle hears: *Ding, ding, ding!*

'What's that noise? Lynne, can you hear that noise?' he asks.

His wife shrugs: she doesn't know.

Ding, ding, ding! The noise won't go away.

They turn to face Nanna, who is supposed to be waiting on the raised platform of the tram stop – and there she is, sitting on the tracks, her wheels stuck in the grooves, with a great big Melbourne tram looming down on her, dinging at her to get out of the way!

Later, my uncle asked her why she didn't yell out for help.

'I didn't like to be a bother,' she replied.

Nanna loves the Commonwealth Games. Because of her wheelchair, she gets special access and front-row seats, and she tells me that she feels like a princess.

We don't know it at the time, but this is the last chance Nanna will have to see me swim at an international meet. In 2013, she will be gone, at the age of ninety-five. After she dies, we will find a stash of newspaper clippings of my races, which she has kept for the past ten or so years, each one lovingly cut out and pasted into a scrapbook. Nanna's scrapbook includes a clipping from Melbourne 2006, along with a photo of the two of us there together.

~

Following my 50-metre victory, Nanna is back at the pool again the next evening, to see me repeat the trick in the 200-metre event.

I swim this one on adrenaline, I swim it with purpose, and I come in almost four seconds ahead of Kirsty Balfour from Scotland, easily taking out gold.

I am stoked: I'm on top of the world.

So what comes out of my mouth in my post-race interview surprises me more than anyone else.

'What is going on with you? You are a new woman!' It is Nicole Livingstone from Channel Nine and we are live, straight from the pool deck. I am still huffing and panting, catching my breath.

A new woman? I think. *Yeah, I suppose I am.*

Even now, two years later, the Athens 2004 Olympics are still very much on my mind. My performance, the public backlash ... Those Games were the single worst meet in my career and some of the worst days in my whole life, but I have tried very hard to put them behind me. I have focused on my sport; I have learnt to shut things out. I don't read my press; I don't listen to my detractors. Since 2004, I've stopped giving a fuck about anything else. I am here to swim; I am here to win.

Most of all, I've changed my attitude. These days I'm trying hard to be positive, and to be a little kinder to myself. So yeah, I suppose I am a new woman.

I don't say all this to Nicole, of course. For one, you can't say 'fuck' on television. Instead I smile graciously and thank her, and then I give my coach my most heartfelt thanks for all his help. I honestly wouldn't be doing so well without all of Stephan's help.

But Nicole is not letting it go. She wants to know more.

I shrug. 'It has been a new year and ... there's been a lot of tough changes for me to make, especially with my attitude and how I swim,' I admit. I try to think how best to explain it. In the end, it comes down to this: 'I love racing and I think, through my swimming, it showed. So the changes have paid off. And I'm actually loving the person I am now,' I venture.

'You're an absolutely sensational role model for the sport,' Nicole says.

At this, the crowd goes wild. They cheer, stomp, whistle and yahoo. 'They love you!' Nicole says.

Do they? I wonder incredulously. I am stunned by the noise. I have always had wonderful support from the people closest to me – Mum, my coaches, my friends and my training partners. But beyond that? I could never tell. My brain is crowded with thoughts of Dawn Fraser, of the criticism I've received in the media, and of that woman on the street in Brisbane at the welcome-home parade.

But Nicole is talking and I need to listen. 'Tell me about the race itself. What were you trying to think about?' she is asking.

I tell her I was so nervous my stomach was churning. Then,

before I know it, I'm telling her about my mantra. 'Throughout the race you could probably have heard me saying, "This is my office, I know what to do. This is my office, I know what to do." So I just trusted myself and let it go.'

Perhaps she can see me opening up, perhaps she can see my guard is down, because Nicole leans in now and makes a grab for my heartstrings.

'Let me ask you about your mum, a single mum . . .' she is saying. 'How much of an inspiration has Rosemary been?'

'She's been an enormous inspiration . . . Being a single mum, having to raise a swimmer and getting up at five o'clock in the morning is tough.' I sit. 'My family's gone through bankruptcy, we've gone through everything, so it's been tough on my mum.'

I turn and grin and wave at Mum. She's so thrilled with my win that she doesn't realise she's on national television. She doesn't have time to get nervous or flustered. Instead, she looks relaxed and happy, just like she does in the kitchen at home. We've all got our guard down tonight.

'And that's some of the emotion that's been behind you for the past five years, isn't it?' Nicole says.

And now the floodgates open. 'Yeah, and it was tough to deal with, especially as a fourteen-year-old at the Olympics. And I don't think people realise that. I think they're very quick to criticise and that has been really tough. But I've decided to . . . you know, people have their opinions and that's fine,' I say. 'If I love myself it doesn't matter.'

And that's it. It's a wrap. 'We love you!' Nicole says. 'The crowd here loves you!' They fade to an ad break, but before they do, my friend, commentator Duncan Armstrong can be heard in the commentary box upstairs saying: 'She's just matured so much into a beautiful young lady.'

~

A couple of years ago, back in 2004, I held the 200-metre breaststroke world record for a staggering three whole days. Three days. That must be some kind of record in itself. On Saturday, 10 July 2004, I swam 2:22.96 at a meet in Brisbane, bringing the old record down by 0.03 of a second. It was the first time I had ever held the 200-metre record. Then, on Monday, 12 July, in Long Beach, USA, Amanda Beard swam 2:22.44.

'Three days!' I had complained on the phone to Mum at the time. I was gutted. I stormed around the car park at the Queensland Academy of Sport, looking for car tyres to kick. 'I finally get the 200-metre record and she steals it away from me three days later!'

My mum responded as only she can: 'That's what records are there for, Leisel,' she reminded me.

Great, thanks, Mum. 'That's what records are for.' Are you serious? Who are you, the Dalai Lama? I hung up the phone to go and fume about my lost days of glory.

This year, though, I have finally clawed it back. At Commonwealth Games trials in Melbourne last month I broke the 200-metre world record with a time of 2:20.54, shaving almost two seconds off Amanda's record. And now at the Games themselves, and with Nanna in the stands, I set a Commonwealth record of 2:20.72.

It feels like it's all coming together. I've won the 50-metre and 200-metre events, so suddenly there is an awful lot to swim for in my final race.

Triple gold is within my reach.

~

The evening of the 100-metre final, the pool is sparkling; it's crystal. It looks as though someone has sprinkled it with diamonds. Maybe Melbourne's frost is finally melting? Or maybe I'm just seeing things differently now.

Whatever it is, it feels like a different place tonight. A new pool. A cool pool. I am ready to rock.

Mum and Nanna are front and centre as usual, enjoying the best seats in the house. Mum is used to being in the nosebleed section, but thanks to VIP Nanna and her wheelchair, she's enjoying an upgrade for the first time in her life.

It's an easy race in the end. I am smooth and relaxed. It is meant to be. Even so, I am surprised when I take it out in a time of 1:05.09. That's a PB. A world record! It's 0.62 seconds faster than the world record I set at trials last month and is ridiculously close to a 1.04, which has never been done in the history of the sport.

When I see the scoreboard, I pump my fist in pure ecstasy.

It's not usually my style to celebrate this way. I'm not that person, not so confident. I'm always excited – don't get me wrong – but I'm also usually shocked, unsure and busy squinting at the scoreboard to try to work out what the hell just happened. *Where's my name? Where's my name?* It's confusing and frenzied after a race, and it always feels like it takes forever to find my name and position. Then, once I've figured out what's going on, I'm often at a loss as to what to do next. *Do I shake my competitor's hand? Can I congratulate you, over there in the next lane?* I am awkward, hesitant and terribly uncool.

But not tonight. Tonight I'm fist-pumping like the best of them. I am totally in the moment, lapping it up. I have beaten Brooke Hanson and Tarnee White, the girls I have been pegged against for so long. Tonight, in a fraction over one minute and five seconds, I have silenced them for good. They simply aren't in my league. They are not in the finishing frame. 1:05.09. Almost a 1:04 ... I am body lengths ahead. This race has separated me from the other girls once and for all. I am the fastest in the world.

Years later, I will find a newspaper clipping of that instant, that exact moment when I threw my fist in the air. The photo is also tucked away carefully in Nanna's precious scrapbook, and it becomes one of my all-time favourite photos.

~

Melbourne may not have started out as a great meet, but it sure ended up that way. I walk away from the Games with three individual gold, the 100-metre world record, and also a gold and a second world record for the medley relay. My Nanna had a ball. Mum is chuffed to bits. I even had a great time with my roommate, Brooke Hanson.

In fact, Melbourne capped off a pretty awesome year for me. Aside from the Commonwealth Games, I set world records in the 100-metre and 200-metre events at trials in March. I broke the 100-metre short course world record at Nationals twice. I gained my seventh straight 200-metre title, seventh overall 100-metre crown and my maiden 50-metre win at the national swimming titles in Brisbane. I also won the Swimmer of the Year award in Brisbane.

But the thing that means the most to me? That's easy. On 10 December 2006, I win swimming's People's Choice Award, as voted by the Australian public.

I didn't realise it at the time, but my on-deck interview with Nicole Livingstone at the Commonwealth Games, just moments after I won the 200-metre event, was something of a career turning-point for me. It couldn't have been less calculated or less scripted if I'd tried. I never intended to open up like that. And maybe that was the key. Maybe people could see I was being completely honest. Until then, I had always been very strategic and structured about what I said publicly. I had been closed.

But in that short interview, I opened up; I just talked. I was brutally honest and I spoke from the heart. Athens in 2004 was such a bitterly hard time for me. It knocked me, just as many things in my life up until this point had knocked me. My dad leaving, our bankruptcy... these things had affected me much more than I realised.

I was learning I was not as mentally tough as I'd thought I was.

But to come out and say these things to the Australian people? I'd never meant to do that. These were off-the-cuff comments. There was no agenda. I'd been honest in the past, but the wrong sort of honest – the sort that shows disappointment at the end of a race and gets you in hot water.

Now, though, I had a different message: it's okay to not be okay. And the Australian people responded to that.

I am touched, honoured and really surprised to become the first female swimmer to win the Telstra People's Choice Award. I might be walking away from 2006 with a ton of gold, but the support of my country? That's priceless.

15

Blast from the Past

In the kitchen, I lean on the open fridge door, deliberating over what to put on my sandwich. Cheese, ham, tomato and lettuce. Avocado, that's a given. But salami too? Can you have ham and salami? I have been training since 5 a.m. and, although the clock doesn't quite say eleven, my stomach says lunchtime. My stomach says ham and salami is fine.

There's a knock at the door.

Weird, I think. *Maybe it's a delivery?* But I don't remember ordering anything. I pad down the hallway, barefoot and still in the daggy t-shirt and shorts I threw on at the pool. I answer the door to a blonde woman I don't recognise. She is shorter than me, even in spiky black heels, and she's heavily made up, with red lips and kohl-rimmed eyes. She is holding a sheet of blank paper in one hand and something small and silver in the other. A phone? An iPod? I can't quite make it out. I squint into the sunshine.

'Hello?' I say tentatively.

'Leisel Jones,' she says, as if it's her name not mine. She is confident and loud, and something makes me wish I were back in the kitchen with my sandwich.

'Yes?'

'I'm from the *Mail*.' She pauses for a moment to let this sink in. *The* Mail? *Does she mean the* Courier-Mail? I wonder what business a reporter has with me.

'Your dad has approached us about doing a story. He wants you to get back in touch with him. The story will be front-page this Sunday, so I'm here to see if you would like to comment.'

I'm floored.

'Would you like to comment?' she asks.

I collapse against the doorframe and stare at this woman. A reporter. At my house. The front page.

I open my mouth to speak but nothing comes out.

'Leisel, would you like to comment?' she asks again, and this time she thrusts the silver thing – a dictaphone – in front of my face.

I just stare. Even if I wanted to, the words won't come out. I don't even know where to begin. My dad wants to get in touch. So he's contacted the *paper*?

'Uh, no. No, I'm not commenting,' I say, finally. And I step back and start to close the front door.

But this woman won't let me be. 'Really?' she says to me. 'And how do you think that will look? Your father is reaching out to you and all you say is "No comment"? Because the paper will run that as your response, you know.'

'Excuse me? Who do you think you are?' I say. I am mad now. Mad at her, at my dad, and at the position I am in. 'No, I'm not commenting! No, it's not any of your business. And if my father has anything to say to me, he can come to me directly and not go through a newspaper.'

I try to close the door again, but before I can, she flips out a sheet of paper.

'Look at him, Leisel.' She holds up a photo of my dad, like that will tug at my heartstrings. *Listen, lady*, I want to say. *See that photo? That's the closest I've been to my dad in years! That photo's paid me more visits than my dad ever has! I haven't spoken to my dad in years, and that's not because he's forgotten my number.*

Instead, I say, 'This is an intrusion of my privacy. How did you get this address?'

Then it dawns on me. 'Did you follow me home from training? You did! You followed me home!'

For a moment, the reporter has the decency to look almost sheepish. Then she's asking again for me to make a comment.

'No!' I say, my voice rising in distress. 'No. This is none of your business and I won't make a comment. If my dad has anything to say then he can try talking to me! Like a normal person would!'

I slam the door and stand inside shaking. I have never felt so invaded in my life. She is still outside and is not going anywhere, so I run down the hallway and phone my manager, Dave Flaskas.

'She's already got the story ready to go,' I tell him. 'Dad's given her quotes and photos and everything.'

'Don't worry about it. You leave it with me,' Dave assures me. 'Just lock the door and get yourself feeling safe and leave it up to me to sort out.'

~

This is not the first time this sort of thing has happened. When I qualified for my first Olympic Games in Sydney back in 2000, my dad started phoning up local radio stations and doing interviews about me and my swimming career. He was out there seeking credit in the media for his supposed part in it. But not once had he ever driven me to training. Not once did he come and watch me compete. Hell, I didn't even know he'd noticed I could swim. I'd always felt like my dad had never showed any interest in me, never cared about me, never provided a thing. Even when he lived with us, I felt like I barely saw him, and then he walked out and left me and Mum stony broke.

In 2008, I learn that my father is sick. Very sick. In fact, he's dying of cancer. Again, I learn this through the media. An article comes out saying that my dad has been diagnosed with cancer – lymphoma – and I guess it must be true. To be honest, I find it hard to care. He discarded our relationship many years ago and this public performance is no way to try to reach out.

It embarrasses and distresses me and – as previously – I decline to comment publicly.

There is Dad on the front page of the paper. 'Talk to me,' he pleads, and I have to assume he's talking to me, although his message goes out to 700,000-odd readers across Queensland, so who can be sure?

I know plenty of people have issues with their fathers. I understand that. But not many of them have their relationship smeared across the front page like this. It's humiliating. It's disgusting. The way he's acting is shameful.

'I would love to give her away when she gets married,' he tells the paper. And I roll my eyes and think: *You gave me away years ago, Dad.* I'm not gullible enough to believe that he suddenly cares. I know he's only reappearing because I've done something with my life. Why else would he go about it this way? He didn't love me when he walked out, and he doesn't love me now. My dad didn't want to know me when I was twelve, when I was just an ordinary kid.

But that's not the thing that gets to me the most. You want to know what does? The thing that makes hot tears burn in my eyes at 3 a.m. in the morning? It's that after all these years, my dad is still hurting my mum. It's not just me he left high and dry when he walked out all those years ago. He deserted Mum too, and now he's hurting her all over again by embarrassing her in such a public way.

Mum is fiercely private. Obsessively so. She never gives interviews; she won't pose for photos. She is shy and reserved and doesn't like being seen. It's almost funny the way my parents are so different. Their attitudes to the media – much like their approaches to parenting – couldn't be more opposite. And now Dad is roping her into a public spat, and I will not forgive him for being so cruel.

The article says that Dad wants to talk. Maybe so. But I am not ready to listen.

16

Matters of the Heart

It is the lead-up to the World Aquatic Championships in Melbourne in 2007, part of my long-standing redemption campaign after Athens. And of course I go and do the worst thing a self-respecting athlete could do ahead of a World Championships: I fall in love.

It begins with a phone call from my friend Louise Tomlinson. Louise is my training partner with Stephan, and we have been friends for a very long time. At the time, I don't see what's coming my way. How could I? Because it's Louise who's head-over-heels in crush.

Louise: So, LJ, I have the hots for this guy called Marty.

Me: Marty. Cute. Talk me through it.

Louise: So he's twenty-one.

Me: Tick.

Louise: And he's tall, dark and handsome.

Me: Tick, tick, tick.

Louise: And he plays AFL for the Brisbane Lions ...

Me: Whoa, stop! Back up the truck. He plays AFL? Bah-bow! Red light! Do not get involved.

Louise: No, this guy is different—

Me: No, no he's not. He's an AFL player. Read my lips: stay away from AFL players. From footy players, full stop. They are bad news.

Louise: But I didn't even know he was an AFL player when I met him! I met him at work and he's such a nice guy . . .

Me: Again, no, he's not. He's not a nice guy, Louie. He's an AFL player. Trust me, you need to stay away.

Advice administered, I think nothing more of it until about a month later, when Louise mentions Marty again. She's been giving it some thought.

'Good,' I say. 'So you've decided he's not right for you?'

'Not exactly,' she admits. 'I've decided he's right for *you*.'

For me? Huh? But I thought Louise liked him? Why would she try and fob him off to me? Was it my low opinion of footy players, my derision before I'd even met the guy, that gave me away? Is that why she thought we might hit it off?

Louise laughs. She isn't trying to fob him off to anyone, she assures me. It's just that she's gotten to know him a little better and she can't help thinking that he and I might be really good together.

Coming from anyone else, I might be sceptical, but not from Louise. She is the sort of person who would pass on a guy she really fancied if she thought her friend might be happier with him. That's the sort of person she is: mates before dates and all that.

But still, it's not that simple.

'Rightio.' I say. 'So you want me to go out with this guy, even though a) you like him, and b) I already have a boyfriend.'

Oh yeah, that's the other thing: I already have a boyfriend.

Mitch Spencer and I have been going out – on and off – for two years now, although at times it feels much more off than on. Mitch and I met at a post-match function for the Brisbane Broncos, where his dad was the team trainer, but things have been rocky between us for a while. Real rocky, in fact. And lately he's taken to emotional blackmail, saying things like: 'I'll tell everyone it was your fault if we ever break up' and 'If you break up with me, I'll put a framed photo of you on the road and run over it with my car.' Nice. Real nice. Someone needs to tell Mitch that if he wants to keep a girl, this is not the way to go about it.

So while Mitch and I are doing the break-up dance, Louise suggests that she and I have a girls' night out. 'Have a few laughs, have a few drinks,' she says. 'Oh, and Marty will be there too.'

I find this strange. And not just because it was meant to be a girls' night out. No, it's odd because I know Louise really likes Marty and yet she's still trying to set us up.

'Just meet him,' she assures me. 'It'll be fun.'

In the end, I relent and the three of us go for drinks at the Bavarian Bier Café, and what I discover is: Louise is right. Marty and I hit it off from the start.

Marty is such a nice guy. He's warm and friendly, charming and sweet. He's just about the funniest person I've ever met. Plus, he's Maltese, so he's as tall, dark and handsome as Louise described. Marty and I have a ball that night – so much so that a few weeks later we arrange to see each other again.

This time we meet at Friday's, a nightclub in the heart of Bris Vegas.

'I must really like you,' I say to Marty. 'And not just because I've come here.' I gesture towards the dingy décor. 'But because this is way past my bedtime!'

It's Saturday night and I don't have training in the morning. But even so, I am always so exhausted after my week of training that I am in bed by 10 p.m., even on the weekend. But now it is fast approaching midnight, and Marty and I are still on the dance floor.

'Should I be worried? Will you turn into a pumpkin?' Marty jokes.

'Are you saying you don't like my fake tan?' I joke back.

We dance for ages, until well past twelve o'clock. And over the noise of the music, I don't hear my mobile when Mitch rings thirteen, fourteen, fifteen times. Even if I had, I wouldn't have answered it. Tonight I am happy and having fun. I stay out late, and kiss Marty goodnight. I am done with Mitch and feeling miserable all the time.

He and I will have to break up ...

~

The next morning, I am sitting on the couch with Mitch, reading the Sunday papers, when I turn the page to find myself staring at a double-page spread of—

Marty!

He's being interviewed about his latest try, or score, or whatever it is they do in AFL. (I don't know! I'm from Queensland, where real men play Rugby League and AFL is for Victorians.) There's Marty, splashed across the sports pages and looking even more amazing and ripped than when I left him last night. I blush and turn the page so fast it almost rips in two.

What a bitch I am! I think. Here I am, snuggled up on the couch with my boyfriend, eating eggs and toast and reading about the guy I have a crush on. This is so out of character for me. I feel dreadful. Two-timing – even thinking about two-timing – is not something I've ever done before.

But I can't help it. I can't think straight. I'm so wrapped up in Marty.

To put us all out of this misery, I break up with Mitch.

And I move seamlessly into a relationship with Marty straightaway. At my twenty-first birthday in August, I had Mitch on my arm, but by the time New Year's Eve rolls around I'm watching the fireworks with Marty. It's fast and strange, and it's not how I would have scripted it. Yet I couldn't be happier. Marty and I have so much fun, and soon we find we are deeply in love. Embarrassing-nicknames-in-public in love. (For the record, I am 'Bubba'.) We have a great time.

We are always together: inseparable from the start. This is not easy given that we both live at home with our mums, but somehow we find a way to make it work. At my place, Mum lives quite independently. She has the upstairs bedroom, I have the down. But at Marty's, things are a little more cosy. Marty is a typical Maltese boy and he's very close to his mum. They live together in a teeny-tiny apartment, in adjoining bedrooms with paper-thin walls, and I blush when I think about what she must hear. Neither of our living situations is ideal. We can never seem to find as much privacy as we'd like. But we're having too much fun to mind too much. As long as we're together, we really don't care.

Marty is playing for the Brisbane Lions when I meet him. Very early on in our relationship, I go along to a match with Jodie Henry from my squad. Jodie is going out with Marty's teammate, Tim Notting. During the match, Jodie has to explain absolutely everything that happens on the pitch. Or the field. Or whatever it is they call it in this code.

It's an eye-opener for me – all of AFL culture is – so when Marty mentions several weeks later that the draft is coming up, I have no idea what he's talking about.

'Draft?' I repeat.

'Yeah, you know, the draft. The pick. I could end up anywhere.'

'Oh,' I say. 'For what?' I'm imagining a training camp, like event camp. Or perhaps some sort of team activity.

'To play. To live!' He laughs at my ignorance.

Wait – he could end up living anywhere? I'm stunned. I had no idea this was how AFL worked.

And sure enough, a few weeks later Marty is drafted to the Western Bulldogs Football Club in Footscray, Melbourne, about 18,000 kilometres south of where we are, lying on Marty's couch, when we find out. I am gutted. But Marty is more philosophical: 'Ah well, babe. It's closer than Perth.'

This is true, but it's not much consolation. Not when I really like this guy. Not when my life is contained in about a 20-kilometre square radius here in Brisbane. I'm still training with Stephan in The Valley, still studying at Stones Corner. I own our house on Wollundry Place in The Gap. And, sure, life isn't perfect here – I'm not loving swimming right now, and Stephan and I have been clashing more and more in the past few months – but ever since I met Marty things have been good. Really good.

'I like you,' I say quietly. 'And I want to be with you.'

One month later, Marty moves to Melbourne.

~

Those first few weeks after Marty moves are awful. I miss him like crazy, and it shows at training. My attitude is bad; my headspace is worse. And there is tension between me and Stephan. I start to wonder if I want to do this anymore.

Then one night I wake up at 3 a.m. in terrible pain. I can't breathe. My chest is collapsing. I feel like someone is sitting on my chest, like I'm being crushed. Like my ribcage is squeezing the life right out of me.

Oh my God. I'm having a heart attack. I am – no joke – dying of a heart attack right now.

My heart feels like it wants to pound right out of my chest, but my ribs are holding it in; they are gripping it tight. I can't breathe. The air is stuck. I am gulping and flailing and drawing ragged breaths. I'm drowning. The room is going black.

I try to stand, but my legs crumple underneath me and I slump uselessly to the bedroom floor.

Have I been training too hard? Have I done this to myself? I am twenty-two years old and I'm dying of a heart attack.

I drag myself across the bedroom floor. The pain in my chest is searing; it's alive. It's grabbing my ribs and cracking me open for the world to see.

I crawl on my elbows, dragging my legs behind me, pulling myself towards the stairwell and towards Mum. Towards help. Didn't Flo-Jo die of a heart attack or something? Didn't she roll over in bed and die just like that? *I am Flo-Jo. I am dying.*

I make it as far as the bathroom.

'Mum!' I yell. 'Mum, we need to go to the hospital. I'm having a heart attack!'

Silence. And then: 'Leisel? Where are you?' There is the ruffling of bed sheets and a thud as her feet hit the floor. 'Leisel?' I hear her clatter down the stairs. 'What do you mean "a heart attack"?' she calls. 'Are you sure?'

Seconds later she is by my side.

'Yup, I'm dying. I'm actually dying,' I tell her.

'We need to get you to a hospital,' Mum says.

But I dither around, not wanting to call an ambulance. Not wanting to call an ambulance but dying all the same. *What if it's not a heart attack? Who has a heart attack at twenty-two?*

But then why is my chest being ripped apart? I recall all the messages I've ever heard about heart attacks: minutes count; just get help; it doesn't matter if it's a false alarm.

'Okay. Let's go,' I agree.

'I'll drive you,' Mum says, pragmatic as ever. 'That way, we won't have to pay an ambulance call-out fee.'

We won't have to pay an ambulance call-out fee? Is she kidding?

Maybe she's trying to keep calm. *Yeah, that's it, she's trying to stop me from freaking out.*

Or maybe she's in shock. I know I sure as hell am.

Mum bundles me into the car and heads to the Mater on Coronation Drive. But on the way there I start to feel better. The pain loosens its grip and my breathing gets deeper. The air is cool and sweet and I gulp it down.

Well, this is embarrassing, I think as we drive. *Perhaps I'm not dying after all.* I'm relieved that it's Mum and not a paramedic sitting beside me.

At the hospital they do an ECG, check my blood pressure and measure my oxygen saturation levels. 'You're fine,' they tell me. 'You're the fittest person here.'

'Are you sure?' I say.

'Positive. There is absolutely nothing wrong with your heart. With any part of you.'

I am embarrassed, but also grateful to be alive. 'Thank you, thank you so much.' I accost everyone I see – doctors, nurses, the guy mopping the hall – and thank them for their help. Mum and I go back to the car. She drives, while I lean my burning face against the window. We slink off home: I'm not dying after all.

A few days later, my aunty asks, 'Have you thought that maybe it was a panic attack?'

'A what?' I don't even know what a panic attack is.

She explains, and I dismiss the idea. 'Nah, I don't think so. I'm not that kind of person.'

She raises an eyebrow, but I don't offer an explanation. I don't need to. Isn't it obvious? I'm not that kind of person. You know, the stress-head kind. The panic-attack kind. The kind of person who's fallible or vulnerable. The kind of person who's human. That's not me.

I am someone who can lift 100 kilos and chin-up thirty-six. Pain doesn't faze me, and neither does hard work. You think I baulked when Ken pushed me into some the hardest training in the country? You think I flinched when Dad up and walked out on us? I am tough. I am a survivor. I am as hard as old nails.

So what if my boyfriend has just moved interstate? I'll live. You think I'm going to fall apart over that? And anyway, the doctors said there was nothing wrong with me. Not with my heart and not with my head.

And so I go on, invincible as ever. A fish out of water, but somehow still breathing.

~

But after my faux heart attack, my heart is slow to heal. Sure, it pumps okay. It does the job. But it aches whenever I think of Marty and how far away he is. I am miserable and alone.

But I stuff all these feelings down and get on with the job. I try to focus on Worlds: the World Championships in Melbourne. Where my boyfriend is.

Our squad heads south with Stephan at the beginning of March to train at the Monash University pool in the weeks leading up to competition. We're in orientation camp again, so I'm staying with the team at the Novotel in Mount Waverley. But I don't want to be here. I want to be with Marty.

Then one day, only a week before Worlds, I have a particularly bad training session. I'm in a bad mood and I have a foul mouth. I want to be curled up on a couch with Marty, not ploughing up and down some boring old pool. The team is in taper, so we're restricted to light sessions ahead of competition next week. Even so, my times are especially slow today. I am frustrated and aggravated, cranky and cold.

'You need to work on your attitude,' Stephan says to me as I vault from the pool.

I rip off my cap and shake water from my ears.

'Pardon?' I pretend I haven't heard him.

'Your attitude,' he repeats. Stephan is all about having a good attitude and giving your best. Today I have given my best, but my times are just awful and my stroke is horrendous. I have given my best but I've given much more besides. I've given lip, I've given cheek, I've given plenty of attitude.

Today, frankly, I've been a shithead.

'I'm over it,' I tell Stephan. 'Over. It.' I grind out the words. 'I'm sick of training. Sick of racing. I am tired of the whole bloody thing. I don't want to do it anymore.'

'Then maybe you shouldn't,' he says calmly.

'Then maybe I won't!'

'Perhaps you should retire,' he says. Just like that. It's so simple, so obvious. Coming from anyone else this might sound like a challenge: like calling my bluff, like winding me up. But Stephan's not like that. He is serious and earnest and he means what he says. He's not trying to provoke me. He's just being honest.

I know this and yet I crack it. Badly.

'Well, maybe I will! Maybe I will quit!' I shout.

Last year was only my best year ever, I fume quietly. *I broke PBs; I broke world records. My times have never been better than they have in the last twelve months. But whatever. No biggie. If you want me to quit, maybe I will!*

I flounce around the pool deck making a big scene out of packing up my stuff. I slap around in my thongs, scoop up my towel, then sweep past Stephan to the showers. But even as I exit stage left, I know I'm in the wrong. Stephan and I butt heads all the time, because we're not necessarily the best fit personality-wise. He is quiet and calm. I am loud and enthusiastic. Plus, he's not always as sympathetic or as understanding as I'd like.

But for all our differences, we work well together. Stephan gets the very best results from me, for sure.

Deep down, I know that today is not his fault. I am tired, fed up and sick of bloody swimming. I've been doing this for more than ten years now, and it's hard to maintain enthusiasm every single day. It will be my fourth World Championships next week and all of a sudden it feels like I've been swimming for a long time. A very long time. It's not fair for me to take that out on Stephan.

But it makes a change from just stuffing it all down.

~

Before I left Brisbane, I woke up one night to discover I'd had a stroke. At least I thought I had.

What's going on? I panic. My face is paralysed and the right side of my body is numb. I can't move my right arm or leg. I tumble from bed and stagger to the door, dragging my dead-wood leg behind me. I can't turn the knob; my fingers are limp. I can't scream for help; my mouth is numb.

Is this a nightmare? Will I wake up? I am desperate and I scrabble at the door with my useless hand. Finally it occurs to me to use my good hand, and I open the door and stagger up the stairs and into Mum's room.

'Mum! Mum!' I grunt. The words loll stupidly around in my mouth, flattened by my dead tongue.

Mum is groggy but alarmed. She sits with me until the numbness fades, till I tingle and burn and my feeling returns. It's not a stroke, then. But if it's not that, then what is it? Something is seriously wrong with me. I know it.

'Go back to bed,' Mum says to me eventually. 'You need to rest and take care of yourself.'

'I can't.' I'm confused. Mum knows I have training.

'You can't train today, Leisel. Just look at you.'

Sure, I might have thought I was having a stroke, but only a mild one, my foggy brain argues. *Nothing worth missing a training session over.*

'Bed,' Mum instructs and I know better than to argue.

I pad back down the stairs and get into bed. Everything feels wrong. I don't like this at all. I think about my body and the way it's suddenly failing me. First chest pain and now this. I think about my mental state and my attitude to swimming. I'm 'train at all costs'. I'm 'get on with the job'. I'm not 'start falling apart and retreat back to bed'. I sink under the covers and try to block out the world.

If I can't train, I don't know what else I can do.

17

Taking Risks

The 2007 World Aquatics Championships are held at Rod Laver Arena in Melbourne, home of the Australian Open and one of the most famous tennis courts in the world. That's right: a tennis court. We are swimming on a tennis court. Somehow, the court is now a sparkling blue pool.

The first five row of seats are submerged under water, and it's lapping gently at the foot of the sixth. It's a stunning sight, it really is – one I couldn't have imagined if I hadn't seen it with my own eyes.

I have a good meet in Melbourne. I win silver in the 50-metre breaststroke, coming second to my friend Jessica Hardy from the United States by only 0.07 seconds. Then I make it a clean sweep by winning gold in both the 100-metre and 200-metre events as well, and setting a new Commonwealth record in the 100 metres. Plus, Emily Seebohm, Jessicah Shipper, Libby Lenton and I win gold in the 4 × 100-metre medley relay, breaking the world record with a time of 3:55.74.

I never thought I would compete at Rod Laver, but when I do I leave with four medals clanking in my bag.

And yet, despite my performance, despite the great pool, even despite the Chapel Street shopping we squeeze in during our days off, I feel unmotivated in Melbourne.

My relationship with Stephan is worn out. It's not that anything has changed – Stephan is as reliable as ever – but I get the impression he's not loving working with me anymore. And if I'm honest with myself, the feeling is mutual. I can't fault Stephan for the training he's providing. But that conversation we had when I was being a diva and he suggested I quit ... somehow that was the start of a downward slide.

I am not enjoying training. I'm not even enjoying racing, which up until now I have always loved. I'm not enjoying anything to do with swimming, in fact. I can't seem to find happiness anywhere, except when I'm with Marty.

'You don't need to feel like this, you know,' Marty says to me one day. We're on the couch at 'home' in Toorak, where we are house-sitting for his business mentor. It's a beautiful house, all clean lines and white tiles, with expensive designer furniture and a sound system that Marty drools over. It's such a luxury to stay here. It's such a luxury to stay anywhere with Marty and not be at the pool.

'Feel like what?' I ask.

'Like this,' he waves his hand in front of my face like whatever 'this' is, is right before my eyes. 'Like: miserable. And frustrated and tired. You don't need to feel like that. Your sport should make you happier than this.'

I stare at him. 'But I am happy. I'm so happy with you. I've never been happier in my life!'

'Sure, I know you're happy with me. But the rest of the time you're miserable. Your training, your swimming: you're not enjoying them. You should be loving your sport. This,' he waves his hand again, 'is not normal.'

Later that night, I lie in bed and think about Marty's words. *This is not normal*, he said. Until now, I hadn't thought there was anything wrong with me. I thought it was totally normal for people to feel like this. To feel sad and tired and miserable and trapped. To feel like they have to get up at 4 a.m. and get on with their job, otherwise how else are they going to pay the mortgage that month? Isn't that how life is? Isn't that what being an adult is all about? I thought it was totally normal for me to not love swimming and to feel trapped in my career; to feel angry and powerless and anxious and bored. I had never thought to question it.

I had certainly never sought help from a professional such as a sports psychologist. I am stuck back in the Ken Wood mentality, where sports psychs are for weak people. And I am not weak. It would never in a million years occur to me to ask anyone for help.

Besides, what help do I need? There's nothing really wrong with me, is there?

But Marty thinks there is, and a few days later he tries again.

'You know, maybe Stephan's not right for you anymore,' he says.

We are back on the couch again. *I'd be alright*, I think, *if I could just train from right here.* I have a vision of myself on the couch, with Marty beside me, floating along a narrow pool lane. The idea makes me feel relieved.

'Maybe it's time to think about a change,' Marty says.

'A change?'

'Yeah. Like a new approach or a new coach. Babe, why don't you move down here to Melbourne?'

In my head, I am still on my couch floating in the pool, so Marty's words slap me like a wave. *Move? To Melbourne?*

'But what about my training? What about Stephan and my squad and Mum and my whole life?' I stutter. Everything I have – everything I've ever known – is in Queensland.

Marty shrugs. 'Start a new one,' he says. 'Start a life here in Melbourne with me, and with a new coach. Start a life where you're happy.' It sounds so simple when he says it.

We write a list of pros and cons.

'You could really do this, you know,' he urges.

Con: The Olympics.

'Write that in capitals,' I instruct. The 2008 Beijing Olympics are less than eighteen months away and I have my eye firmly on the ultimate prize: individual gold at an Olympic Games. It's what I want, what I've been working towards. I have not trained my whole life in order to throw everything away at the last hurdle.

Con: Where to train?

Con: Where to live?

Con: No family support here in Melbourne.

Con: Coach???

'Don't forget the cold weather here in Melbourne,' I say. Then I realise the 'pro' side is looking a little thin.

Pro: 'You!' I say happily to Marty.

Pro: Uh ... A fresh start!

I drum my fingers on the arm of the couch, summoning inspiration.

'Anything else?' Marty asks.

Maybe the list is a bad idea.

Could I do this? I wonder. *Do I risk it?* But one look at Marty and I suddenly decide that I will. I will do this. And I will do it for him. Marty makes me so happy. It's as simple as that. He makes me happy when nothing else in my life does the trick.

'Uh, let's do it,' I say and give him a grin. He hugs me and tells me it will all be okay. Then he walks over to the kitchen bench, picks up the phone and brings it over to me.

'What's this for?' I ask.

'To phone Stephan. Tell him what's going on.'

'What, now?'

'Sure, why not now?'

'Uh, because I've only just decided.'

'So? What are you waiting for? Are you scared?'

'No! It's just I don't know what to say to him yet. I only made my decision, like, two seconds ago.' This is moving too fast. I know I am the ultimate procrastinator – I will do anything to stall – but surely this is moving fast by anyone's standards.

Marty writes my script down for me. He hands me a sheet of paper with the words I should say all laid out. Even with a script, this is still going to be the hardest phone call of my life. I'm breaking up with my coach over the phone.

Stephan is confused when I call; he is on the back foot. But, to his credit, he is as calm and controlled as ever. I tell him I am leaving the squad, and he accepts what I say. I wish he would shout or rant or get mad or do *something*. I tell him I've decided to move to Melbourne, and he rightly points out that I've never even raised the possibility with him.

'I just want a change,' I say to him lamely. 'It's nothing personal.' And then I add: 'Marty is here.'

We hang up and I feel physically sick at the thought of what I've just done. That was a terrible conversation; I went about it all the wrong way. I should have flown back to Brisbane and had a meeting with Stephan, talked to him face to face. I should have explained what I was thinking and how I was feeling. I am instantly sorry. I wish I could change it. I stare at the silent phone in my hands.

But then I turn and smile optimistically at Marty. I've done it. I'm going to move to Melbourne.

'Well done, babe!' He gives me a hug and I know in that instant that we'll make this work. Sure, there might be a bit of self-interest in his encouraging me to move. I know that. He wants me here in Melbourne for his sake as much as for my career. But doesn't that just prove how much he's into me?

I know the cons list is long, while the column of pros is blink-and-you'll-miss-it. I know I am gambling a lot.

I am taking a risk. Don't think I don't know it.

~

The papers go to town over my alleged poor decision. 'What a bad move, Leisel,' screams the headline in the *Sydney Morning Herald*. The journalist describes how Stephan 'transformed' me 'from an anxiety-ridden teenager into an unbreakable machine and a near-certain 100m and 200m gold medallist in Beijing.' They quote my old coach, Ken Wood, who tells them, 'I don't know if it's for the betterment of her swimming that she's moved there.' Then, in case I've forgotten, the papers remind me that the Olympics are only eighteen months away, and they point out that my rivals could all have an advantage over me during this time of flux.

Mum, as usual, is much more measured. While she is adamant that I shouldn't change myself for a guy ('Don't ever let them change you' is her mantra. She adds softly: 'I made that mistake.'), she is quietly cool about my decision. She doesn't like Melbourne and she's cautious about Marty (show me a mum who would encourage their daughter to date an AFL player), but she doesn't say a word against my decision.

I don't go back to Brisbane. I have my stuff shipped down and I say my goodbyes over the phone. I'll visit for sure, I'll be back all the time, but I am a Melbournian now.

I never regret my move. A lot of people criticise me, saying I am throwing away my chances for Beijing, that I should stick with Stephan, that I should put swimming before Marty. I understand where they are coming from, but I know in my heart this is the right thing to do. It's right for me, right for us both. When I'm with Marty, I'm the happiest person on earth, and being so happy can't possibly be wrong. Can it?

If Marty hadn't suggested moving to Melbourne, I don't know what I would have done. I was not enjoying my swimming, but, at the same time, I was never going to quit. No way. Not now. Not so close to winning Olympic gold.

All my threats of quitting, all my flouncing round the pool pretending I might leave: none of it was true. Not really. Retiring is never really an option. I can't go anywhere until I have finished what I started. I can't stop until I've achieved what I set out to do. Winning Olympic gold has been my goal since before the Athens Games, and there is no way in the world I will quit without achieving it.

And this is the last chance I have. I'm not carrying on after the Beijing Games next year – who ever heard of a swimmer going to four Olympics? – so I'm painfully aware it is now or never. If it doesn't happen for me at Beijing, that's it. Beijing is do or die, make or break. It is the very last shot I've got.

And yet I'm not afraid.

Despite having just made the most controversial decision of my career, despite having just risked it all for a boy, I am not afraid. I should be bloody terrified! This could turn out to be the worst choice of my life. On paper it *is*. Just look at my list of pros and cons. Right now, only eighteen months out from the Olympics, I am swimming the very best times in my life. I have a coach who gets results. I must be crazy. But it just feels right.

So I ignore the critics, even the well-intentioned ones (some of the people closest to me do not like the idea at all). I focus, I am committed. I block everyone out. *Say what you like*, I think, *I'm going to make this work.*

Following my heart to Melbourne takes every bit of courage I have. But I don't dwell on the fact that it could be disastrous. I just look forwards and focus on my goal. And underneath, I am a little bit proud that I am choosing to do the right thing for me. I know it's a risk. I know others think it will fail. But I take pride in always doing my own thing. I'm going to go for it and I'm going to make it work.

I will make moving to Melbourne the best decision of my life.

~

At first, life in Melbourne is bliss. I have four weeks off training after the Melbourne Worlds, so Marty and I spend April 2007 mooching around the city, stupidly in love. We move into an apartment in Moonee Ponds, à la Dame Edna, and because it's Melbourne we have an awesome cafe downstairs. We shop for furniture. Buy a dog. All that stuff.

The guys from Marty's team often drop in. They're always coming over for dinner with their wives. We play a lot of Balderdash with Jason Akermanis and his wife, Megan. We hang out with Mitch Hahn and his wife, Lana.

Although he was drafted to the Western Bulldogs, Marty is playing for Werribee right now, so after I finish training on Saturday mornings I drive forty-five minutes or so out to Werribee to watch him play. Sometimes I even drive as far as Ballarat, an hour and a half away.

I make friends with a bunch of the wives and girlfriends of the team. Georgia (Travis Baird's wife), Kristy (Peter Street's wife) and Lana and I sit in my car during matches, escaping the freezing Werribee wind, drinking hot chocolate and reading trashy magazines. We freeze our arses off and pretend we're watching the game. Then, when the boys pile into the car after the match, we act like we haven't missed a minute.

Them: 'Did you see that goal in the third quarter?'

Us: 'Uh, yeah, sure. You had a great game.'

Them: 'We lost.'

Us: 'Oh yeah, that. That one. But still, great game, huh?'

We are so not into the AFL scene. We are uncool – not glamorous at all. We are the plebs in the car park, the bottom of the rung. We couldn't be further from Rebecca Judd and all the other AFL WAGs if we tried. But we have the best time together – we're such great mates.

Melbourne is hard for Marty and I, though. It's tough making new friends, tough finding our feet in a new city. Our schedules are hectic. By the time I'm home from my morning training session, he's already at the club for training. But we are so very much in love that somehow everything else just melts away. We manage to have our evenings together and we're very happy in our little unit on Shuter Street.

~

In the days and weeks after my move, I approach several swimming coaches. The obvious choice is Ian Pope, a high-profile coach to all the big names. Grant Hackett, Giaan Rooney, Massimiliano Rosolino: they all train with Popey.

When I meet him, he's friendly enough, but also a little vague. 'Sure, come join us if you want,' he tells me with a shrug. Then he's back off to the pool and his throng of champions.

I call Rohan Taylor. He is not my first preference (that was Popey). It's not that I've heard anything bad about Rohan, more that I haven't heard much about him at all. He trains Sarah Katsoulis, who is a great girl but who has never swum at Olympic level. And beyond that? I couldn't tell you. Rohan doesn't have the credentials or the star power of Ian Pope. But he agrees to meet me, and for that I am very grateful.

We arrange to meet at Lil Kitch cafe on Puckle Street on Friday morning. As usual, I get there early. Maybe it's because of all the 4 a.m. starts. Or because Ken always told us, 'If you're not ten minutes early, you're late.' But I can't seem to go anywhere without being at least ten minutes ahead of everyone else. I settle into a table at the back and order the Anzac breakfast: two fried eggs, hash browns, baked beans, bacon and sausage. When Rohan arrives he proves to be a fairly nondescript-looking guy. He's in his early forties, I'd guess, and is a little stocky, with a crewcut and a polo shirt and not much to distinguish him except that he looks quite American, although I can't pinpoint exactly why.

He looks at me, then at the plate in front of me. 'Not hungry today?' he asks.

'On a diet,' I reply.

We both laugh. *Perhaps*, I think, *this just might work*.

Rohan is meticulously organised. He comes to our meeting armed with folders full of schedules. He's got training programs, gym programs and spreadsheet columns stacked full of data. I am seriously impressed with his preparation. He has ideas for this and plans for that. And every sentence that comes out of his mouth seems to start with: 'What I can do for you is …' He speaks with a soft American accent, and he tells me how he grew up in the States, how he went to university in Las Vegas and Hawaii, and how he is heavily influenced by the US college system when it comes to swimming. 'We have a real US attitude to training at our squad,' he says. 'We work hard, we play hard, and we encourage each other all the way.'

'We're a young squad,' he says. 'A vibrant squad. You'll have a lot of fun if you train with us.'

I tell him I don't doubt it. I like the way he says 'we' a lot.

'We'll cop some criticism for this, you know,' he says.

I raise an eyebrow.

'This is controversial, this plan I've proposed. This style of training, this stuff.' He presses one finger into the manila folders spread out in front of us. 'Not to mention the fact we're less than sixteen months out from Olympic trials now.'

He doesn't mention the elephant in the room: the fact that he is not an Olympic coach. Rohan is a good coach, a keen coach, but he has never successfully coached anyone to an Olympics before. To go with Rohan will be a massive gamble on my part.

'But,' he goes on, 'I don't want you to think about any of that. Your job is to have fun.'

'To work hard,' he adds quickly. 'But to have fun, too. And I think we can have a great time together.'

I look at the folders. I look at Rohan. I like what this man has brought to the table. Literally, in the case of his detailed plans. But also in terms of his attitude to training.

'Rohan, I like your style,' I say. 'I like you and I like your style.'

We agree to start on Monday.

While Rohan may not have the credentials of coaches like Popey, I am again convinced I have made the right choice. We hit it off, Rohan and I, and opting for him feels right. Lately, I've become a believer in listening to my gut instincts. I'm on a bit of a roll. Sure, I've always done my own thing and made up my own mind. But recently it feels like I've been making braver choices than usual, and this decision to go with Rohan – just like my decision to move to Melbourne with Marty – is a choice I'm convinced will pay off. I am determined to make it do so.

At the weekend, Marty and I do a drive-by to check out the Bulleen pool where I'll be training with Rohan.

'So it's called "Bulleen Swim Centre",' I read hesitantly, twisting the map to orientate myself. 'Carey Bulleen Sports Complex, off Bulleen Road.'

'Here?' Marty says and he swings the car into someone's drive. Trees line the sweeping drive, which wends its way towards an austere red-brick building in the distance. A pristine blue and gold sign reading 'Carey Baptist Grammar School' stares disapprovingly down at us. Carey is one of Melbourne's largest private schools.

'Uh, no.' I squint at the map. 'No, this can't be right. Chuck a U-y and we'll go back to that last roundabout.'

'You sure?' Marty says. 'That sign says Bulleen pool.'

I follow his finger towards another sign. It says 'Bulleen pool' in gold and blue. I shrug, and Marty guides the car further down the driveway and past a lush oval and an imposing pavilion, towards a domed building.

It houses the Geoffrey Stevens pool. When I see it, I almost die.

'Where's the rest of it?' Marty says. And no wonder.

Not only is the Geoffrey Stevens pool part of a high school, it is – I swear to God – only 25 metres long. Eight lanes wide, and hip-deep at the shallow end, the pool is only half the length of the regular Olympic version. There are no flags at the 10-metre mark, no diving blocks to be seen, and there is a learn-to-swim poster sticky-taped to the door.

Oh. My. God. What have I done?

I think about Popey and his squad training down at the Melbourne Sports and Aquatic Centre, where they held the Commonwealth Games last year. I think about Stephan and his squad back at the Valley pool. Then I look at the Carey high-school 25-metre pool and I want to cry. I could be back at Burpengary, with its dinky pool, back in Col's backyard shed with its corrugated roof. At least Col had a barbie.

What have I done? I panic. This was my big chance, my last shot at individual Olympic gold. I am starting to feel hysterical. I will be training for my third Olympics in an indoor 25-metre pool? With the learn-to-swim kiddies?

I phone Rohan.

'You train indoor twenty-five, are you kidding me?' I say as soon as he picks up. 'This is a school pool. This is absurd!'

On the other end of the line, Rohan is unperturbed.

'Sure,' he says. 'This is Melbourne. We have to train indoors. Except a few times each week when we do outdoor sessions.' My delicate Queensland blood shivers in my veins.

'Yes, yes. Indoor is fine. But twenty-five metres?' I cannot get past this.

'Nah, the outdoor pool is the full fifty,' Rohan says, misunderstanding me. 'We also use the one at the VIS sometimes, but we have to share that with Collingwood.'

The VIS is the Victorian Institute of Sport. I picture myself trying to train while the Collingwood Football Club boys walk up and down in the lane beside me comparing bruises and talking boofy footy talk.

Holy crap. What have I done?

I run through my options. Go back to Popey and tell him I made a mistake? Go back to Stephan and tell him I made a mistake? Go back to the drawing board and find a new coach? Can I really do that? After I've hit if off so well with Rohan?

I look at the pool and I gulp down hard. *Screw it*, I think, *I will make this happen*. Whatever it takes, I will make this work. I have risked too much. I have come too far. I can't back out now. Not when so many people are waiting to see me fail.

And who knows? Swimming in a half-sized pool might just be okay. At least I'll have a chance to work on my turns ...

~

I start with Rohan in April 2007, sixteen months out from the Beijing Olympics. It is a busy time, there is a lot going on. And yet as soon as I get started, I know I've made the right decisions. The right decision choosing Marty. The right decision choosing Rohan. Aside from Rohan's too-short pool, life in Melbourne is pretty near perfect.

What would make it completely perfect is an individual Olympic gold to add to my collection. I have two silvers and a bronze for individual events, and a silver and a gold for the medley relay. It's the thought of a gold in the 100 metres or 200 metres that gets me up and out of bed in the morning. It is my focus, my world. Everything I do revolves around this.

Rohan is focused on the 100-metre rather than the 200-metre event, as he thinks this is my best chance in Beijing. So all my training is geared towards it. Of course I'm fit enough to win the 200 metres too. I have enough training under my belt that I hope to take out both. But to return home with one shiny gold medal: that would make my life complete.

Training with Rohan is loads of fun. Just as he promised back at our first meeting, his squad is young and vibrant and they are loud. Like Stephan, Rohan is all about having a good attitude at training, but a big part of that here is encouraging one another. Rohan likes his swimmers to be vocal and to have team spirit, so we cheer and shout and make a racket at training each day.

'C'mon, guys, this is the last one hundred!'

'Last effort! Dig deep! You can do it!'

We try to propel one another up and down the lanes with sheer enthusiasm. And it works. I dig deep. I find the energy I need. I get so much more out of myself in a squad like this. There is a good atmosphere, a good vibe. We're all in it together: I like that feeling.

And the sense of community doesn't finish at the pool wall either. We're good friends, all of us. We're always going out for breakfast or to the movies together. Rohan encourages us to socialise outside of training. This is very different to the way things were back with Stephan in Brisbane. Back then, I was lucky if I went out for breakfast with Mel Schlanger and Jo Fargus once or twice a week. These girls were amazing but they were my only close friends the whole time I was there. Here, I am always hanging out with friends – either from my squad or Marty's team – or I am round at Rohan's with him and his family.

Rohan and his wife, Jodie, have two small girls, and the door to their home is always open to anyone in the squad. Marty and I have dinners there, chatting with Jodie in the kitchen and playing with the kids before bedtime. It's unlike any relationship I've had with a coach before. Rohan is very professional, but also very welcoming too. I feel like I can say anything to him, tell him anything about how I'm feeling or what's going on in my life. He really cares. And it's not long before his family becomes my family in Melbourne too.

By now, Marty's training in Footscray, while I'm out at my minipool in Bulleen. We're still living in our apartment in Moonee Ponds, which is at least forty-five minutes' drive from the pool, so by the time we both get to and from training each day we only see one another in the evening for dinner. And yet we are so close. We totally get one another, Marty and I. He is incredibly supportive of my swimming, my crazy hours, my heavy training, my strict eating and my deep sleeping.

Marty does all the cooking and makes sure my meals are super healthy (and super delicious). He is going to cook our way to Olympic gold. And after four hours in the pool each day, and a couple more in the gym after that, there is nothing more special he could do for me than cook. *Am I the luckiest girl in the world, or what?* I wonder as I eat another amazing casserole, another steak, another chargrilled lamb chop. *What did I do to deserve this?*

Then one day my friend Louise calls me to tell me she thinks Marty is cheating on me. Twenty seconds into Louise's phonecall, I am slumped on my bedroom floor, phone in one hand, head resting in the other. I feel as if someone has punched me in the stomach.

There are stories going around. Rumours. Someone says he's sleeping with this girl. He was seen kissing another. Someone else heard he gave some woman his number. *What did I do to deserve this?* It's lies, all of it. It must be.

Even so, it's weird. Why would Louise say all these things about Marty when she and Marty have been friends for such a long time? It was Louise who introduced us in the first place. Now here she is, bad-mouthing him? I can't think why she would make any of this stuff up.

I am on the floor bawling my eyes out when Marty comes home.

'LJ? What's happened?' He drops his footy bag and rushes to my side.

I sob and hiccup and bury my face into his chest. 'Louise told me ... It's just that she said ...' I give him an abbreviated version of what I have heard.

'That's absolute shit! That's horseshit!' Marty is furious. He flares up in an instant. 'Do you believe her? Do you? Do you? Answer me!' He is ranting again before I can answer, shouting and slamming his fist on the floor. 'I can't believe you would trust her word over mine. Why would you believe her? She's making up stories. It's bullshit! All of it!' He stands and kicks his footy bag across the room. Then he storms back out into the corridor, shouting over his shoulder as he goes. 'Don't you talk to that girl ever again!'

When he's gone, when the apartment is quiet again, I sit in the fading light and pick at the threads of the bedspread.

Winston, our dog, will be scratching at the door for his dinner soon. I should go and defrost something for him. I don't feel like eating anything – don't want to eat ever again. I'd rather just sit here in the gloom. Louise is such a good friend to me – she's always had my back – so I can't understand why she's making up stuff now.

I don't blame Marty for being so furious. I would be too, if someone accused me of cheating. But doesn't he know that I trust him? That I always believe him?

I sit and wait for him to come home. I sit and wait in the purple dark.

I later learn that what Louise had heard was made up by someone else spreading rumours.

18

Crashing

It is spring 2007 and Melbourne is thawing out. Slowly uncoiling. Freesias push through the grass in gardens and on kerbsides. Spring Racing Carnival fever has taken over the city, and there are flags flying on every council flagpole, and posters and pictures in all the stores.

I am cruising down Bridge Road, past the Epworth Hospital, past Schnitz restaurant ('You love Schnitz, we love Schnitz, we all love Schnitz!'), to my training at the Richmond Recreation Centre. We've been training here a lot lately. Maybe Rohan is finally taking my hints about a 50-metre pool. It's handier to home, a bit less of a commute, which gives me more time to spend with Marty, of course. We've been trying to make a real effort lately, trying to see one another as much as our schedules allow. Louise's accusations have shaken him, I think. They have shaken us both, although I don't believe a word.

The traffic is slow today but I don't mind, because I'm in my beautiful Holden Astra convertible – a sponsor car – with the top down and the windows low, so the light breeze ruffles my hair. I could sit in this traffic all day long. Up ahead, the light is green, but I go slowly. I know this intersection and I know there is a speed bump ahead of the traffic lights. My car is low-slung, the bump is high, and the combination needs careful negotiation.

I must be going about 40 kilometres an hour when I enter the intersection, but then somehow – suddenly – I am stopped. It's as if a giant hand reached down and pushed me with its palm. *Stop.* There is a crunch. A terrible noise. And a car has materialised in front of me. A metal speed bump, crumpled and groaning.

I have T-boned another car. Across my smashed bonnet, I watch as the car shudders, reverses and tries to get through the intersection for a second time. The guy I've pranged is driving away. *He's driving away?* But there's traffic, there's a mess. There is glass and dangling bumpers. He can't get through.

A face appears where my window used to be. A girl. She is talking to me. Someone else has pulled out a phone.

'What the hell was that guy thinking?' I shout out to them.

Back when I first met Rohan, just about the only thing I knew about him was the name 'Lori Munz'. Lori was a Commonwealth Games gold medallist who swam with Rohan, and she was on track to make the Sydney Olympic team – his first Olympian – when she had a terrible car accident just two months out from trials. She had her legs pinned in the wreckage and broke both knees: the accident ended her career.

Now, eight months out from the Beijing Games, I phone Rohan with the news he never wanted to hear again.

'I've had a car accident,' I sob down the line. His golden girl. His Olympian.

For a split second there is silence. There is nothing coming through.

Then: 'Holy shit! Where are you? What's happened? Are you okay?'

I sob and ball my fist into one eye. My nose is running. 'My car's broken, Rohan! I broke my car!'

'What?'

'I broke my car and it doesn't belong to me. It's Holden's and now I've broken it and I don't know what to do, Rohan!'

'Leisel, where are you?' he shouts.

I pause and look up stupidly. 'I'm outside.'

And I am. Having wound my way through peak-hour Melbourne, I have had an accident less than 100 metres from the pool. I can see the car park from here. I laugh, and this unnerves poor Rohan even more.

'Don't move!' he tells me. 'I'm on my way!'

When Rohan arrives at the scene, he finds me sitting on the grass on the side of the road, still in tears, still worried about Holden. From the rear, my car looks pristine, but when you walk around and view it from the front there is only thin air where the engine and the bonnet used to be. 'You were bloody lucky,' Rohan says grimly to me later. For once he says 'you', when he usually always says 'we'. But I know that he still means 'we'. We were bloody lucky.

The other driver – an unlicensed driver – ran the red light. There was a witness: the girl who tapped on my window. And the Richmond police station, like the pool, is nearby, handily placed for her to give a statement.

I feel so scared to tell Holden that I've messed up their car, the beautiful convertible they loaned me. I'm normally so good about looking after things. It's still a novelty for me to have expensive things, so I have kept the car spotless. I have taken it to get detailed every second week and made sure it's always garaged. And now I am ringing Holden to tell them I've written it off. I had to leave it in two pieces, abandoned at an intersection. 'They're probably used to their footballers doing that. Not their swimmers,' Marty jokes.

But if I feel bad about Holden, I feel worse about Rohan. I've clearly scared him so much. He is in shock all morning, I can tell, even though he pretends it's business as usual. I still train the morning after the accident, still get straight in the pool. I'm sore. I have some whiplash that feels like it will hurt in the morning. But it never occurs to me not to train. Just like it never occurs to me that my Olympic-grade legs might me more valuable than a Holden car.

Besides, if I don't go swimming, what else will I do?

~

Several days after my accident, I am back in a car again, but this time Marty is behind the wheel. We are off to the Yarra Valley for a little wine tasting. A surprise romantic weekend. I could not be more uncomfortable if I tried.

'You're sure Rohan said it's okay if I miss training this morning?' I ask. It is Saturday morning and I'm not in the pool.

'Yes, already. I asked him the other night when we were round there for dinner.'

I want to say: *Yes, but why were you asking my coach if I could have time off – without telling me*, but I don't. *He's being romantic. Suck it up. Enjoy it*, I tell myself.

'So, wine tasting, huh?' I say for the umpteenth time in our short car trip. We are not usually wine tasters. I drink about one glass of wine a year.

But we go and it's fun. We taste a few wines, matching them with cheeses. It's cool-climate wine country down here in the Yarra, and yet things with Marty seem hotter than ever this weekend. He is sweet and romantic, and more affectionate than usual. Was it really just a few weeks ago that Louise thought he was cheating on me?

There are forty or so cellar doors in the region and by the end of the day my head feels as though I have drunk at every one. We have dinner at a fancy-pants restaurant on one of the rolling estates (more wine), then drag ourselves back to our B&B. We are staying near the Dandenong Ranges and the view from our cottage, stretching all the way down the Mornington Peninsula and towards the bays, is pretty spectacular. This morning I could have looked at it all day long. But right now? I'd settle for a couple of Gaviscon and a good night's sleep. That last pinot noir and the chocolate mousse for dessert finished me off. I am rifling through my bag looking for something to take for my groaning stomach, when Marty emerges from the bathroom.

He doesn't say a word, just walks dramatically to the centre of the room, gets down on one knee and with a flourish produces a small black box from behind his back.

'Will you marry me?' he asks.

Wha– marry him? My eyes widen. Blood pumps loudly in my ears. I can feel my pulse race. Then I break into a big silly grin. 'Of course!' I cry. 'Of course I will!'

I stoop down to kiss him just as he is getting up, and we bump into one another awkwardly halfway. Marty asks, 'So, was that a yes?'

'Yes!' I shout. 'Yes, I will!'

He pulls out a ring and slips it onto my finger.

'Oh,' I say in surprise. 'It's yellow gold?' Then I immediately curse myself for having said it. *Idiot*, I think. *Who says that?* You're supposed to say 'thank you' or 'I love it'. Not 'Oh, it's the wrong colour'.

But it is the wrong colour. I hate yellow gold; I only ever wear white. And Marty knows this, because he asked me months ago what sort of ring I would like if we were ever to get engaged. I said white gold, and something simple. Those were my only criteria. And now he's here with a yellow-gold extravaganza.

'Yeah,' Marty says. 'My mum thinks white gold looks cheap so I got you yellow instead.'

Oh? Cheap? And so you bought what your Mum wanted and not what I like? I try not to show how insulted I am.

'Cool. That's really nice. Thanks, babe.'

'It is, isn't it?' he agrees.

~

Later, we are lying in bed. The chocolate mousse in my stomach weighs heavily, the ring on my finger even more so. *You're engaged*, I tell myself sternly, *to the man you love! Stop acting like the colour of the stupid ring matters. Why do you even care about this now?*

But it's not the colour, or the style, or any of that. It's that Marty asked what I wanted and then decided he knew better. Worse than that, he decided his mum knew better.

'Hey, babe, we should tell people that we got engaged,' Marty suggests and I realise that I am actually embarrassed.

'What, now?'

'Yeah, why not?'

Because I am twenty-two years old and I'm not sure I'm ready for this.

Because my stomach is churning and it's not just the mousse.

'Okay, sure.'

Marty reaches over and takes my mobile phone from the bedside table.

'You're using my phone?' I ask.

He doesn't reply. Instead, he types out a message on my behalf, then sends it to everyone in my address book. It's not long before my phone starts pinging in reply.

'No way!' replies Sarah Katsoulis, my friend from swimming.

'Oh, congratulations!' replies my cousin. 'BTW that's the weirdest message I've ever got from you.'

I scroll up to see what Marty wrote – then I cringe – from

embarrassment. 'A romantic thing happened to me today in the Yarra Valley,' the message gushes. 'Marty asked me to marry him and I said yes!'

This is so not what I would write. To my friends, I would say, 'Suckers! Guess what? I got engaged!' Something like that. Never: 'A romantic thing happened to me today...'

I feel embarrassed, and then I worry about feeling embarrassed. *It is not a good sign to be starting this way*, I think.

I phone my Nanna and she is underwhelmed. 'You did what?' she asks from back in Woy Woy.

My mum, I learn from Marty, already knows. He asked her permission and she said it was 'fine'. But 'fine' is hardly the joy I hoped she might feel. Or *I* might feel for that matter. I re-read Marty's text message and feel awkward again. I can't shake the sense this is all about him. Like he's tied me down. He's got bragging rights now. To what, I'm not sure. But already I feel like this engagement is nothing to do with me.

I think about the slip of paper with some girl's number on it that I found tucked carefully in Marty's jacket once, after he'd come home from clubbing. We were living back in Brisbane at the time, and he promised me it was an old number. One from ages ago, before we'd met. But even that small slip of paper seems enlarged in my mind tonight.

Marty is still lying beside me, propped up on one strong arm, his eyes closed as he lazily rubs his free hand back and forth across the base of his head. I love this man, I really do. I love him so much I wouldn't change a thing. But that's the problem: I wouldn't change a thing. I'm not ready to be engaged. Not ready at all. At twenty-two I'm certainly not ready to start planning a wedding. In any case, I have never been the kind of girl who dreams of white dresses and a lavish wedding. Even the thought of 'announcing' I'm engaged makes me want to puke. But how do I say that? How do I press pause on our relationship? Could it survive if I put it on ice? I shouldn't have said 'yes', but then, I could never have said 'no'. If I lost Marty I don't know what I'd do.

And on some level, though I don't admit it to myself, what I really fear is screwing things up ahead of the Olympics. Beijing is the biggest campaign of my life. It's only five months now till trials and the last thing I want is to go through a messy break-up, to have to move out of home, to have to change things. I am happy and settled and more focused than ever, and I'm not going to throw that away in a hurry. It's ironic, after all the bad press I received over Marty. 'He's a distraction', 'she's lost her focus', the papers all accused. Yet now here I am, getting engaged to him – at least in some small way – in order to keep my Olympic campaign on track.

I glance back down at my yellow-gold ring, then across to Marty again. And like the whiplash I felt after my car accident, I am nervous this engagement will hurt in the morning.

19

Beijing Blues

On Monday morning at 4 a.m., I am back in the pool. Six and a half kilometres. Up and down, up and down. The repetition is good. It's soothing, all this blue.

My yellow-gold engagement ring is tucked carefully away inside a cotton purse, which is hidden inside my sports bag, inside my locker, inside the change rooms at the far end of the pool. A babushka doll of security. I feel lighter when I'm not wearing it, more able to concentrate on my swimming, as if shedding that 3/4 carat will shave microseconds from my times.

As I swim, I do the maths in my head. I have five months till trials, then another five after that until the Beijing Games begin in August. I'm training six hours a day, for six days a week. That's thirty-six hours per week, and it gives me roughly 1560 pool hours until I have to be ready. 1560 hours. Ten months.

Up and down. I count strokes, breaths, laps, time. Ten months to get ready. Ten months to be perfect. Then the rest of my life to dwell on the results. This is what my whole career has been for. My self-worth depends on it.

I am training like a demon; I am sleeping like the dead. I have never worked so hard in my entire life. Rohan has me doing lots of dry-land training, in addition to my work in the pool. 'Very experimental,' I say. 'It's what all the Americans are doing,' he explains. And so my gym coach, Jeremy Oliver, gets me working up a sweat in the weights room. Or doing bike training at the velodrome. It's cool: I've never done anything like velodrome work before and I enjoy the challenge of trying new things. Most of the time it's just me and Jeremy. Sometimes swimmer Shayne Reese comes along too. We cycle for hours and, to lose weight, I also wear a 10-kilogram vest. Or we pull metal sleds. I watch Jeremy stack my sled with 40-kilogram weights. 'Forty?' I ask. There will be gymnasts on the Olympic team who weigh no more than this. 'Forty,' he says. And so I wobble away on my bike, hauling my sled across the grass behind me.

Then one day Jeremy suggests I replace my evening meal with soup. 'No biggie,' he assures me. 'It's just you might swim faster if you were lighter.'

Ouch. The words sink like lead. They sink like an Olympic swimmer who's overweight.

Lighter, huh? What exactly is he saying?

But Jeremy is so smart, he has so much knowledge when it comes to fitness, that I tell myself to get over it and just take his advice.

'Alright,' I tell him. 'I reckon I could do that.' And I go home to google soup recipes.

Marty is amazingly supportive about my diet. He is still chief cook in our house and even though he only ever cooks healthy stuff for us anyway, he relinquishes his role now, in order for me to make soup for our dinners. I cook a big batch each Sunday and then we eat it all week. 'Whatever you have to do, I'll do it with you,' he tells me. And I am grateful to have him by my side.

So now I'm as disciplined with my eating as I am with my training. More so, in fact. I am a woman on a mission, a calorie-counting quest. For breakfast I eat one cup of high-fibre cereal with diced fruit and the lowest-possible-fat milk. For lunch I start out eating chicken and salad, or a sandwich, or tinned tuna, but it's not long before I cut back to a single red apple. Dinner, of course, is the soup de jour. Often it is minestrone, sometimes pumpkin or tomato. And there is no bread allowed. No croutons, not even a little shaved parmesan on top. I only eat dinner if it can fit through a strainer. My teeth start to forget what I ever used them for.

I drink no tea, no alcohol, no soft drink. Just the odd coffee and sometimes a protein shake after the gym. It goes without saying there is strictly no snacking. In fact, except for my apple and my bowl of soup, nothing passes my lips after breakfast. I am still training six hours per day, most days of the week. And I am starving. I am stomach-achingly, head-spinningly famished.

Even as I am doing this, I can see that I have taken things too far. I know I'm being irrational about food. I am warped: obsessed. It's all I can think about. The less I consume, the more I am consumed by it.

But I get too much satisfaction from dieting to ever stop now. It is powerful – it's addictive – this ability to control. It feels like if I can restrict what I am eating I might be able to dictate everything else in my life, too. I am desperate to win; I will win at all costs. I've got it into my head that I am too fat and if I can just lose more weight then I will win the 100-metre event for sure. Then this pain will all be worth it.

My focus now is different to the way I was before the 2004 Athens Olympics. Back then I was obsessing strictly about swimming. This is broader and bigger. This is everything. I am determined to be the best athlete I can be. If I can just win gold, the rest of my life will fall into place. My relationship with Marty. With myself. Everything will be perfect if I can just win one race.

It is no-one else's fault that I am so hungry, but that doesn't stop me taking it out on everyone. I am grumpy at training, and at home when I'm with Marty. I have no energy and my metabolism is screwed. I struggle at squad. I have to keep getting out of the pool to vomit from hunger and exertion. I am swimming on nothing but stubbornness and thin air.

Jeremy organises a bike ride for us one day. We're doing a lot of rides and hikes these days, uphill, for long distances and wearing that 10-kilo vest. 'Sure you want to wear the vest today?' Jeremy asks me. It's going to be a long ride today. 'Think I can't do it?' I reply. If there's an extra challenge, an extra step, I'm always willing to take it. I am the only one making myself do all of this.

I strap the thing on and grimace under the weight. It's only 10 kilos but that feels like a lot these days. Damn thing weighs more than what I eat in a week.

I am super-hydrated this morning. Jeremy warned us the ride would take us a few hours and that hydration would be important, and so, me being me, I've drunk four or five litres. More is more. The more extreme the better. I am taking everything way too far.

I say goodbye to Marty, who is out in the front yard talking to our new neighbours. We've recently left our flat and moved into a house on Davies Street in Moonee Ponds, and I haven't yet had a chance to meet the couple next door. Marty has. He says they're really nice. I wave and hurry off to several hours of gruelling training. Hurry, so I'm not late for the pain.

We do the ride and I don't feel well. That's no surprise, given that I have several litres of water sloshing around in my stomach.

I'm going to be sick, I think on the way home, and I wind down the window and vomit down the side of my car door. Then I bunny-hop all the way home to Moonee Ponds. Drive. Stop. Vomit. Drive. Stop. Vomit.

When I get home, there are strangers in the lounge room; Marty has invited the new neighbours over. I smile weakly but don't stop to ask their names. I just stumble on through to the bathroom and vomit some more. I lie on the couch after they've gone.

'Eat something.' Marty waves a muesli bar under my nose, but the smell of the oats makes me nauseous again.

I vomit again, even though my stomach is empty.

A few days later, my physio comments: 'Wow, you've toned up.' I smile grimly and nod my head. But I haven't really gained much tone. I haven't gained much at all.

Here's what I've lost though: my healthy metabolism, my energy and my perspective. Ironically, the one thing I haven't lost a whole load of is weight. Yeah, I've shed a few kilos, trimmed down a bit. But it's nothing I couldn't have achieved a lot less painfully – and a lot more healthily – if I had done it slowly and properly over eight or ten months. I look fit now, and I'm probably the weight I should be going into an Olympics. But I'm still not skinny. Not lean. I guess I'm just not made that way.

So even after all my dieting, after all my angst, I have not transformed into someone new. I have wasted so much time trying to be something I'm not. I've spent hours torturing myself in training and I've bypassed thousands of calories, trying to magic myself into some super-skinny stranger. And by the end of it I am worn out and sick.

But I am obsessed. I am living and breathing Olympic gold. I am victory or bust. I am win-or-die-trying. I keep slurping that damn soup and dreaming of success. And by the time I reach trials at Sydney in late March, I refuse to even consider I could lose. I qualify comfortably for the 100-metre and 200-metre events for Beijing, then get back to the business of being obsessed.

~

At Beijing, for the benefit of US television ratings, the Olympic Committee has decided to reverse the scheduled times for the heats and the finals. Normally we swim heats in the morning and finals at night. But now, at the request of the NBC, they have turned that on its head so that finals coincide with prime time in the United States. They want Americans to be able to watch Michael Phelps win live when they settle down after work with a beer in front of the box.

'We're flipping our training,' Rohan advises us. 'Hard sessions in the morning, easy in the arvo.'

We are one of the only squads in the world to do this and I don't know why no-one else follows. It's smart and experimental. We're adapting for our conditions. Rohan has us gearing up to do our best work before 10 a.m. in the morning, whereas at any other Olympics I'd barely be out of bed at that time.

But changing your whole program is very difficult. In the lead-up to the games, when we are in taper, I am off to the gym by 6 a.m. Jeremy has me doing a light session to get activated before breakfast, then it's on to the pool by 7:30 a.m. From here, I will train hard for the next few hours, except, of course, on race days, when I'll be preparing to compete. My body adapts quickly to the upside-down regime, but my mind less so. I am aggro and wired. I am highly strung 24/7. A cat on a tin roof with the temperature dialled to blazing.

Marty is good for me. He is stable and calm. But he has problems of his own. A few weeks out from Beijing he is dropped by the Western Bulldogs and his footy career is suddenly over. Retired, involuntarily, at the ripe old age of twenty-three. Now, in the days before we leave for China, he spends his mornings in bed reading the jobs pages and trying to look upbeat. He will still be travelling to Beijing to support me and act as cheerleader. Even though a sports stadium – as a spectator – is probably the last place on earth he wants to be.

Beijing is big. It is oversized, overdone. A caricature of an Olympics. And I love it. First, there's the Bird's Nest, the National Stadium, which will hold almost 100,000 cheering fans and which sits inside its tangle of twisted metal twigs, a latticework of imagination. Then there's the Water Cube, the National Aquatics Centre, which is a fantastic blob of luminous bubbles that looks like it could wobble, bounce once or twice, and then drift away on the breeze.

When I first arrive, I am dazed by the sights. I wander around feeling dwarfed and insignificant. Then I shake off my awe and refocus my mind. I'm not here to be a tourist. I have a job to do.

'After you've finished racing, come and see the Great Wall with me,' Marty says. He has never been to Beijing before either.

'Sure, later. When this is all done,' I tell him. When I've won, then he'll understand. When I've won, he will see. After I win, we'll be together and my fiancé will love me more than ever. These are the things I tell myself.

I skip the Opening Ceremony and stay in my room at the village instead. I have still never been to one of those things. I am rooming with Shayne Reese and even though she's not out marching round the stadium either, she is giving me plenty of space tonight. Just what I want. I don't need any company. I don't need any distractions, not this close to the finish line.

These Olympics are the most expensive on record, the papers tell us. The biggest too. Beijing will be the most-watched Olympics in history, perhaps the most-watched event in history, the media reports breathlessly. But I skip the spectacle to stay in and focus. The world might be watching us, but I am navel-gazing.

Mum and Marty stay just outside Beijing, Marty in a hotel and Mum in a serviced apartment. It is someone's home but it's the size of a shoebox: tiny, dark and jammed into a towering unit block that's identical to every other block on the street. It couldn't be more different from my home for the next few weeks: the Water Cube.

Every time I walk past the Water Cube, with its hundreds of bubbles, I can't shake the feeling it might just float away. Apparently, as a building, it's incredibly robust. Each bubble is placed in just such a way that it's so strong you could stand it on its head and it wouldn't collapse. But it looks pretty shaky to me. Like one strong gust of wind might send it tumbling.

I've been in my own bubble these last few months, my own self-designed exile from the world. Isolated and self-contained, but much stronger because of it. Strong and tough and bubble-slick. I like this building. I will do well here.

I have a tough schedule at these Games. If everything goes to plan and I make all of my finals, I'll swim in eight events over seven days: back-to-back races with only one day off. I am fit enough, of course – fitter than I've ever been in my life. But by this stage it's equally about being able to put it together mentally on the day.

I cruise through the heats of the 100 metres on Sunday night, then back it up in the semis the next morning. I am the fastest qualifier in the heats (1:05.64), then again in the semi-finals (1:05.80). I am the only person to swim a 1:05. Rebecca Soni from the USA is the only one who can touch me now, and even she only manages a 1:07.07. This gold is mine. I cannot lose. I will shake off my hoodoo this time. I just know it.

But things get weird the night before my race. It's after 9 p.m. when my phone rings, just when I'm winding down, ahead of my big day. Shower, teeth, double- and triple-check my bag for tomorrow. My stomach flip-flops with nerves (or is it because of the liquid dinner?). I sit down cross-legged on the bed to talk to Marty.

'Hey, babe. Is everything okay?' I ask. I'm concerned. Marty knows better than to call me when I should be in bed.

'I don't know. You tell me,' he growls.

'Huh? Marty? Are you alright? Where are you?'

'I know what you've done,' he mutters.

But I'm clueless. I have no idea what he's on about.

He launches into a tirade. He accuses me of sleeping around. Specifically, of cheating on him with other swimmers on my team while I am inside the Olympic village.

I am gobsmacked. Baffled. It is such a bolt from the blue.

'Wha– Are you kidding?' I stammer. 'When have I ever given you the idea I would cheat on you?' My mind races back through the past few days for any sign, any gesture, that may have given him the wrong impression. I draw a blank.

But Marty is adamant. He will not be placated. He is shouting, then I'm shouting, and things are getting out of hand.

'This is absurd. You're being absurd!' I tell him.

'I'm not the one who's having sex with other people!' he spits.

'Seriously? You seriously think that? I'm swimming the biggest race of my life in the morning and you seriously think I have time to be sleeping with anyone? Who in their right mind would do that?' I am getting wound up now. 'I have trained my whole life for this! I am swimming six hours a day and eating nothing but fucking soup! How would I even have the energy to sleep around!'

From down the hallway I hear a thud that sounds suspiciously like a shoe hitting a wall. 'Oi! Keep it down or I swear I will throw that phone out the window!' It's my friend, KP (Kylie Palmer), and it's not hard to tell she is seriously pissed. My roommate, Shayne, has retreated into the bathroom, but there's only so long someone can feign being on the loo.

'Look,' I hiss into the phone. 'No-one, no-one is going to be sleeping around before a major meet. As if anyone in the village would be doing that. These people are racing. This is the biggest meet of our lives! Besides, babe, I love you. Why would I ever do that to you?'

I spend the best part of an hour on the phone trying to reassure him. It's ridiculous and damaging. I am disturbing so many people and I feel terrible. I am wasting so much valuable energy on his totally baseless fears.

Yet I stay on the line. I feel bad that my fiancé is feeling so bad. I could just switch off my phone and say 'screw you, I need to sleep'. But if he's hurting, I'm hurting, and I want to try and make him feel better. *He's been so supportive*, I tell myself. *This is the least you can do.* And I stuff down the thought that perhaps his insecurities are rearing their ugly heads now that it's me – and not him – in the spotlight, for the first time in our relationship. He has never been to an Olympics with me. We haven't known one another long enough. And the last few days, with their merry-go-round of media interviews and autograph signings and special events has been an eye-opener for Marty, I'm sure.

But I am loyal to a fault. So I sit on the line and listen to his fears and soothe and cajole and stay up late.

The next morning at the pool, Rohan confiscates my phone. 'You don't have the energy for this. You need to focus,' he admonishes me. He is not impressed. No-one who roomed near me last night is, and I feel awful that I've disturbed my teammates.

Then I walk out through the tunnel, onto the exposed pool deck, and I feel even worse. There, on either side of the pool, towers of supporter-seating rise up in all directions. There are only press photographers in here now, but soon these stands will be packed with journalists, fans, family and friends: all coming to watch us perform. All expecting the world.

And these people won't know I've had a bad night. They won't understand that I've had a fight with my fiancé, that I'm feeling upset. How could I explain all that? That's behind-the-scenes stuff, the stuff no-one sees. To the rest of the world, we only appear every four years, step up onto the blocks and swim 100 metres. It's what we're trained to do, what we do every day. So how hard can it be to do it again today, right?

Unfortunately, life happens for us too. We're human, and we have problems just like anyone else. But when we have a bad day, we let down so many people. Our coaches, our teammates, our families and friends. And the spectators, the Aussie fans. When I have a bad day, I let down you guys at home in your lounge rooms watching. How do I make it up to you when I have an off day?

Marty was still texting and calling me when I handed my phone to Rohan. I pass it over feeling like that kid in the back row who's been caught sending messages in class. But I don't care. I'm happy to be rid of the stupid thing. I don't want to think about it, don't want the worry. I don't want to deal with my fiancé right now.

I am mad. No, wait: all of a sudden I am red-hot furious. I am ready to explode. How dare he do this to me when I'm at the last hurdle? The night before my race? How dare he accuse me, distract me and disturb all my friends! And after everything I have done for him! I moved to Melbourne and changed coaches: I risked everything for him.

'Forget it,' Rohan tells me, and he gets me in the water and training. Up and down, up and down. Back on track. Thinking of gold.

Forget about Marty, that's what he said. Forget that you are hurting and your fiancé thinks you're a cheat. Forget that you've just turned twenty-three and you're head-over-heels nuts about a guy. You must focus, must be clinical. You must be single-minded.

So I am. I do. There's less than two hours until I'm due in the pool, till I'm back to the business of being an Olympian.

I have less than two hours to prove what I'm worth.

20

Relief

Thinking back, I can still remember the relief. Sheer, cool, white relief. Relief so palpable I could wear it like a blanket. Relief so real I could smell it.

I feel good going into the race. I stand on the edge of the pool and splash myself with water to lessen the shock of the cold when I dive in. Despite the events of the last few hours, I feel calm and relaxed: quietly powerful. I am one hundred per cent in the zone. Around me is a circus of colour and light. There are blue bleachers and blue banners; the blue of Beijing 2008 is everywhere. There are flags of every nation, every colour of the rainbow, swinging from the rafters. And there must be 17,000 people in here today, all shouting, laughing, waiting and hoping. But I block them out, I don't hear a thing. The only voice I hear is the one in my head speaking softly and gently for once.

This is my office. I know what to do.

Every moment has led to this. I know how to do this. I don't think about anything but where I am in this instant.

I am standing behind the blocks. I am here in the moment. I am now. It's as if the more I have to block out, the more present I feel.

The first whistle blows and we're ready to start. I think about what I have learnt over the years. From Rohan and his enthusiastic, US-style cheers. From Stephan: 'Let's control the start. We can't control the last 25 metres, because we're not there yet. Let's control the start and get the best one we can.' *This is my office.* I am bouncing and windmilling my arms. I am blowing out air. I think of Ken and his advice: 'Just swim bloody fast.' I think of Col back in Burpengary with his backyard barbie and his Mars bars and his bloody besser brick. I hear Mum speaking to me now, with her simple mantra: 'Do your best, Leisel.' That's what she always says: just do your best.

I will do my best. I will control the start. I will swim bloody hard. I will do them all proud. I will get that gold.

The second whistle blows and I step onto the blocks and arrange myself for my two-footed start. I shift and blow out, and wriggle my hands.

I wait for the whistle. I have waited my whole life.

A pause. Then the whistle. Away we go!

I'm off and I'm in, and oh it feels good. I break the water and head into slipstream. Hands up, palms down. *Think slick, think slick.* I feel smooth and beautiful. I feel easy in the water. This is how it's meant to be.

The water doesn't gush past today. Instead, it surrounds me and takes hold of me. It is carrying me along. I press my hands down and slide into my pull-out, breaking smoothly at the ten. Control, control. Don't rip, don't rip. I ease into my 42-stroke rate as easily as slipping a car into gear.

Easy, easy. Today it's so easy.

This is my office. I know what to do. This is my office, and today it is easy.

Today I am a fish. I am at home. I am feeling the water. Holding it. I am sleek and slick, smooth and light.

Three long strokes and I'm 25 metres in. Now is the time I begin to build. Build, build, build. I shift up a gear. Build, build, build. I am feeling it now.

I am the first to the 50-metre mark, and the first off again as well. I hit the wall fast but with absolute control. Hands to feet, hands to feet. Hit, flick, swish. I am gone. All those hours in Rohan's mini pool have paid off. I pull up and turn faster in the water than most people could on dry land.

I am 0.2 of a second off the world-record split at the turn. But I don't need a stopwatch to tell me that. Today all of the elements are working together. I glide off the wall. Slick and smooth, long and lean. I am where I am meant to be.

But then it's time to build again. Pull, breathe, pull, breathe. Build, build, build. I shift up another gear. I can feel the burn. I can feel the fire.

I explode into the final 25 metres. Build, build, build. My lungs are on fire. Build, build, build. Pain engulfs me. My forearms are burning; my fingers are stiff. My legs feel as though they are made of dead weights.

Build, build, build. I am burning alive. I can hear myself breathing. I am ragged and old.

But I am steaming home now, powerful and strong. I am coming home fast. I am gasping and burning. I hit the wall hard.

I am empty: done. I have given all I've got.

I breathe hard and I cannot see. I turn and blink. I am blind.

I squint to see if my life has changed.

It has.

I've got gold. I've done it.

Ugh, thank God. Thank God for that.

Relief floods my tired brain. It seeps from my ears and out every pore. I've finally won the gold. It's unbelievable.

Oh. Thank. God. For. That. I've won.

I smile, I think. *Did I manage a smile?* I am still gasping to breathe in air. I single out Mum in the crowd and I give her a wave. Next to her, Marty pumps his fist in the air. I lean on the lane rope and hug Mirna Jukic from Austria. She came second and is grinning from ear to ear. I hug Rebecca Soni from the USA after that. She is third and I couldn't be happier for her. I thump her back in congratulations, flashing my racing-red fingernails.

I spring from the pool, calm now. I'm relieved. I do my media interview, talking to my friend Dan Kowalski, in a light-headed daze.

And then I see Rohan and I run up for a hug. He squeezes my shoulders and pats my back. 'You did it. You did this,' he says to me.

'I feel bad,' I tell him. 'All I can feel is relief.'

It's true. It's as if I have no other emotions. I'm not happy, not even excited. All I can feel is relief. Sheer, pure relief.

'Yeah, but you did it. You got that monkey off your back.'

Monkey? I turn to my coach and this time I smile for sure. 'Rohan, that was no monkey. It was a silverback gorilla.'

21

Fallout

ABC radio reports my win: 'Another gold medal in the pool in Beijing, and this one was a long time coming. Leisel Jones has been the dominant women's breaststroke swimmer in the world for most of the last eight years. But there's been one thing missing from her trophy cabinet: an individual Olympic gold medal ... Now that has changed. Leisel is lethal! She's finally got that gold. It's 1:05.17, outside the world record. But who cares? Finally, Leisel has done it! She's got the full set!'

The full set. That's what I have now. The full box and dice. The kit and the caboodle. But most importantly, I finally have peace. I've done it. It's finished. I've answered the question. I don't have to justify or explain any more. I have nothing left to prove, no more races to swim. I don't have to go to another Olympics again.

I soak in every minute of the medal presentation. I absorb it, relish it, cling to it tightly. *This is why*, I tell myself as I stand on the podium. This is the reason for all the 4 a.m. starts, the hard kilometres in the pool, the weight vests, the chin-ups and all the bloody soups. It was all for this moment: it must be worthwhile. It has to mean something. *I'm so grateful. It has to be worthwhile.*

This is for the hard work, the hard times. For all the times I have come second. It's for every time I've had to stand in second place and hear the American national anthem!

I've waited my whole life for this. Other girls dream of their wedding day or of being a princess or something. But all I wanted was this: the green and the gold. Especially the gold! But just as a wedding day whizzes by fast, so does a medal ceremony. I try to take it all in, but it flies by. I want to bottle it so I can open it up and taste it any time I like.

But I do feel earthed, in the moment. I do not waste a single second. I sing our anthem and I swell with pride. This is for something greater than me.

I am composed and complete: in control. I walk around the stadium, waving and thanking the fans. But then I spot Mum in the crowd and she's run down to the front of the stands. She is hanging over the fence and she's waving like a dag. Like a POO. *God, I love that woman.* And this is when I lose the plot. I am bawling – she is bawling – we are a silly, wet mess. Mum leans down and I touch her hand. It's the only way I can say how much she means to me, how much she has done for me. Say thank you, thank you, thank you some more. For all the driving, all the cooking. All the everything. Ever.

And in this moment, this one right here? This is when it's all completely worth it.

~

After the 100-metre event, I have less than forty-eight hours to turn myself around for the 200-metre heat. I rest, train and rest some more. I leave my phone with Rohan. I can't see Marty (or Mum, or anyone else for that matter) until I have finished racing, so I don't do anything to celebrate my gold medal. I just get back to work.

I qualify for the 200 metres just behind Rebecca Soni from the USA. But when the Friday morning final rolls around, I feel off. To be honest, I just feel exhausted. I'm not myself at warm-up and I can't do my 4 × 50s (descending) like I usually can. After the elation of winning the 100 metres, and the emotional turmoil of my week with Marty, when I hit the water, I just don't feel like me.

It shows in my race and I come second to Rebecca Soni in a time of 2:22.05. I am numb when I finish. Not elated, not disappointed. Not anything at all. I exit the pool and do my poolside interview.

Then I stagger away and collapse on the deck.

Everything goes black and for a few moments there I'm worried I will lose consciousness. But, although the room wobbles and swims in front of me as though this giant bubble really might float away, I manage to hang on.

'I'm fine. I'm fine,' I insist, as a crowd gathers around me. 'I just dug so deep in that last 50 metres, I kinda forgot to breathe.'

This is true, in part. I did forget to breathe. But I'm not wobbly and faint and feeling sick to my core just because I am short of breath. If I ate a decent meal once in a while; if I didn't have boyfriend dramas; if I was nicer to myself occasionally; then maybe I wouldn't be laid out on the tiles for the world to see, hoping the TV cameras don't get a shot of my swimming-tog wedgie.

I am done. Physically, emotionally, mentally wrecked. I start to feel pretty gutted I didn't win the 200 metres. *I should have won it – just think: I could have been in the running for three gold at one Olympics.*

But then I realise I just didn't have it in me. I have nothing left in the tank. And that is some consolation. I tell the press later that I gave it everything, I couldn't have done any more; it just didn't happen for me on the day. So I don't feel like I lost the gold: I feel like I won the silver. I decide I'm not disappointed, just relieved. Relieved it's done. Relieved I survived. Relieved that this week is almost over.

~

Almost over. First, of course, there's the medley relay and our chance to give our old foes, the USA, a good spanking.

I love the relay. It's always so much fun. But today, as Emily Seebohm, Jessicah Schipper and I are in the marshalling area waiting for Libby Trickett (formerly Libby Lenton) to arrive, things start to go pear-shaped. Libby's not here yet because she's out in the race pool, swimming her heart out in the 50-metre freestyle final. This is Libby's event, her big chance to shine, but instead of winning gold she fails to medal at all. This is bad. This is very, very bad.

'Right,' I say to the girls. 'Libby will be coming in here in a minute and she will be angry. She will be pissed. She will be absolutely filthy after that race.' I train with Libby. And I know when she comes into the marshalling area she will not be skipping. Who would be? I sure as hell wouldn't.

'What we're going to do is actively change her attitude,' I tell them. 'We're going to sing, we're going to dance, we're going to be absolute idiots. We will be over-the-top and loud and ridiculous and fun – and we will turn her around and make her happy. You in?'

'Yup,' says Schipper.

'Let's do it,' says Seebohm.

The American team are deadly serious. In their hoodies and headphones, they are here to win. They don't talk, don't smile, don't communicate at all among their team. *Do they use telepathy?* I wonder. *How are they so silent?*

We are the polar opposite. We are loud and proud and not afraid of bad singing. When Libby arrives, she is just as I predicted, but we are determined to lift her up.

'Forget about it,' I tell her. 'I get it. You're pissed. I would feel exactly the same.' She shoots me a black look.

'But that race was so ten minutes ago. Leave that shit at the door, Trickett. And prepare to have fun!' She raises one eyebrow sceptically.

But to Libby's credit she does a complete one-eighty. It's not easy to change your attitude like that, in such a short time, but within minutes she is singing and dancing and being as obnoxious and rude as the rest of us. It's big of her.

And dammit, we have fun. 'Screw you guys,' is the message our bad dancing sends to the USA. 'Screw you,' we say with our sprinklers, our moonwalking and our mashed potato. You and your serious attitudes. You who are so cool. We're Australian and we're loud! We're here to have a good time!

We are Australian and we are here to be ourselves.

The USA get off to a flying start with 100-metre backstroke gold medallist Natalie Coughlin, and we are back in fourth place at the end of the first leg. But I am having none of that and I swim my guts out and bring us up to poll position. By the time Jessicah Schipper finishes the butterfly leg we have a three-metre advantage over the Americans, before Libby brings it home in her usual style.

We win the race in world-record time. We win the race *our* way.

Aussie-style. Aussie-*girl* style.

Oh, yeah: all six of Australia's gold medals in the pool at Beijing are won by its women.

~

As soon as I finish racing, I check out of the Olympic village. I'll be back for the Closing Ceremony. (Yes, closure, Mum, closure.) But that's it. I'm in a rush to see Marty, to spend some time with him and sort things out, so he and I move into the shoebox serviced apartment with Mum. She stays for only a few more days, and then finally Marty and I are alone.

And then the real fights start.

Never have 50 square metres felt so tight. Marty and I are constantly at one another's throats: arguing, bickering, driving each other mad. There is one moment when he threatens to go home, and I am so angry and so stubborn that I agree that, yes, he should. But he doesn't go through with it.

During the week after my wins I'm required to do a lot of media stuff. Interviews and signings. Marty knows the deal. He's been there and done that a hundred times himself. And yet he puts pressure on me to skip my commitments and hang out with him instead.

'This is my time to shine,' I tell him. 'I finally made it.'

But he sulks when I tell him I've got interviews to do, and I can feel myself being pulled in two very different directions.

Make that three. Because I'm missing out on time with my teammates, too. The rest of the Aussie contingent are back in the village and I'm keen to see them, to hang out with them. Especially my relay team girls. I want to party! Let my hair down! Gold, schmold: the best part about the Olympics is the parties. Put 10,000 fit, ripped, mostly twenty-somethings together – twenty-somethings who are on a high, who are having perhaps the greatest experience of their lives and who have been working their arses off for the last four years to be here; who have been denied alcohol and fast food and going out and doing all the things that twenty-somethings do – put these people together in a village for two weeks and see what happens.

And did I mention everything's free? Marty and I go to one party – the Speedo party – and the food, the booze, the whole shebang is free. They're handing out stuff left, right and centre. Freebies. Gift bags. And this is common. All the major sponsors are doing it. Red Bull, Omega, Nike. It's huge. It's chaos. It is so much fun.

But I skip most of that to hang out with Marty. I pass on going out with my teammates and going nuts, being stupid. Pass on dancing and drinking and losing my shoes at 3 a.m. All that dumb stuff everyone does as an eighteen-year-old but that most athletes never have the chance to do because we have to be up for training at 4 a.m. the next morning. But now, quick! Here's your chance! Here's your chance to go crazy!

I stay home to spend time with my fiancé instead.

Mum is disappointed. She doesn't say anything; that's not her style. But before she heads home, she wants a photo with me, in the apartment, holding up my medals. I can tell she's unhappy with the result. I'm smiling, but somehow I still manage to look sad in the photo. Sad and subdued. Not what you expect from someone holding three Olympic medals. In the photo, I have my arm around Mum. But when later we look at the pic together, I can see that she knows something's just not right.

But if Mum knows what it is, I wish she'd tell me. I lie in bed at night wondering what's wrong with me. *You've done it*, I tell myself. *You've won the gold! Achieved your dream! This is the part where you're ecstatic. You should be over the moon!*

It doesn't feel at all like I expected.

The week together in Beijing is a difficult one. Marty and I try to do all the right things and give it our best shot. And there are moments when he is so lovely and thoughtful that I think everything will be okay after all. One day, he organises a car to take us to see the Great Wall, and as we walk a section of the great monument together he surprises me with a beautiful diamond necklace.

This sure is more romantic than the way my friend Mel Schlanger sees the Wall. She was corralled into doing so, along with the entire Aussie Olympic contingent, by Laurie Lawrence. Laurie told them they were going on 'a bit of a wander' and so Mel walked sixteen steep kilometres of short, sharp steps in thongs. She told me later she was at the very back of the pack, with Laurie leading the charge, and all she could think was: 'What has my life come to?'

But Marty and I do the Wall our way and it's fun and he is sweet and I really do think we'll be fine. So what if we fight sometimes?

Doesn't every couple? And I don't even really know what we're fighting about.

I'm not as happy as I expected to be – as he expects me to be – and this is hard for both of us. But I can't help it. I'm just not happy. As proud as I am of my medals – and as grateful as I am for the support I received to win them – winning gold isn't all it was cracked up to be. Which leaves me thinking: *Well, if this doesn't do it for me, what on earth will? Why don't I feel amazing? What is wrong with me?*

I am angry at myself and I take it out on Marty. This dream of mine – this thing I worked so hard for, that I did 12,600 tough hours of training to achieve – what does it mean? Winning individual gold is the highlight of my career. Technically, I've swum better in the past (at the Melbourne 2006 Commonwealth Games, for a start). But this is what I've worked for, what I have sacrificed so much for. I think about all the soup, all the dry-land training. All the pressure of the past, all the times I failed, all the times I came home with silver. This is what Beijing has been about: putting my past behind me. All my near-misses, all the times I was slated in the press. The times when our family was poor. When my dad walked out. All those things I've stuffed down so deep. In Beijing I got past all this. I got on with the job. This is what it was all for.

I did it. I won. I'm the best in the world. That's what the Olympics means. And I'm not complaining, don't get me wrong. Not complaining at all. But it hasn't solved all the problems I expected it to.

Even as a gold medallist, you still have to get up in the morning. You still have to eat your Weet-Bix and brush your teeth. Life goes on. It was stupid to think all that would change. Yet somehow, I now realise, I thought things would be different now. That life might be smoother. I thought my friends would like me more and my fiancé would love me more. And most stupid of all? I thought I might even like myself.

I thought winning gold would make me feel fulfilled. That there would be balloons and streamers and media interviews galore. (There's nothing worse than winning silver and discovering the press don't want to know you.) I thought my self-worth would go through the roof. That my psychotic efforts in the lead-up to Beijing would be worth it. What I lost would be worth it because of everything I would gain.

But it wasn't. It just wasn't.

It's a warped way of thinking, but that's honestly what I believed: when I get that gold medal I'll be happy. When I win, everything will be okay. You know the line: 'When I get that job, meet that guy, buy that car, have those shoes...' When my life changes, when it's different from how it is now, then I'll be happy. We lie to ourselves like this all the time. Why did I think my lies would hurt any less?

And have I looked at my medal again? Have I even got it out of the box? Not really. Do I take it out and hold it and think: 'Wow, I'm one pretty amazing human being.' You're kidding, aren't you?

Sure, I'm proud of my hard work. Of the fact I stuck with it. And you bet I'm eternally grateful for all the support I received.

But beyond that? Beyond that, I'm crazy for thinking it would truly change things. 'A gold medal is a wonderful thing. But if you're not enough without one, then you'll never be enough with one.' Isn't that what they say in the movie *Cool Runnings*? I need a little Rastafarian wisdom in my life as Marty and I board the plane home from Beijing. He is not in a good place when we leave. Not a good place at all. It must have been hard for him, so recently retired, to watch me win gold and then see me struggle so much with it. I'm at the very peak of my career while he's at the bottom. And we're finding it hard to meet in the middle.

After Beijing, a bunch of my teammates go on holidays together. Some go to Bali, others to Thailand. Me? I pack my bags, say my goodbyes, and then head home to Melbourne to break up with my fiancé.

22

The Lonely Days

After we fly back from Beijing, things between Marty and me unravel quickly. We fight for a while, and then we stop fighting, but only because we stop talking altogether. This is a silent war. I feel betrayed and I don't think things between us will ever be the same.

I am in the study one Tuesday night when Marty wanders in with our bulldog, Winston, trailing behind him. They sit on the floor and look up at me together.

'This isn't working, is it?'

'Nup,' I say.

'We should break up, shouldn't we?'

'Yup,' I say.

And that is the end: as simple as that. It's utterly clean cut.

I move out and stay with my friend Sarah Katsoulis. I am miserable and heartbroken. It's really kind of Sarah to put me up, and I am grateful to her. But I hate it there. I stay in my tiny bedroom, avoiding her cat (I am not a cat person). I feel like I have fallen very far from the high of the Olympics just a few short weeks ago.

Rohan is as supportive as ever. He is understanding at training and gives me the space I need. But Jeremy, my gym coach, is much more brutal. 'Saw that one coming,' he says when I tell him about Marty. Then it's straight back to training. Enough talking about emotional stuff.

Mum is not terribly disappointed Marty and I have broken up. She tells me that I was never myself when I was with Marty. 'You were a dulled-down version of yourself. You seemed self-conscious. Just not you,' she says.

'Then why didn't you say anything?' I ask her. But I already know the answer. Mum couldn't tell me; nobody could. I was in love and I thought it was the greatest thing ever.

But after Marty and I break up, I wonder to myself: *Did he ever cheat on me? How many times?* I have flashbacks to finding a girl's number in his jacket pocket, right at the start of our relationship. I truly believed Marty when he said it was from before we started dating. I *wanted* to believe him, just like I wanted to believe that he was different to other footy players. I needed Marty to be the man I'd never had in my life. He was so wonderfully supportive. He cooked for me, ate the same restrictive diet as me, and came along to all my races. He did, in short, all the things my dad never did. He loved me and supported me and stayed right by my side. So I ignored other things. I refused to consider that maybe it was too good to be true.

~

I last one month with Sarah before I go out and buy myself a townhouse in Mitcham, just east of Melbourne's CBD. I do it because I need to get out of Sarah's quick smart. It doesn't occur to me that living on my own might not be the answer.

I am lonely in Mitcham – even more so than I was at Sarah's. There is no cat to avoid for a start. And I don't have my dog, Winston, either. I had to give Winnie away when I broke up with Marty. I really miss him. I miss everyone. I miss my old life. I miss it so much.

After the dust settles and we have untangled our lives, I never speak to Marty again.

I lose a lot of friends when I split up with Marty, as you do after any break-up, I suppose. Most of our friends are footy-related, and without footy in my life – when I'm no longer driving out to some far-flung football field to sit and shiver and gossip and read trashy magazines with my friends – I don't have a lot to fill my weekends. I spend a lot of time sitting at home by myself.

I also don't have swimming eating up my days anymore; it's no longer chewing up my mornings and afternoons, feeding on my whole life, leaving me exhausted. I take four weeks off after the Beijing Olympics, but this stretches out, until soon it is eight. I decide to take a year off international competition. I don't want to see a pool, don't want to go near one. I have no passion to get back in the water.

'You could be the first Australian swimmer to go to four Olympics!' Rohan says.

Cool, I think. *But that's not enough.* That's not enough to keep me motivated for the next four years.

Four years is a long time to keep swimming if you can't see the point. All those thousands of kilometres in the pool, all those early morning starts, just to get a record? I'm getting older, getting bored; I'm not passionate anymore.

'Besides,' I tell Rohan, 'that's never been my goal.'

My goal was individual gold and I've ticked that box. I've done everything and got everything I wanted.

So why does it feel so crap then? I wonder.

I have worked so hard, given up so much. But where did all that hard work get me? Winning doesn't feel as awesome as I dreamt it would. Winning feels empty. I am empty. So why would I do it all over again?

'But if you don't swim, what else will you do?' Rohan asks.

And it's a really good question. It's the question I've been asking myself during the long, cold hours before dawn most mornings. *What will I do? What can I do?* I am twenty-three – still young – so why does it feel like my life is over?

'I haven't got that far,' I tell Rohan. 'I could get a job?' But we both know my heart isn't in it.

I could sit around all day at home, like I am doing now. I could stay stuck and lonely and sad, like I am now. I have lost my way, lost my purpose. I am disillusioned about winning and I've lost my passion. I've lost love. I've lost my friends. It's all gone. But worst of all, I seem to have misplaced my self-worth as well. I feel worthless now.

Professionally, of course, I am in a great place. *At the peak of my career!* I think bitterly. But what's the point of professional success if your personal life is falling apart?

The days and weeks after Beijing – when I sit around the house feeling like Marty couldn't even love me when I won gold – are some of the worst weeks of my life. *What's happened?* I wonder. *Where did my life go?* A few weeks ago I was in the Olympic village, feeling on top of the world. Now I'm alone and it feels like I'm starting at the bottom again. I feel like the lowest of the low. I feel like shit. I am in a really unhealthy place, mentally.

And I'm not in great shape physically either. Rohan coaxes me back into training – slowly at first, then a little more and a little more. I start with three sessions a week, but soon it's four, and then it's five. I hate it, but it keeps me sane. It makes me get out of bed each day.

I am headed for a World Cup competition in South Africa. It's not like a football World Cup – not a big international competition; it's just a short-course meet, for a bit of fun. It's also a chance to win some money, because most top swimmers don't bother with world cups.

But just days before I am due to fly out, I get sick. I miss the comp. I stay home on the couch by myself, with a raging sore throat and my temperature sky-high. I have no-one to look after me, no-one to bring me flat lemonade. Mum is at home in Brisbane, and there's no-one else. I need to vomit but I don't make it to the bathroom in time and I am sick all over the lounge-room floor. I have to crawl to the laundry for a mop to clean up the mess myself. There is no-one else to do it.

'You need to get yourself to a pharmacy and get your temperature checked,' Mum says worriedly.

I drive myself there, shivering. When I walk into the store, the pharmacist stares. I am white and shaky; I look like death. My temperature is over thirty-nine degrees. 'You should really go to a hospital,' the pharmacist tells me.

But I don't. Instead, I go home and feel sorry for myself. No-one comes to help; nobody cares. *My God, what has my life become?*

My temperature fades, but the loneliness stays. I slide further and further into depression.

~

Despite everything, I don't consider going back to Brisbane. I love Melbourne; it's my home. So I decide to stick it – whatever *it* is – out here. Who knows what's next for me? Who knows what I should do? I am aimless.

I step up my training to eight sessions a week, but only because I have nothing else to do. I have decided that this year I will not do any major international competitions, such as the World Championships in Rome in July, but I still go to trials for Rome and qualify for the team.

'Sure you don't want to go?' Rohan asks me yet again.

'Sure,' I say.

And it turns out to be a good decision. Rome signals the advent of the 'super suit' era, with many athletes trialling new high-tech swimsuits. The suits, made of polyurethane, among other things, are not supposed to be performance-enhancing, but forty-three world records are broken in Rome, and championship records are bettered in thirty-eight of forty events. Events are being won by people I've never heard of, people who are (relatively) crap. I'm glad I'm not there for that.

I don't watch Rome on TV. I'm not interested. I can't pretend to care. But the strangest thing happens while I am at home not caring: I discover no-one else cares very much either. My neighbours don't watch it; the girl at the checkout is nonplussed. The world, it seems, keeps on turning, even when there is a swimming meet on. Who knew? The sun keeps rising; the traffic is still terrible. Nothing grinds to a halt because someone, somewhere, in a pool on the other side of the world, has got a silver medal instead of a gold. Nobody cares. Nobody cares! This is something of a revelation for me.

Then my friend Meagan Nay, who is away competing in Rome, receives news that her brother has died in a car accident. It's terrible news. I feel so much for Meagan and her family. And I recognise more than ever that being an athlete doesn't mean you're immune to real life. There are no guarantees that the lives of elite athletes will be happy.

The perspective I get from missing Rome is good for me. It is the slap in the face I need. I realise I need to step away from competitive swimming for a while.

But being an outsider is also lonely, and so, after spending so much time in my own company, I spiral down and down. I spiral in on myself. I hate my sport, but I have nothing else. I keep training, keep plodding, because what else am I going to do? I'm not working. I have no alternatives.

This is something my mum constantly points out. So does Rohan. I feel pressure from both of them to keep on swimming.

But swimming doesn't make me happy. Nothing like it, in fact. I hate training and don't like my squad. I feel flat and directionless. Ever since I won gold in Beijing, I have had nothing on the horizon. Nothing to wake up for. I can't find my hunger. I'm a different person to the passionate, happy Leisel of the past. The Leisel who was focused, who was committed to her goals. The Leisel who took risks like moving to Melbourne – who did anything to achieve her golden dream. Now I plod along, paralysed by my own inaction. I do nothing, say nothing. I don't know how to help myself. And the monotony of my days almost drives me mad.

I am studying beauty therapy again, this time at Elly Lukas College on Flinders Lane, and around this time I start going to parties with my beauty therapy friends. *Screw it*, I think. *I may as well get on the social scene. What else am I going to do?* I go out to bars and clubs with the girls I meet. I am looking for fun at the college – for anything that will snap me out of this low.

And it *is* fun and my friends are great but it's still not enough. When I go out, I have the same attitude as when I'm at training: turn up, get the job done, go home. Repeat.

Nothing makes me happy; nothing picks me up. I'm only twenty-three and I have lost my hunger for life.

23

Opening Up

The following year, 2010, I am back on the circuit, competing in international competitions. FINA has banned all high-tech bodyskin suits this year, so it's as good a time as any to dip my toe back in. I train for the first half of the year; then the second half is all about racing experience.

I go to the Pan Pacific Championships in California in August and I get three silver medals and a bronze, coming in behind the Americans in all events.

Then it's on to the Commonwealth Games in October: this year they are being hosted in Delhi.

'Delhi? Really?' I ask Rohan.

I am unconvinced this is a good idea. I don't think I'll regain any of my hunger in Delhi. I'll get constipation, maybe. Diarrhoea, possibly. I reckon I'll experience the whole colourful spectrum of Delhi-belly during my eleven days there. But nothing that resembles hunger.

Also, I have some serious misgivings about safety in Delhi. In the lead-up to the Games, there have been reports in the media of security concerns – rumours of a terrorist attack. This is nothing new (there seem to be threats made at just about every Commonwealth and Olympic games these days), but with Delhi it feels somehow more sinister. More real. Like something is lurking beneath the surface. In Delhi, it doesn't feel like the threat is under control, and I am fearful something bad might actually happen.

'I'm not going,' I say.

'You'll be fine,' says Mum.

'You'll be fine,' say the head coaches from Swimming Australia.

'Let's talk about how you're feeling,' says Rohan, and I love him for it. He always says exactly what I need to hear.

In the end, I am persuaded to go and the security is fine. In fact, it's very efficient. Our buses are escorted by armoured cars to the pool each day and there are guys toting machine guns, wearing bandanas and army boots, riding alongside us in the trays of white utes everywhere we go. We are chaperoned in and out of the pool and the athletes' village. I have never felt so safe in my life.

But it's not long before I decide I'd rather take my chances outside with the terrorists than in the athletes' village. Inside, things are far more dangerous. For a start, there are balconies with no guardrails, and we're on the fifth floor. There are bandaids in the pasta (Alicia Coutts finds one and returns her bowl to the kitchen, where the kitchen staff promptly stir it back into the communal pot!). And there is God knows what lurking in the cloudy swimming pools. My feet are always filthy: a big deal for me. Dirty feet is my biggest nightmare, my strangest phobia. And, just as I feared, the food here is so bad that we have swimmers diving into the warm-up pools at one end, getting out at the other, vomiting and then getting back in the pool again. It's so gross.

Everyone is sick and exhausted and still trying to compete. I swear I've never had so much Imodium in my entire life. We are instructed by our team managers and nutritionists to avoid all fresh fruit and vegetables because of what they're washed in. For almost two weeks in Delhi I eat nothing but baked potato wedges, because I figure at least the germs should have been slow-roasted to death. It's a restrictive diet, and not one that I would recommend. And I have never been so constipated in my whole life.

But somehow I win three gold medals and a silver at Delhi, making me the third Australian in history to win ten Commonwealth Games gold medals. Susie O'Neill and Ian Thorpe are the only other Australian athletes to do this. I am joining some esteemed company.

But honestly? As I board the flight home from Delhi, I think I'll just be happy when I can poo again.

~

As well as a return to racing, 2010 marks the beginning of a couple of new professional relationships for me. The first is with Lisa Stevens, a – gasp! – sports psychologist. My friend Marieke puts me on to her and, to start off with, she is just someone to chat to. A friendly ear. But we don't talk about swimming: we talk about life. Lisa works out of her home, a beautiful house in Port Melbourne, just outside the city centre. We catch up every few weeks, and each time we meet in her downstairs office, a room tastefully decorated with pictures of horses on the walls. Lisa was a show jumper and an Australian champion at one time. She tells me stories about her horses, and about competing and what that felt like for her. I listen, enthralled, when she talks. It's such a relief. It's all so familiar. When she tells me about the pressure, about her perfectionism, about always striving to be better and better, I think, *Oh – that! Yes, that. You felt that too? It wasn't just me!* I want to cry when I realise I'm not alone.

Lisa is so inclusive, so generous. I am never given the sense that I'm crazy or strange or isolated in what I'm feeling. I tell her I've been feeling the strain of the pressure for years.

'You've been sweeping a lot of things under the rug,' she observes. 'A lot of dust. One or two crumbs. Maybe even a mouse under there.'

'Lisa, there's a whole *moose* under the rug,' I say with grim humour.

Lisa just gets it. We have so much in common and it's so easy when we talk. Plus, she is the only person I've ever met that loves shoes more than I do.

Lisa has a dog called Stewart, a gorgeous Blue Heeler-cross-Collie. During most visits, Stewart has to stay upstairs and I can hear him clattering across the floorboards while Lisa and I chat in the office below. But sometimes he's allowed downstairs with us, and I love it when he is. Lisa jokes that Stewart would make a better psychologist than her because her patients' moods always improve when he comes to say hello.

The other person I meet around this time is Anthony Barnes, who becomes my new flatmate. Barnsey is a fun-loving psychiatrist and he is responsible for introducing me to such things as traditional Jewish family dinners on Friday; Yiddish words; a repertoire of practical jokes I could never have dreamt of; and shopping and coffee on Chapel Street, *dah-lings*.

The first time I meet Barnsey is at D.O.C. Pizza Place in Carlton, when a mutual friend realises we both need a flatmate. We shake hands and I sit down.

'Just so you know,' Barnsey says by way of a conversation-starter, 'I like to have a bath with my housemates once a week. To just get naked and get all our issues out.'

This is his opener. And I'm straight onto it.

'Sounds good to me,' I say. 'I'll bring the wine. And the soap. You scrub my back and all that . . .'

Our friend looks faintly aghast but Barnsey laughs. 'We're going to get along just fine, you and I,' he says to me.

And we do. We rent a place together just near Chapel Street, and for a while life begins to look up.

Barnsey and I are like ships in the night. I'm up and out at 4 a.m., and by the time I'm back at 9 a.m. he's already headed to the office. In the afternoons I'm hard at training when he gets home, but we meet afterwards and go out to the latest popular fancy-pants restaurants. He takes me to Jacques Reymond for my birthday, and we both nearly die because the serving sizes are so small. (We have to have a second dinner of toast when we get home to our flat.)

But despite the expensive restaurants and the shopping – even despite the Jewish family dinners – by the end of 2010 I am feeling worse than ever. I am not well at all.

For the life of me, I can see no end to this depression.

24

The Depths in the Heights

In 2011, I head to a high performance sports centre in Sierra Nevada, Spain, with my squad from Nunawading. Sierra Nevada is ridiculously beautiful. A spectacular freak of a mountain range, erupting on the wrong page of the atlas, its snow-heavy peaks popping up at the southernmost tip of Spain, right where the country is slipping on its togs and plunging into the Mediterranean Sea.

Being here makes me think of where I was born. Strange, because the Northern Territory is nothing like this. The landscapes couldn't be more opposite. They're from different hemispheres, different planets. But I have the same sense of displacement. If I was a fish out of water in the desert back home, then how will I go in the snow?

We are here to do altitude training. It's fifteen to twenty per cent harder to swim at altitude, and this place sure does offer height. Much of the mountain range is 3000 metres or more above sea level. We step out of the airport and straight into the sensation that we're breathing through straws. Gasping for air.

It's going to be impossible to do the same sets here that we do at home: it's just too hard. Walking – even sleeping – will be a workout, we're told. And as a result our coaches expect we'll all shed some weight. Up to a kilo a day, even. I look up at the glowering sky, heavy with clouds and grey as my mood. The weather forecast is foul, we have been warned. I shiver and hurry onto the bus.

I'm still shivering later that day when we sit down for lunch. I can't get warm in this place. Everything I touch is cold and dead. It's like my fingers are numb right through. And I can't remember anyone's name either. I can't shake the sensation that my brain is numb too.

I am foggy, cloudy; I am not myself at all. And worse, I am teary and fearful and I don't know why. When the woman at reception hands me my room key and tells me to enjoy my stay, I am overwhelmed by the sense that this place is not going to end well for me.

Why? I think, as the elevator pulls me even further into the thin, thin air. *What's your problem? Get a grip.* I give myself a shake and tell myself to get on with the job.

And yet when I walk down the corridor and into my room, I am full of blank dread. It is a bare room, with twin beds, a TV and a single desk that runs along one wall. There is a large window that looks out on an empty running track and the mountains in the distance. There are mountains in every direction, in every vista in this place. Mountains looming down at me whenever I turn around. I dump my bag on my bed and begin to unpack. It's cold in here; it's like a cheap motel room. I'm rooming with Ellen Gandy, a UK swimmer who is new to our squad, but there's no sign of her yet. I try to remember if I saw her at the airport. Try to remember any details from my morning. Landing, going through customs, the bus ride out to the sports centre, even the flight – all twenty-five and a half hours of it – it's just a blur. *Focus*, I chide myself. *C'mon, Leisel. Who did you sit next to? You must remember that.* But my brain is as thin as the air around me.

This visit to Sierra Nevada is the first time I've tried altitude training. We've been told it will affect every physiological system in our bodies – cardiovascular, nervous, endocrine, the works. 'Even your mental state will be affected,' we're advised. 'Training will be hard and that can screw with your head.' That must be why I'm feeling so horrid, I think. I ignore the fact I was feeling like this long before our plane touched down at Málaga on Tuesday.

The idea behind our camp is that we train up here for a couple of weeks, and then when we return home, when we come down from on high, we will swim like gods. We will redeem Australian swimming glory. It's been a quiet couple of years in the Aussie swimming camp, after the golden era of Sydney and Beijing, and the powers that be at Swimming Australia are prepared to do anything to stop the rot.

But altitude training is not just for swimmers. There are runners, footballers, basketballers, even gymnasts here, too. Cadel Evans, the Aussie cyclist, is staying in a hotel nearby while he trains for the upcoming Tour de France.

One day our team goes on an excursion to a nearby coastal town. We are rocketing down the side of the mountain in our van, heading for the flat below, when we see Cadel Evans riding on the road ahead.

'Maaate!' Michael Klim has wrenched the door of the van open and is yelling out to Cadel as we rattle down the mountain. 'Mate, how are ya?'

Apparently Michael and Cadel go way back. Cadel sidles up alongside and reaches out his hand. He grabs on to Michael's arm and the two of them cruise happily along, chatting away, shooting the breeze like they're not hurtling down one of the steepest mountains in Spain at 80 kilometres per hour. Cadel is flying along, really picking up speed, and he's yakking away, telling Michael what he had for breakfast. Crazy cyclist. I'd like to chat with Cadel properly while we're here in Sierra Nevada. I've met him before, at an Olympics somewhere, and I've always been a fan. Maybe there'll be time to chat to him when he's not pelting down a mountain.

From day one, training is a slog. It's slow and tiring and terribly frustrating. My lungs burn, my muscles ache, my body won't do what I want it to. Everyone else seems to be enjoying themselves; there's a buzz, a good vibe among the team. And I try – God, I try so hard – to be happy. To fit in, to keep up, to keep the laughs coming. Because no-one wants to hang around with someone who's dragging their feet. But nothing seems to work.

One of my friends takes a photo of me in the lunchroom when I'm pretending to wear a banana for a smile. We laugh and muck around, but behind my fake smile I am desperate, hollow. I can't find a real smile for the life of me. I am using what little energy I have to try and be pepped up and positive and fun and myself. My old self. Wherever she is.

Even my friends can't break me out of it. My good friend Tay Zimmer, a backstroker from Warrnambool, can't get me to crack a smile, and Tay is the funniest person in the world.

Get over it. Just get over it! I say to myself as I plough up and down the pool. *It's not forever; you'll be home soon. You need to stop feeling sorry for yourself and make the most of this.* But that's not it either. I'm not feeling sorry for myself. I'm not feeling anything at all. I am cold and exhausted and empty and grey. I'm disappearing into the landscape. I am drifting away.

I call Lisa daily from Sierra Nevada. I skype her in Melbourne when it is early morning for me and late evening for her. As always, she is patient and kind. She wants to know how I am feeling, how I am coping. I tell her as much as I dare to let out.

'We are going for a hike in the mountains tomorrow,' I say. 'Jeremy's got us walking twenty kilometres to some mountain.'

'Do one thing for me?' Lisa says.

'Sure. Anything.'

'Try and take in your surroundings. Really take it all in. I want you to notice everything, all the details, then report back to me what you saw. Don't skim over anything. I want to know how it smelt, how it sounded, what the air felt like on your skin. Everything.'

'Okay,' I say slowly. 'I think I can do that.'

The next morning we assemble for our hike. 'Pack your ski goggles?' Jeremy, our gym coach, asks us on the way out of camp, by way of a pep talk. Apparently there will be plenty of snow and ice.

'I've got mine!' Tay shouts and twirls her swimming goggles round her finger in the air. That gets a laugh from just about everyone. Everyone except me.

'Forget the goggles: you need a bloody snorkel,' I mutter. The air today is thinner than I could ever have imagined.

We trek for four hours and being outdoors is good, but I'd still rather be at home on my own. It's all I can think about: getting home. Some of my friends have been playing soccer in between training sessions during the last few days, and they can't understand why I don't join in. Usually I would. Usually, I'd be the first person out there, organising teams, assigning dumb nicknames, revving people up, stirring the pot. But now I can barely remember how.

I shake my head and try to forget all that now. Try to look around and soak it all in. Try to absorb all the details to tell Lisa tonight.

~

'Everything was blue,' I tell her on Skype that evening. 'Blue and crisp and clean and fresh. I could smell pine and hear the sound of rocks and ice crunching under my shoes.'

'That's good,' she says. 'That's all really good.'

'Oh, and there was this family of goats. A dad, a mum and two baby goats. Just standing there on a rock watching us as we headed out of camp.' These goats are the only animals I have seen since arriving in this place and suddenly they are important, they are crucial, they are so vivid in my mind. I describe them to Lisa for a few more minutes and she listens quietly.

'This thing, this awareness thing, this is so that I forget about my problems and just live in the moment, isn't it?' I say eventually.

'Sort of,' Lisa agrees. 'Not exactly that you'll forget your problems but, yes, it might help you to focus on where you are right now. I don't want you to feel like we're trying to suppress your worries or your anxieties. Not at all. We've swept so much under the rug again while you've been away because we just haven't had time to talk about everything yet. But we'll recap on those things when you're back home in Melbourne.'

'Oh yeah, the dead moose under the rug,' I say. I picture a cartoon moose under a red Turkish rug, its antlers poking out. 'That thing's starting to smell!' I say.

It's true I haven't been dealing with my emotions. Not in Sierra Nevada. Not ever, really. I just keep stuffing everything down and hoping it won't all explode in my face. Just because I now *know* I'm suppressing things doesn't mean I can stop doing it.

'Just look on the bright side,' Lisa says, signing off. 'There's a lot of material here for when you write your book one day.'

We both have a laugh at that.

~

As well as treks and other dry-land training at Sierra Nevada, we do daily weigh-ins at the pool. Each morning, before we hit the water, we have to stand on the scales and see how much weight has slipped off us in the night thanks to the wonders of altitude training.

But despite all the promises of weight evaporating into the thin air up here, my weight is not budging. If anything, it's going up. I'm eating less, training harder and somehow I'm putting on weight, while others around me are dropping up to a kilo overnight. *What's wrong with me?* I want to scream. I'm working so bloody hard just to wake up in the morning and I'm not even losing any weight. *C'mon! I'm working so hard here, people. So damn hard.*

Every day it gets worse and worse. For the life of me I cannot sleep. I don't want to eat. If I can't go home, then all I want to do is sit in my room and be alone. I spend hours in there. Whenever I'm not in the pool, I'm in my room. Sitting, staring; wishing I was somewhere else. Wishing I was someone else. Wishing this whole thing would end. The room is as bare and as stale as when we first moved into it. Aside from some of Ellen's clothes and a few books that are lying around, there's no real sign that anyone is living in here. My stuff is still inside my bag, ready for a quick getaway. Ready for an exit of any kind. And even though the room is so unremarkable, I feel like I am moulding into it. Like it's alive, like it's yawning and stretching and swallowing me whole. It's an animal, a monster. It's one of those terrible mountains outside, towering over us, casting its shadow. Making everything dark.

I am not seeing eye to eye with my gym coach right now either. Jeremy and I have always had a difficult relationship, but up here things seem more strained than ever. He can see that I'm sad, down, whatever you want to call it, and yet he never cuts me any slack. He is so hard, so unforgiving, and I leave every gym session in floods of tears. His attitude to life is to 'suck it up', so he refuses to acknowledge how much I am suffering. *I am not well! I am not well!* I want to scream at him. But then, that's not my style. Acknowledging weakness, asking for help: none of these things are very 'me'. And if I was going to seek help, the last person I would go to is Jeremy. Jeremy who pushes, Jeremy who won't see. Jeremy who drives me to tears again and again and again. After one session when he has told me to get the job done, I go back to my room and scrawl in my diary: 'Jeremy is a fucking asshole.' My tears spill on to the page and make the words bleed.

I do not want to be here. I don't want to be anywhere. This is the worst feeling in the world and I just don't know how to break out of it. I phone Mum in tears and tell her I need to come home. 'You'll be right,' she says. 'Just stick it out.' If only she knew what was going through my head. If only I could tell her somehow. I try listening to music, watching movies: all the things that usually make me happy. I watch *Curb Your Enthusiasm* (starring Larry David, the co-creator of *Seinfeld*), which is a show I normally love, but now even this can't make me laugh. Nothing will break me out of it. I want to shake the feeling. I want to shed my skin. Pull out my black soul so I can feel light again.

I'm not well. I am spiralling. I am mentally, physically and emotionally done. I want this to end so badly that I will do anything – *anything* – to make it all stop. I swim up and down, thinking about suicide, about ways I can kill myself. I'd rather shoot myself in the head than go on like this. I'm tired of swimming, and just so terribly sad. I hate my life, I hate myself. I just want to quit. I shut down every time I get in the pool.

What else can I do? Who am I if I'm not a swimmer?

There isn't an answer; I am nothing without it.

I don't exist without swimming, and I don't want to exist with it. I wish I was dead. I want to go to sleep. I want to die.

And so one hollow, grey Tuesday afternoon in Spain, while the snow outside is beginning to whirl and dance, I sit down on the bathroom floor with sleeping tablets and plan how I will steal a paring knife from the hotel kitchen to try to kill myself. I will start with my legs, with the big veins in my thighs. Then I will slash at my arms, at my pale white wrists. I shake as I think about it.

The room smells like every other cheap hotel I have even been in. Like a room constantly being deserted.

I imagine the knife and how I will run its blade gently over my skin, scrape it across the smooth skin of my wrist – then go further, do what I need to do.

I am bawling my eyes out now. It's coming from my guts. It's all coming out, I am sobbing so hard.

Then I get a text on my phone. *This is it!* My heart lurches. This is the message that could yet save my life.

I click it open and stare in disbelief. It's from our team sports scientist. 'Having a coffee downstairs with Cadel Evans, if you want to join us.'

Fucking what? Are you serious? I want to kill myself right now, I'm planning to cut my legs and arms open, and she's telling me Cadel Evans is downstairs! *You think I give a shit? How insensitive!* I am irrational and frenzied. I am on the edge. I hit 'delete' and slump to the floor.

~

I sit in the bathroom for a couple of hours. On my own, on the floor. Sobbing and trembling and trying to let go. *I can do this, I can. I can fix everything. On my own, by myself. I will do it my way.*

But then suddenly I am not alone. Someone is knocking.

I peel myself off the floor and stagger to the front door. Who would be knocking? Who could possibly know?

'Leisel? Leisel! What's going on in here?'

I open the door and find myself falling. The carpet feels warm and alive after the cold tiles of the bathroom. I don't speak – can't speak – I just sit on the floor bawling, and my coach waits beside me for as long as it takes.

In the end he speaks first, and all he says is: 'Leisel, we need to get you some air.'

25

The Comedown

It is not the end of me, but it's the end of Sierra Nevada for me. I am shipped off home at 4 a.m. the next morning, in a shroud of secrecy, when the sky is low and cold, and dark as congealed blood.

Nobody knows I planned to kill myself. The papers don't get hold of it; my teammates aren't told. Even Mum has no idea. My coach, who found me, and my psychologist, who has to fix me: these are the only people who know. The only people in the world who have any idea how close I came to going through with it. 'How did you know what I was doing in there?' I ask Rohan.

He shrugs. 'I didn't. I just came to see why you weren't at coffee.'

So it was a fluke. Just a coincidence that Rohan dropped by. The casualness of it all sends a shiver down my spine. And at the same time, I really feel like Rohan was my guardian angel that day. It's as if someone sent him just for me.

I arrive home from Sierra Nevada and immediately disappear. No training, no racing, no leaving the house. I'm in lockdown: I cannot face the world. I see no-one, go nowhere. I do nothing except try to want to live again.

In June I am supposed to compete in the Barcelona leg of the Mare Nostrum series in Europe. I am scheduled to fly to Spain again, along with seventeen other Australian swimmers, within weeks of returning from Sierra Nevada. But Rohan doesn't even discuss it, doesn't entertain the idea. He immediately pulls me from competition. 'Expected starter Leisel Jones will no longer swim in Barcelona after her coach, Rohan Taylor, decided she would benefit more from a home training environment following three weeks of altitude training in Sierra Nevada,' reports Swimming Australia.

'Following three weeks of altitude training in Sierra Nevada ...' If only they knew. If only anyone knew.

Following her intended suicide in Sierra Nevada. Following her plan to drug herself and then slice open her wrists and legs, to go at them with a knife as if they are nothing more than slabs of meat and muscle, slabs of tendon and sinew waiting to be dissected. Slabs of meat made for swimming and racing and winning, and later bleeding and dying. But never really designed for living.

I sob and sob and shake and sob. I don't want to swim, but I have nothing else. I don't want to die, but I hate living, too.

~

In July, despite everything, I go to the World Championships in Shanghai. In a fog, I win silver in the 100-metre event, just behind Rebecca Soni, but I don't compete in the 200 metres. I will never swim that race again.

In November 2011, after Mare Nostrum in Barcelona, there is yet another trip planned to Spain. *I should just buy a bloody villa in Majorca and relocate already*, I think bitterly. This time a bunch of the Aussie contingent, plus their coaches (including Rohan), are heading south for three weeks. Back to Sierra Nevada.

Over. My. Dead. Body.

And this is exactly what Rohan is terrified of. There is no talk of me going; we don't even mention it. Because Rohan knows – and I know – it would kill me for sure. Instead, I head to Queensland for three weeks to train with local coach Michael Bohl for a bit. He's a big deal up there. He knows Olympics and Olympians; he knows the drill.

I will lob up at Bohl's instead of going back to Stephan's, because I still feel really bad about the way I left Stephan all those years ago. Every time I think back to that phone call I made – when I rang Stephan from Melbourne and told him I wasn't coming back – I feel awful all over again. I'm sorry for the way I treated Stephan back then. It was a terrible conversation and that was my fault. I should have flown back and had a meeting with him, told him face to face. I handled it very poorly and I regret that I did. After all he'd done, all he'd given me . . . I never performed better than when I was under Stephan.

That's not to say I regret the move to Melbourne. I don't. Not for one second. Even after Marty and I broke up, I still maintained that taking that chance, taking such a huge risk to relocate just months out from the Beijing Olympics, was one of the best decisions of my life. *The* best decision of my life. It was gutsy, gung-ho and totally right for me. And I don't think I would have won at Beijing if I hadn't done it my way.

But now I head to train with Michael Bohl in Brisbane for a few weeks. Back to Queensland, to my roots. Back home to try and remember who I used to be. Back to Bris Vegas and back to Mum's for some support and some home-cooked meals.

I have just started taking antidepressant medication. Lexapro. The word bounces around in my brain, all nervy and jittery and too keen to get off the blocks. Lex. A. Pro. Lexapro. Be a pro. Turn yourself into a professional human being! No tears, no feelings: no nothing at all.

I wander around in a fog and lose hours, lose days.

Mum doesn't know I'm on meds. She doesn't know I've started seeing a psychiatrist. (One with a dingy office in Carlton, all dark and uninspiring. His solution is drugs, always drugs. Lisa sent me to see him after I got back from Sierra Nevada. 'This is bigger than me now,' she said.) But most of all, Mum has no idea I planned to kill myself. It would break her heart if I told her that.

I lose a lot of time over the next six months. Lose time, lose myself. Just wander in my fog. By the end of the year I am as miserable as I've ever been. I'm in a black hole, no matter how hard I dig.

And I've tried bloody digging, believe me. I've tried sports therapy, psychotherapy. I'm taking my meds. I've tried working hard, and tried working less hard. I've tried going out with friends. I've flown to New York with my friend (and fellow swimmer) Matt Targett. We went there on holidays for two weeks on the way home from Worlds in July. But even the Big Apple couldn't give me back my hunger. At least not my metaphorical one.

My physical hunger – my actual hunger – seems to be alive and kicking these days though, and I am drinking a contraband full-fat latte when I phone Rohan with yet another idea to try to be happy. I am back in Melbourne, in my car, stuck in traffic, while half the city seems to be in Yarra Park just beyond my car window, soaking up the summer sunshine.

'Okay, what about this?' I say to Rohan. 'How would you feel about me switching gym coaches – train with Matt's coach instead of with Jeremy?' Matt Targett suggested this while we were away in New York. He reckons his coach and I would get on like a house on fire. 'He's a respected gym coach; he's a name in the business,' I say.

And I'm pretty sure he won't make me bawl at every session, like Jeremy does.

'Nope,' says Rohan, as if that is that.

I try again a few days later at training: 'Look, I can't train with Jeremy anymore. It's no good for my health. I've called Matt's coach, I've organised everything. He's happy to start working with me starting Monday.'

'Nope,' says Rohan again.

'But why not? This could be just what I need, Rohan! Just the thing to get me back on track. Just the thing to help me feel a bit more positive about training.'

'Jeremy's an excellent gym coach.'

'Sure, fine. But he's not excellent for me. I'm no good when I train with him. I'm crying after every session with the guy, and it's not because he's working me too hard. It's because he makes me miserable. He makes me feel like shit. When I train with him I don't want to be here.'

But Rohan has got a bee in his bonnet about it.

'Leisel, you train with Jeremy.'

'I want to train with Matt's coach.'

'But I don't know Matt's coach.'

'Yeah, but you didn't know Jeremy a few years ago, either,' I point out. 'What difference does it make, anyway? I don't want to work with Jeremy.'

'You train with Jeremy or you don't train here with me.'

'You— what?' I am pulled up in my tracks. 'Did you just give me an ultimatum?'

'The decision is yours,' Rohan says.

'Don't you *ever* give me an ultimatum, because I will always choose the option you don't want! I'm not going to train with Jeremy!' I say, my voice rising. 'I'm just not!'

Rohan simply holds out his hands, palms facing upwards.

'Fine!' I shout. 'I'm leaving! I'm going to train with Bohly in

Brisbane. He's happy to have me!' I am bluffing. Bohly knows nothing about this. And it's a dumb thing to say, because Rohan and Bohly are great mates, too.

Rohan doesn't flinch. But I am stubborn and gutsy, and stupid to boot.

'You leave me no choice, Rohan. I am not training with Jeremy. Pure and simple.'

And I leave Rohan's squad for good that day.

~

I still don't know what went wrong with me and Rohan. How we got to that point. Sure, I was bloody-minded about it: that's me. If you give me an ultimatum, I will choose the option that will piss you off. But it was more than that. It was something else. It was almost like Rohan had had enough of me and he was using Jeremy as an excuse to end our partnership. I can't think of any other explanation. Why else would he be so insistent I train with Jeremy, the guy who made my life a misery. Jeremy was so bad for my head. Rohan saw me in Sierra Nevada, for Christ's sake. And yet he insisted I stick with him? I still don't get it.

When I leave the pool that morning, my hair still wet, my skin reeking of chlorine, I thank Rohan for everything he's done for me. Things are pretty awkward. We're like polite strangers. But we're on speaking terms at least and I know eventually we'll be fine. Not great, not like we were. But Rohan and I will never lose touch. We've been through too much together for that.

And so I pack up my stuff and I move back to Queensland. Back to the Sunshine State to let a little light back into my life. A bit of routine, a bit of control. I move into my old house at The Gap, where Mum is still living upstairs. I catch up with friends I haven't seen in a while. Go out for pasta. Do a little comfort eating.

I turn up at St Peter's Western and throw myself at Michael Bohl, beg him to let me join his squad. Bohly is confused. Bemused. He doesn't even coach the 100-metre breaststroke event.

But he's my only option. I've got no-one else.

'Can I join?' I ask bluntly.

'I've got too many people, Leisel. I don't think I can do this.'

He's being kind. What he means is:

I don't do 100-metre breaststroke.

I don't do 26-year-old dropouts.

I don't do miracles, and the Olympics are only six months away.

'Bohly,' I level with him. 'Either you take me in or I retire. You're the only thing saving me from quitting the sport.'

And Bohly, thank God, takes pity on me. I start that day. I've got no doubt that Bohly lets me join his squad out of sympathy. But I am grateful that he does. And even more grateful that he doesn't say so.

And for all the awkwardness about the way it happened, for all my falling out with Rohan, who I admire, there's something cyclical about being back in Queensland for my final Olympic campaign. For my last roll of the dice. There's something nice about returning to where it all began.

I've come a long way since I left. I've learnt an awful lot. But at the same time, I haven't really changed at all. I'm still little Leisel from Burpengary, little Leisel who'll tread water for a Mars bar. Still Leisel who will try and try and try again, do anything to win. Six months ago in Sierra Nevada I planned to take my own life. In the coming six months, I will try to qualify for the Olympic Games. My fourth Olympic Games. By this stage in my career, I might not have regained my hunger to win, but I haven't lost my stubbornness either. I will qualify for the London Olympics. You know I bloody will.

So I get back in the pool to get on with my job.

~

Michael Bohl's squad, at St Peter's Western Club at Indooroopilly, Brisbane, is the biggest elite swimming squad in the country. When I join in November 2011, Bohly already has three Beijing Olympic gold medallists in his squad (Australians Stephanie Rice and Bronte Barratt, and Korean Park Tae-Hwan), plus half a dozen other Olympic hopefuls. The squad is big, slick and intimidating. It is the worst squad environment I have ever swum in.

The first few weeks are not too bad. Everyone is welcoming at best and only indifferent at worst. Fine, whatever. I don't need a red carpet. I'm just happy to be accepted and keen to get on with the job. We do some fun stuff; they are pretty good at being social. We play barefoot bowls, have barbecues at the weekend. But from the beginning there are signs that I don't quite fit in here. I am loud. I am vocal when no-one else is. 'C'mon, guys! Last one! Last effort!' I shout, as the squad buckles down to do our final splits of the day. But my encouragement is met with awkward silence and sideways glances, and I soon learn that's not the way they do it around here.

Bohly's squad is competitive. We are not one big team. We do not encourage one another or look out for each other the way we did at Rohan's. Most days we don't even talk to one another. These people are here to win and anything else is wasted energy. These people are not here to be my friend.

Except for one person: Stephanie Rice.

Steph Rice is an unlikely ally, I'll admit. She's not the first person I expected to hit it off with. When I move to St Peter's, I don't know much about Steph, except that she has a reputation among the swimming fraternity for being a bit of a showpony. That, and she can swim a pretty impressive individual medley. But within days of meeting, we are fast friends. Steph is so welcoming and helpful. She is as nice as pie to me. She shows me which showers are the best ones in the change rooms, and which cafes nearby do the best brunch. She introduces me to her friends, invites me to her parties; we go for coffee, catch up for wine.

I say to Mum in my first few weeks: 'You know, I feel Steph Rice is a bit misunderstood. Like, she gets a bad rap and she doesn't deserve it.'

By now Steph has insisted I share her gym coach with her ('You'll love my coach!') so we're doing all our workouts together, spending all our gym and pool time together. And yeah, I think she is a bit of a showpony, but you know what? Good on her. If that's what floats her boat, if that's her style: good for her. She's not hurting anyone.

Training seems easier now I have a friend. I'm doing a lighter load these days: four or five kilometres per session, nine sessions each week. I get Friday afternoons off. The rest of my squad are still training like a much younger squad would: ten sessions per week and up to seven kilometres each time they hit the pool. Knock yourselves out, kids! I've earnt my stripes. After thirteen years, and more than 50,000 kilometres in the pool, I reckon I deserve my Friday arvos off.

But despite all my experience, around this time I start to doubt myself. What am I thinking, acting like I can make an Olympic team one more time? Why have I wasted my life for the past three and a half years, pretending I can be an Olympian again? My weight is starting to sneak upwards, my motivation spiralling down. Olympic selections only take the fastest two people in the country in each event, and even then you have to make qualifying time. And I think I can do that? In the state I'm in? Look at me! I'm a mess, a wreck. I'm on antidepressants, and I am still living at home with Mum. I'm on the phone to my sports psych, Lisa, once a week. I've just started at a new squad, in a new state. And I think I can make the Olympic team in four months?

But there is something I am even more afraid of than failing – something that haunts me: the prospect that I might succeed. Do I really want to make another Olympic team? Can I do that to myself? Because qualifying means more effort, more pain, more training. Qualifying for the Olympics means more swimming.

The thought drives me to 7-Eleven to pick up a donut. And then another. Last week I ate a whole pack of mini-Mars bars. This is my plan. I will self-sabotage to make sure I don't qualify. Only, because I'm training so hard, my attempts at self-sabotage don't amount to much. Any poor eating choices I make are like tapping the brake while I still have one foot on the accelerator, going full speed.

26

London Calling

In March 2012, I find myself at the Adelaide Aquatic Centre for the Australian Swimming Championships, which double as the selection trials for the London Olympic Games in July. Of course I'm here. You think I'm going to miss this? No way.

I am here because I have come too far not to be. I am too stubborn to let myself just drift away.

I am not bothering with the 200-metre event at London. It's 100 metres or nothing, 100 metres or bust. I don't really want to be at trials. I don't want to be anywhere much. I am still struggling to get through the days, still struggling to be happy, to be my old self again. But I'm here and I force myself to commit. *Let's do this. Let's get this job done.*

I feel a strange sense of relief at trials: as if whatever happens now, things are out of my hands. Win or lose. Qualify or not. I can't control these things. It's no longer my decision. Whether I go on or not is not up to me. My job is just to give this thing one last go. My job is just to give it a crack.

And I do. I swim my heart out in the heats and make it to the semis. Then I win my semi and progress to the finals.

I am stoked, dazed. I feel woozy with relief. Then just woozy. I stagger and hold a hand to my forehead. I feel like my brain is swimming in fluid. I feel the way you do when you have a virus. I wave to my coach and call him over to help me. Something's not right. Something's definitely wrong.

Inside the medical rooms, a doctor I've never met before tells me she needs to run some tests.

'We should probably do a blood test because you're very overweight,' she tells me.

Sorry, *what*? I'm very overweight? I'm currently the number two breaststroker in the world and I'm swimming at the Olympic trials. How overweight could I possibly be?

'There could be something wrong with your thyroid,' she adds quickly, sensing my mood.

Really? Very overweight, did you say? If only you knew what I've been through to get here, I think. Sierra Nevada flashes through my mind.

'Thanks, but my thyroid is dandy,' I say.

No-one knows I'm on antidepressants, and that's the real reason I'm putting on weight. No amount of donuts could cause this weight gain, not with the distances I'm swimming every day. Not to mention all the dry-land training I'm doing. This doctor is not the first person to notice my changing physique. But what do I say? Do I tell them how I have been depressed for years? That things got so bad I was going to kill myself? Or do I let them think I've just had one too many desserts?

I'm not as strict as I used to be, but this is my fourth time round at the Olympics and I'm not doing another bloody soup diet. I am sick of being disciplined, sick of being unhappy. Even so, old habits die hard and a 'bad' diet for an athlete is still pretty amazing by normal standards. Throw in forty-odd kilometres in the pool each week, plus five or six gym sessions, and you could hardly blame much of my weight gain on indulgence. No, most of it is down to depression and antidepressants. But I'm not prepared to tell anyone that.

I am still woozy with a virus when I swim in the final. But I don't feel too bad once I hit the water. I swim a good race, my own race. I am happy with that. When I come second to Leiston Pickett and my time, 1:07.64, is under qualifying time, I am stunned.

I made it? I made it! I am off to the Olympics again. I look around at the screaming fans in the stands in astonishment.

'You did it!' Lisa cheers down the phone to me later, when I'm back in my hotel room. 'Just look what you can do!'

'Look what you can do even when you're scraping the bottom of the barrel,' I joke. I am happy; I can joke for the first time in weeks.

'Yeah, when you're really, really desperate!' Lisa laughs.

And it's true. Everyone competing at trial is in peak physical condition. They're all prepped, primed and ready to go. They're young, hungry and out to win, whereas I just feel grateful to still be alive. I am so underprepared, so underdone compared to these kids.

'Ninety-nine per cent of the population couldn't make the Olympic team at their best, and here you are qualifying at your near-worst!' jokes Lisa. 'I'm proud of you,' she adds. 'Look at what you can do.'

And for a moment I am proud of me too. I'm pleased I had the guts to stick it out this far, and I'm chuffed I've made the team. I've booked my ticket and that's all I had to do. Mission accomplished. I'm stoked.

This baby is off to the Olympics, again.

~

I go back to Brisbane and work hard. I work my butt off. And there's plenty there to work with, if the gossip back at squad is to be believed. 'Too fat, too slow,' that's the word on the street. What, you don't think I hear the other girls talking in the change rooms?

Before trials, things at St Peter's Western were pretty tough; afterwards they are just horrible. There are cliques and 'in-crowds'; there is social exclusion. There are rumours and narky comments and there's bitching galore. I try to just ignore it, to get on with the job. I am too old and too tired to be bothered with this.

But one day I swear I will confront the ringleader of it all. If she pushes me too far, I will have it out with her. That's my style. That's how I do things. I'd rather say it to your face than talk behind your back, any day. So I will wait until she is alone, until she's not protected by her little gang of followers, and then I will confront her and ask her: why? Why the hell are you making my life such a misery? What have I ever done to you?

Ah, but I can already guess what will happen. She will look at me blankly with those doe-brown eyes of hers, as if to say 'Who me?'

Yes, you, Stephanie Rice.

I've been told it is Steph who is saying nasty things behind my back and bad-mouthing me to my coach. She has dropped me completely since those early days at squad, when she was my BFF. Now she seems hostile and it's making my life at training a misery.

I don't care if people like me or not. That's their prerogative. Not everyone is going to like me, and I'm fine with that. But the sort of bitchy behaviour Steph Rice dishes out is unnecessary and hurtful, and I won't stand for that. I'd much rather have it out with her if she has an issue with me.

But I don't say anything to her now. I bide my time. Instead, I watch as the rest of the Aussie contingent leaves for London while I stay behind. They're going three weeks ahead of competition, which is too long for me. I'll fly later in July. Besides, I have doctors' appointments at home to attend. I see specialists: gastroenterologists. I have bleeding stomach ulcers that will not heal. I stay in Brisbane and endure the indignity of colonoscopies.

27

Toxic Team

I arrive in London and discover our Australian swimming team could also use a colonic. The whole thing could do with a cold hose down.

We have a new head coach for the 2012 Games, or an acting one, at least. Leigh Nugent is officially in charge (having been acting in the role since 2009), and this is his first Olympics since he was head coach at Athens in 2004. Back then, he was only in the role for a short time before he left to resume working with the youth squad. Now he's back in the top job after Alan Thomson took leave.

The other difference in our team is that it's packed full of newbie swimmers, many of whom have never been to the Olympics before. Not that you'd know it. With their sense of entitlement and their obsession with fame, these Gen Ys are acting as if they've long ago earned their stripes. It's funny, given that there were much bigger names on the Aussie team in years gone by and they never acted like they owned the pool: people like Hackett, Thorpe, O'Neill and Trickett. Serious stars. Back then we all encouraged each other; we pushed each other to be better athletes. Hackett and co. had every right to be full of themselves – there was something to be full about! – and yet they always remained all about the team, not just about themselves.

So our new-look Aussie team feels anything but fresh. It feels rotten. Gone bad. Decidedly *off*. There's no camaraderie, no team spirit. Not much sense of a team at all. The culture is terrible; people's attitudes stink. This squad needs a clean out. This swimming team is toxic.

In London, Aussie swimming is all about the individual. It's about *my* performance, *my* sponsors and *my* horde of Twitter followers. About selfies, image and 'This is my Games, don't you know?' Our team is ruled by a small elite of big personalities; everyone else is pushed to the narrow periphery. There's no sense of encouragement or support. And there aren't many friendships here either.

For a start, we can't use the term 'rookies' anymore for the new members of the team. Rookies is politically incorrect, it's offensive, we're told. We must use the more obscure 'tyros' instead (which sounds like a very American way of saying 'novice' to me). And Rookies Night is thrown out too. When I think back to how we dressed up and poked fun at ourselves during Rookies Night back in 2000, I feel sad that these kids are missing out on the fun. But these new tyros are too special to have a laugh at themselves. It's too embarrassing, too uncool. Better to do Stilnox initiations instead.

Also out the window is the expectation that we will support one another during competition. In the good old days, whenever you weren't swimming you were required to sit in the stands and watch your teammates swim. Heats, semis, finals, whatever. You attended and you cheered. We supported each other and we were happy to do it. We did what was right by the team. In 2012, however, things have been updated. We no longer have to go along and watch our teammates swim if we think we have somewhere better to be. Somewhere like bed. Or the games room. Or wherever else we might feel like being. People are skipping sessions, or turning up halfway through after deliberately missing the bus. And nothing is said or done, no-one is punished in response. It is poor form. During the Don Talbot era we would have been berated if we dared to try something like this. Back then there were standards – gold standards – and we all knew exactly what they were.

Worse, however, than those swimmers who don't turn up are the ones who come along and then cheer for other countries. That's right: there are people wearing the green and gold who are sitting in the stands gunning for the USA, for Britain or for Japan – for anyone but Australia to win. I cannot believe my eyes. When Emily Seebohm lines up to race Missy Franklin, Steph Rice nearly shouts herself hoarse cheering for the American girl to win. It seems we're uncool compared to the States.

But then James Magnussen steps onto the blocks and suddenly everyone is doing it. There's a whole bunch of Aussie swimmers cheering for Maggie to lose. And yet the Australian swimming management doesn't say a word.

Prior to racing, we have a special ceremony inside the Aussie swimming camp. It's an initiation of sorts, our version of handing out the baggy greens, and it happens at the start of every Australian swimming Olympic campaign. This year the ceremony takes place in a darkened basement, deep underneath the Olympic village. Here in the low light, to the strains of *Waltzing Matilda*, each swimmer – old or new, medal-cert or up-and-comer – is met by Laurie Lawrence. He shakes their hand earnestly, congratulates them on being chosen to represent their country, and presents them with the pocket square from the team blazer, showcased under glass, in a hardwood frame. The pocket square is only small. It's forest green, edged with green and navy grosgrain ribbon, and it bears the golden embroidery of the Australian coat of arms – the kangaroo, the emu and our Federation star – along with the Olympic rings and the place and date of these Olympics: 'London 2012'. The frame has a plaque for the athlete's name, and receiving it is one of the proudest experiences you could ever hope to have.

Even after four Olympics, the ceremony still gives me goosebumps. It's a beautiful occasion – and a proud one too. What greater honour is there than representing your country?

We have a team photo taken, and all sing the national anthem together. And then it's over and we're back upstairs, standing blinking in the daylight again. It takes, maybe, forty-five minutes all up.

This year, Steph Rice and James Magnussen (Maggie) and I are due to have a press conference together immediately after the ceremony, so I hang around in the foyer to wait for them to come up from the basement. But then Maggie saunters in from outside the building.

'Maggie, were you in that meeting?' I ask.

'Nah.' He walks past, distracted, looking for someone else.

I trail behind him. 'Why not?'

He can't see who he's looking for. He seems frustrated. 'Huh?'

'Why weren't you at the meeting just now?' I ask.

'I didn't want to go.'

I can feel my blood boiling. 'You didn't want to go?'

'Yeah, my coach said I didn't have to go if I didn't want to. That I could rest instead.'

'Since when was that the rule?' I ask loudly. 'I've been to a few of these things now and that's never been the rule. In fact, the general consensus is that this is a bit of a proud moment and that receiving your pocket is one of the greatest privileges there is as an athlete. Most athletes would kill for it. And you couldn't be bothered because you're too tired?'

Maggie looks at me like I'm crazy, like it's none of my business what he does. Like we're not on the same team or something. The papers have taken to calling me 'mother hen' on this trip, because of the way I'm looking out for the younger kids. Right now I don't feel like a mother hen. But I do feel like I'm doing some hen-pecking.

Hen-pecking that Maggie could do without, apparently. He shrugs. 'Yeah, well. We've been travelling and stuff and I thought . . .'

'You thought what? Who do you think you are? We're all fucking tired, buddy. This is my fourth time around the block. You think I'm not tired? If anyone's going to be fed up of these things, don't you think it might be me? But no – I'm proud to be here. I'm proud for our team to come together and to sing the national anthem and to shake Laurie's hand and to get my pocket square. You shouldn't *have* to go along. You should *want* to be there. You should want this thing! This is your first Olympic team and it's a fucking privilege to do this, buddy!'

Maggie rolls his eyes and slopes away. What does he care what I think?

Why do I care so much? I can't help it: I do care. I care a lot. This team is important to me. And the fact that our gold-medal hopeful can't be bothered turning up to this ceremony is pretty pathetic. People are taking it upon themselves to bend the rules here and do whatever suits them, not what's best for the team. And I hate it. All Maggie had to do was turn up and look interested. To sit on his arse for forty-five minutes. That ceremony makes the hairs on my arms stand up, it makes me swell with pride. With Aussie pride. This is us taking on the rest of the world! And he couldn't be bothered? What a terrible attitude. During the Games, wherever the Olympic flag is displayed throughout London it must fly higher than the Union Jack. (This is a requirement of the International Olympic Committee as a sign that the Olympics is bigger than any one nationality.) I think about James Magnussen's attitude towards being an Australian representative swimmer. No-one is asking him to choose between seeking Olympic glory and being an Aussie. He can do both. James Magnussen is not a flagpole; he doesn't have to put one higher than the other. And yet he still puts himself before the rest of the team.

What's more, he's not the only one.

~

I eat alone in the Olympic village. I am fed up with them all. I read, listen to my iPod and relax on my own.

Then one afternoon I see Stephanie Rice on her own in the change rooms. It is the first time I have seen her without her posse. I see my opportunity and I'm not going to pass it up.

'Ricey?' I start. 'What the hell is your problem with me?'

She looks up in surprise.

'When I started at St Peter's you were as nice as pie to me,' I say. 'What happened? What changed? I've heard that you're spreading rumours behind my back. What is your problem? What is it? I'm not competing against you. I've done nothing to upset you. I'm no threat to you in any way. We don't like the same boys, don't swim in the same races. So what is it? Do you just not like me? Do I annoy you? Is that it? Well, that's fine. But for God's sake just leave me alone!'

She studies the floor, her nails, her gear bag. She looks everywhere in the room except at my face. 'Huh? What do you mean?' she asks impassively. Apparently she has no recollection of the last few months, no memory of making comments to the other girls about my weight, my clothes, the way I walk or the way I swim. She can't remember bitching to my coaches about me or reporting on what I've eaten that day. What, she thinks I'm stupid? She thinks I don't hear? Yeah, it's small-scale, petty stuff, but it's not what being in a team is about.

I say all this to her and she leaves in a huff. But she cannot look me in the eye when she does.

But if I thought the girls back home in Brisbane were bad, the behaviour of the boys here in London is ten times worse.

Over the course of thirteen years and three Olympic Games, I've seen plenty of shenanigans among the Australian team. Piss-taking, practical jokes: our team has been there and done it all. And I am the first to admit to getting stuck in. I like a good practical joke better than anyone. I don't think I've ever laughed so much as the time Skippy (Geoff Huegill) dared me to eat a spoonful of 'avocado' at a Japanese restaurant during one of my first ever television interviews. The Nine Network was filming a bunch of us during our 'down time' after training, and I was only fourteen and it was long before I'd ever heard of wasabi. It was hilarious.

During the reign of people like Travis Nederpelt, Grant Hackett and Geoff Huegill – back when those guys were in the team and causing trouble – we all had a lot of fun. No-one got hurt and no-one got offended. But there's a different vibe now: a nasty vibe. What some of the boys are doing in London isn't funny: it's bullying. They're berating people. It's brutal. They're picking on anyone they identify as a weaker target: the newbies, the rookies. Anyone who can't defend themselves. They are singling people out and then ganging up on them, three or four against one, and it is not cool. Not cool at all.

One of their 'jokes' is to get in the elevator and press all the buttons and then, when the doors open on a random floor, they push someone out. When they do it to someone like me (which they do), I don't mind. I get it. But in some instances it feels much more malicious. When they do it to the younger kids, the kids who aren't confident and who don't know their way around the village, kids who have enough to worry about without getting needlessly lost, I feel it stops being funny – it seems cruel.

Their favourite target for this – and for all their other jokes – is poor Jarrod Poort. Jarrod is a 1500-metre swimmer and a newbie on the squad. He's only seventeen, and this is his first national team, so it's hardly a fair fight.

Team management in the Aussie camp are aware of what's going on, but no-one does anything to stop the bullying. The culture in the camp is rotten. Some coaches allow the issue to be swept under the rug, whereas previous coaches such as Don Talbot would have sent the offenders home immediately.

I speak out in the press to say I won't tolerate bullying, but I refrain from naming names. Everyone involved is still racing and nobody – bully or not – deserves that kind of distraction while they're competing. It wouldn't be fair. Instead I watch and wait for my opportunity, but all the while my fury is building.

28

Breaking Point

London. 5 a.m. Four days until D-day. Four days till I race for the last time.

'LJ? You awake?'

I am now. I roll over and groan and consider throwing a pillow at my mate, Mel Schlanger, who is lying in the single bed across the room from me. She is holding her phone above her head, absorbed in reading something. The low glow from the screen casts an eerie light across her face. Schlanger is always on her phone at this meet; she can't seem to find sleep no matter what she does.

'LJ?' More urgent now. 'LJ, I think you need to see this. It's important.'

She has my attention now. 'Is it Mum?' My first thought, always, is that something has happened to Mum. 'Is she okay?'

'There's a story, LJ. And it's not very good.'

'What story?'

'Look, there's some jerk saying some horrible things. But don't listen to him. Don't listen to any of them; they're just jerks. You're better than that, okay? You're better than all of them.'

So I crawl out of bed to read on Schlanger's phone that the

Herald Sun is running a story that seems to question whether I am too fat to swim. They are comparing photos of me over the years, under the headline 'Leisel is relaxed, but is she ready?' Alongside it is a terrible photo of me diving into the pool. It's horrid. It's taken from an unflattering angle, evidently intended to make me look bad. I am pale and leaning forward, gravity doing me no favours. In another image, I am standing completely at ease, back swayed, stomach relaxed. In reality I look exactly how lots of people would look in private, standing in front of their bathroom sink at home, say, in bad light and if they didn't suck in their stomach for the camera. But I am mortified.

The article quotes my press conference two days earlier, when I'd said: 'I'm so relaxed and I'm just really enjoying everything about these Games and the lead-up.'

'Some would say too relaxed,' muses the reporter, 'with coaches privately frustrated at her condition.'

Really? Which coaches?

Although the article doesn't actually use the word 'fat', it says my figure is in 'stark contrast to that of 2008' and includes half a dozen photos of me to drive the point home. Oh, and they're running a poll asking readers whether I'm fit enough to compete. The implication is clear. Bloody hell!

'I thought you should hear it from me first,' Schlanger says, and I am grateful in that moment that I have a friend.

I have a sudden urge to throw up, but I swallow hard. I hand back Schlanger's phone and my hand is shaking.

'Oh my God,' I say finally. And then: 'Right. What do I do? What do I do? I don't even know what I'm supposed to do.'

I want to cry; I want to laugh. I want to crawl under a rock and die.

Who would do this? Who did this? I snatch back the phone and squint at the screen.

'Paul Kent? Who is he?'

I stare at the photos again. They truly are horrid. *Is that really how I look? When was this taken? When did they do this?* I feel violated at the thought of these photos being taken. And furious. Sure, I don't look like my eighteen-year-old self, but I'm not eighteen anymore. I'm twenty-seven.

My phone pings. A message. Then another, and another. I check my inbox and it is jammed with messages. It is mid-afternoon in Australia and everyone back home has had all day to pick up a copy of the paper and find me there. All of me. So much of me. I am mortified and distressed all over again.

'What do I do?' I ask Schlanger again. 'What do I do?'

I tell myself not to cry. I won't give them the satisfaction.

'I can't go back to the pool today,' I say.

'You have so much support,' Schlanger says to me. 'Everyone is behind you. Look!' She holds out her phone, but I wave it away. I've seen enough for one morning. Enough to last me a lifetime.

'I don't care, I can't do it,' I say again. How am I supposed to rock up at the pool today?

But even as I say it, I know I have to. Today is Wednesday. On Sunday morning I swim the heats of the 100 metres, and in the evening, if I'm lucky, are the semi-finals. This weekend could be my last Olympic race ever. I have to train today. I have to get in the pool. I have to face the media dressed in my togs.

And so I get on with it. I go to the pool and I walk out on deck, clutching my gear bag hopelessly across my stomach. It's so obviously my defence, my security blanket, and I must look like a fool. But by this stage I figure I can't look much worse.

There are over 21,000 members of the media at the London Games and it feels like every one of them is on pool deck this morning. There are photojournalists, news teams and film crews galore, beaming my body out to four billion people worldwide. *Is this*, I wonder, *the most embarrassing moment in my life?* I hear the clicks and whirs of the thousands of cameras behind me and, without a shadow of a doubt, I know that it is.

I think about every time I have ever felt self-conscious in my togs, about every time I've ever had a 'fat-day' during competition, about every time I have felt people stare at me with recognition on the street. None of that has prepared me for this moment. Nothing could. It's like that feeling when you strip down to your togs on a crowded beach and for one instant you feel like the world is looking at you. It's like that, except the world really *is* looking.

Here I am! I want to say. *Dissect me now. Pull me apart and leave me here to bleed. But for God's sake make it quick, would you?*

I glance around for a friendly face. For my coach or someone from squad. Even Stephanie Rice would do right now. And then I spy Lachlan Searle, the media manager of the Aussie swimming team. He is sitting on the pool deck with the head coach of the Australian swimming team, Leigh Nugent. I walk over to the two of them and dump my bags at their feet so they have no choice but to look at me.

'Leisel!' Lachlan says, as if the thought has just occurred to him. 'Just so you know, there's something about you in the paper today. But it's nothing to worry about.'

Behind me is the sound of ten thousand or more cameras clicking. A staccato of humiliation.

I pause for a moment to consider what Lachlan has just said. *Just so you know. There's something in the paper.* I kind of figured that out when I woke up to thirty new text messages and I thought my mother had died. It's almost 10 a.m. now and I haven't heard anything from the Australian swimming team management. I'm amazed they haven't come to talk to me about this. I'm shocked.

I nod slowly at him. 'Yeah, I've seen the story,' I manage to say.

Then I put my head down and get on with my session. I swim my socks off in the pool.

~

Just about everyone I know gets in contact with me over the next few days. If they didn't read Paul Kent's piece in the *Herald Sun*, then they read similar pieces in the *Age*, the *Sydney Morning Herald* or the *Australian*. My friends, my family, they all text or call or send a message. 'We love you and we support you,' they all want to say. That, and: 'Paul Kent's a douchebag'.

'Who *is* Paul Kent?' I ask Bohly. I still have no clue who the guy is, nor why he hates me so much.

'News Limited journo,' Bohly says. 'But not one of our usual.' I think of Nicole Jeffery, Jessica Halloran, Wayne Smith, Todd Balym, Rebecca Wilson and all the other journos who we deal with regularly. Journos who I trust and who have always supported me. Nicole Jeffery would never write a story like this.

But Paul Kent? Never met him. No idea what he even looks like. The thought makes me paranoid as I wander around the village. Is that guy Paul Kent? Is that one? If I'd bothered to google 'Paul Kent' it wouldn't have taken me long to discover that the guy has a history of criticising others. He's had public spats with the likes of Anthony Mundine and Matthew Newton. He's won a Wankley Award from Crikey. But I don't google him. I don't waste my time.

I have a race to swim, so I have to put Paul Kent and his comments out of my mind. I have to be brave. I have to suck it up. I have to say, you know what? Screw you. Fine, I'm not in the best shape of my life but I will prove to you that I can do this. That I deserve to be here. A year ago I was lying on the bathroom floor in a hotel in Sierra Nevada, planning how to take my own life. I didn't come back from that – from the biggest battle of my life – to get back in the pool and qualify for my fourth Olympic Games just to be put down by some journo I've never met.

I am an athlete, an Olympian. I am a woman, and I am an Australian. I am all of these things. I am not just my thighs or my stomach. I am not just my BMI or my skinfold test result or any other number anyone tries to tell me I am. I am more than that. How dare you try to reduce me to this?

Of course, I don't say this. I don't say much at all. I decide early on that I won't fight back.

I will be the bigger person. Metaphorically speaking, at least.

This doesn't make me a victim. I just make a conscious decision not to retaliate or take any kind of complaint action. Instead, I let my swimming do the talking. I go out Sunday morning and I swim my heart out. I give it all I've got. I qualify fifth, in a time of 1:06.98. This is a good time for me. And after the race I am interviewed by my buddy Grant Hackett.

'You copped a bit of flak earlier in the week. That's been tough. But it's nice to come out and have a good performance first up,' Grant says.

'I have to say, it's been hard to have journalists saying things – to have my own countrymen saying things about me – before I even start racing. That's been a new challenge for me.' I'll say that, at least. 'But I'd like to think I've proved them wrong by getting out here and swimming fast. It's all I've got to do. I've got to get out here and do my best. Can't ask for anything more.'

'Does it make you angry? Does it make you want to swim fast?'

'It's actually the best thing that could have ever happened to me,' I admit, and I laugh. 'I have never swum faster in time trials in my life before that, so thanks a lot! You've just fired me up!'

I grin and walk from the pool deck. I am fired up; I am ready to go. I may not be as young or as skinny as I was in the past, but I don't think anyone can doubt my dedication. I will do this. I will fight tooth and nail. And I'll need to if I am going to get a spot on the relay team.

The women's medley relay team is my final goal. It is the reason I am here in London. It is what matters. Deep down, I don't care where I place in my individual event, as long as I qualify for the relay team. And that means beating new young Queensland swimmer Leiston Pickett. Leiston and I are in the same semi-final tonight, so the pressure is on. She beat me at trials, and she's a real danger to me. Only one of us can swim the breaststroke leg in the 4 × 100-metre medley relay. But I won't let her take my spot. That spot is mine!

I tell Bohly this as we travel to the pool later that day for the semi-finals. It's just hitting dusk as we approach the Aquatics Centre, with its undulating roof, which looks as if a big wave has just hit and the ripples are still being felt. Out of the window, I can see kids flying kites in the park, and I pause to enjoy the sight. Just to be. I have been chatting to Lisa in the last few days and she has reminded me to observe my surroundings, look out for simple things – like the goats in Sierra Nevada – and enjoy them for what they are. Just be in the moment. I look at these kids with their colourful kites. I could be one of those kids. I still feel like little Leisel from Burpengary.

'I don't care what happens tonight,' I say to Bohly. 'I'll give it a crack, and I'll try and get that relay spot.'

'Well, you better swim bloody fast,' he replies. That makes me laugh, and I think of Ken.

I will swim bloody fast tonight. I will beat this kid. If Leiston thinks she's taking my spot on the relay team – my spot for the past twelve years – she's got another thing coming. I know this game; I know it well.

Actually, Leiston reminds me of myself. Myself from a very long time ago. She's a plucky little thing, skinny and brave. A great kid, actually. I have a lot of time for her. But she hasn't yet learnt to put it together mentally, and I know how debilitating that can be. Leiston is half my size; she is so fit it makes my eyes water. But I have it over her in terms of racing experience. I am weary with the weight of all the experience I have. And if there's one thing I've learnt, it's that racing comes down to mental strength. If only the likes of Paul Kent realised that. The mind is the thing, not the body.

So I get to the pool that night and I beat Leiston Pickett. I come second in my semi, qualifying fifth-fastest overall, in 1:06.81.

Immediately after my race, Mum texts me with the best message ever: 'Job done'. I love it.

Job done. Job bloody well done. This is my job and I know what to do. I'm in the relay team and I've qualified for the finals. This is huge. I am stoked. *Halle-bloody-lujah!*

As for Leiston, she got a time of 1:07.74 in the semis and, while it's not good enough to make the finals, I have no doubt Australia will see more of her in the future.

After my race, I face another barrage of questions from the media about how I feel about my weight being discussed. But nothing can touch me tonight. I am floating on air.

'Look,' I tell them, 'I have been around this game for a long time. I'm not shocked by anything. It's pretty hurtful, sure. But I'm here to swim. And I swim in the pool, not in the papers. I'm here to do my job and I know what that is and I just hope to do it well and to make Australia proud.'

'I've made *myself* proud just by being here,' I add.

And I have. I feel I have triumphed just by turning up today. For me to rock up to these Olympic Games – for me to face each new day when the sun rises – is an achievement right now. I know that.

Even if no-one else does.

I still say nothing to the press or anyone else about my depression or my intended suicide in Sierra Nevada. I would hate for anyone to think I'm using it as an excuse. I am here and I'm alive: that's enough for me. And if Paul Kent had any idea what an achievement that is, he would never have written that article.

Of course, there's a silver lining: if it hadn't been written, I would never have realised how much support I have. Ever since that article was published my phone has been ringing, buzzing and pinging with messages of love and support. People are getting on Twitter, Facebook and talkback radio and saying all sorts of lovely things. It's pretty overwhelming to hear how much everyone cares. I have never had so much encouragement in my life and it touches me deeply.

Our Australian chef de mission, Nick Green, says the reports are 'disgraceful' and 'extremely unfair'. The sports minister, Kate Lundy, calls it 'an appalling attack'. Even Whoopi Goldberg gets in on the action, defending me on her show *The View*. Hearing Whoopi Goldberg – Whoopi Goldberg! – say my name is such a highlight in my life to date that I almost – *almost* – consider Paul Kent's article worth the pain.

But I keep thinking: what if this had happened to someone else? What if they'd picked on some newbie on the team, whose skin wasn't as thick as mine? What if it had happened to someone as green as I was when I joined the team? Imagine if a middle-aged male journo plastered a fourteen-year-old girl in her togs across the papers and implied she was 'fat'! If that happened, I would be livid; it would be unforgiveable. You can really damage people with implications like that, and the thought that it might happen to someone else – someone more vulnerable – makes me angry. I've been around the traps: I can handle it. It was lucky it was me who was singled out.

I spend the next twenty-four hours eating, sleeping and keeping my head down. I do a light swim at the pool, watch a bunch of DVDs, and hang out and enjoy village life for a bit. I go to the games room for a bit and record funny videos with Mel Schlanger on her phone.

~

Finally, on Monday night, it is time for the 100-metre final. I'm in lane two, away from the action. The USA's Rebecca Soni is in lane five and expected to win, although the fresh-faced Lithuanian in lane four, Ruta Meilutyte, has qualified fastest. In the marshalling area, I am relaxed. I feel calm. I have enough butterflies in my stomach to know I am alive, but nothing like what I experienced in Beijing four years ago. *This is my job. I know what to do.* I repeat my mantra over and over, but it suddenly occurs to me that I won't be able to say that soon. *This is my job. I know what to do.* But for how much longer? The rest of the year? The rest of the week?

There is no time to think about that now. We are being called for our race; we are being announced. I walk through the tunnel and out onto the pool deck just in time to hear the voice over the loudspeaker boom: 'Appearing in her fourth Olympic Games ...' But I never hear my name. The stadium goes wild. They raise the roof, screaming and stamping and whistling like mad. I have never been as thankful for the support of the public as I am this week. And never as thankful as I am in this moment. I grin, wave and soak it up. I love these people. I love this sport.

I stand behind the blocks and swing my arms. I have energy to burn. Energy in spades. I will give this my best shot: you know I will. It's strange, because after Sierra Nevada I thought I'd lost my hunger forever. No matter what I did, no matter what I tried, nothing ever felt the same again. But in this instant, staring down the barrel of my lane – in this Olympic stadium, this Olympic final – I feel that hunger again. You can't be here and not feel it.

This is my job. I know what to do.

We are lining up now, ready to go. We are jumping and shaking. We are focused and cool.

But then somebody cracks. There's a splash. Twelve thousand gasps. Breeja Larson in lane six has jumped the gun. She is in the pool. She has made a false start.

The rest of us on pool deck shudder and bounce. We windmill our arms. The tension is back. I look down, look away. Look anywhere but at Breeja. I can't imagine her pain. Breeja qualified immediately ahead of me yesterday. She was one to beat. *One down*, I think grimly.

We step away from our blocks.

No, wait – is that a technical issue? Breeja's back in? Officials swarm around and test the equipment. Rikke Pedersen has put her jacket back on. No, she's taking it off again. We're on? We're on. There was a malfunction with the starting gun, but we're good to go again. Breeja Larson is back in contention.

We line up behind the blocks again, hearts pounding, blood pumping. It's worse than before.

'Take your marks.' The gun fires this time, and suddenly we're into the water.

I'm smooth and controlled. *I know what to do.* I can feel the other girls pull away, but I'm not worried. I will swim my own race, I will do it my way. Mentally, I put the black curtains up along my lane ropes, and ignore what anyone else is doing. *This is my office.* I control the first 25 metres, and then the first 50. I ignore the others and focus on my turn, my pull out. Smooth, controlled. I know what to do.

In the final 50 metres, I come into my own. I am powerful and strong, I am clawing it back. I am gaining now. I am racing them home. *This my office, dammit. I can do this. I know how to do this.* My lungs burn, my arms ache: I feel like I am burning alive.

I hit the wall hard and suck in some air. Gulp it down fast. *I can breathe! I can breathe!*

I have made it, and the relief is immense. I have completed the race. Job done. I knew what to do.

I look to the board and seek out my name, seek out the Aussie flag. Fifth? I came fifth. I slip under the water with relief. Fifth is awesome. Fifth in the world. I am proud and amazed. And I am content.

I congratulate Satomi Suzuki in the lane next to me, then exit the pool and the pool deck. My job here is done.

Rebecca Soni got silver, second by eight one-hundredths of a second. It's brutal, but that's how the Olympics go. I know Rebecca will be dissatisfied with that result. Ruta Meilutyte, the Lithuanian kid, got first, and she can't believe it. Lithuania can't believe it. You can practically hear the whole country cheering from here. It's Lithuania's first medal of the Games and no-one would have put money on it coming from the pool. I'm stoked for Ruta, the new kid. I couldn't be more thrilled. There's some nice synergy in finishing up my career just as a precocious fifteen-year-old hits the scene. The thought of it makes me smile.

'Mission accomplished,' is my response when I am interviewed.

'Aren't you disappointed? To finish in fifth place?'

I shrug and smile. How do I explain to them that fifth is fine by me? Fifth is amazing. Fifth today means just as much to me as first did in Beijing. But they won't understand that.

'I guess you've had a rough ride this week,' the journalist concludes. This is the first time I have failed to win a medal in the 100-metre event in four Olympics and five World Championships. I know it; the journalist knows it. I bet she's thinking the least I could do is give her some tears.

But I'm far too ecstatic for that.

'Smooth sailing doesn't make for a skilful sailor,' I reply sagely. And then I wander off into the stands to go and find Mum.

~

I try to soak it all in during the next few days. It's my last Olympics, my last meet. I savour every minute. I still train hard, but it's bittersweet now. I know this is the end.

I do plenty of talking. Everyone wants a comment, a quote. They want to talk about the 'changing of the guard' in London town. I oblige. I give them what they want. Soon they won't need any more comments from me.

The heats of the medley relay are on Friday morning. And, as usual, we have so much fun. This time the medley relay team is Emily Seebohm, Alicia Coutts, Mel Schlanger, Brittany Elmslie (who swims in the heats only) and me. And we're swimming for pride, doing it for our country. We come first and qualify fastest for the final.

But then we don't quite put it together on the night. Emily is up first, with the backstroke leg, but she can't quite keep pace with the USA's Missy Franklin. Missy is the best in the world. Then, just as Emily comes in to hit the wall, Japan sneaks in ahead of her – so I enter the water in third.

I know this race. I can swim it in my sleep. But today I don't make up the lost ground, and we slip to fourth by the time Alicia gets in the pool. The USA are powering ahead now, they're running away with it.

But wait, Alicia is gaining? She's mowing them down in the butterfly leg. Suddenly we're back in it. We are firmly back in the race. We are second only to the USA, and although they are body lengths ahead of us, we're safely ahead of the rest of the pack.

My mate Mel Schlanger brings it home for us, and in the end we take out silver. The USA get gold, and they do it world-record time.

But I've set a record of my own in this race – the record for the most Olympic medals by an Australian swimmer. I've matched Ian Thorpe's tally of nine, with my three gold, five silver and one bronze. I feel like I have been doing this for a long, long time. I feel like I have been doing this my whole life.

I am relieved when the race is over: proud and excited, but ready to go home. I have given my all; I have nothing left. I have done my job, have worked so hard. And I am feeling very, very finished. I made a conscious effort to enjoy this race. To wave to Mum in the stands and to thank the crowd. But now that it's over, I just feel relief.

After our medley relay final we don't swim down. We never do. It's a point of honour: one small act of rebellion against our coaches. After all the hours of training that have led to this point, we give ourselves a break, a reprieve from jumping back in the pool and warming-down properly, from swimming some more. Instead, we celebrate. We hug and cheer. We make some noise. After all, it's what we're best at.

It means that when I spring from the pool at 8.10 p.m. on Saturday, 4 August 2012, I never get back in the water. I don't swim down. I don't do another training session. I don't go back to squad when I get home.

In fact, I rarely get in a pool again.

Occasionally I'll go for a swim at the beach. Once or twice I'll do laps just to see how it feels. But beyond that? Nothing. It's a line in the sand, and it's how I want it to be. I'll take the sand over the water from now on, thanks. The girl from the desert is back on dry land. I'm heading back to my roots. I want to stay dry and get away from swimming.

But most of all, I want to go home.

~

We pile onto the bus to Heathrow. From here: Dubai (plenty of sand there) and then home. The bus is almost full when I climb on board.

There are only two or three free seats left, so I trudge down the aisle to the back of the bus to take one. I slide into my seat, clutching my backpack across my body. There's not a whole lot of room back here.

And then Jarrod Poort, who has copped a rough ride on this team, climbs on board, and I get a sinking feeling. He spies one last empty space on the back seat of the bus and makes a beeline for it.

'Don't even think about it, fat boy!'

'No way you're going to sit on the back seat with us!'

They start up before he even begins down the aisle.

'Not for you, fat boy!'

'This one's taken!'

The three boys on the back seat jostle and slide over, making it clear there's no room for Jarrod there. Everyone on the bus is aware of what's going on, and Bindi Hocking, who's sitting nearby, calls out gently, 'I'll swap seats with you, Jarrod, if you want?'

Jarrod shakes his head. 'Nah, it's okay,' he says.

But it's clearly not okay. Nothing like okay. With dozens of eyes burning into the back of his head, Jarrod turns back to the front of the bus to sit in a spare seat next to one of the managers, like the kid sitting next to the teacher. The loner. I feel so much for poor Jarrod in this moment. My face is burning hot. How dare they treat him this way? I put my headphones on and slide low in my seat.

We arrive at Heathrow and flood off the bus. Uncorked, we flow fast into the airport. We go through security, passport check, the usual routine. Then my good mate Matt Targett comes up behind me and pokes me. 'Cheer up, Charlie,' he says to me good-naturedly.

I turn to face him. 'What?'

'Cheer up,' my friend says to me again.

'Don't you fucking dare!' I shout at him.

I have had enough. Enough of the bullying, enough of him. Enough of this Australian swimming team. London is our single worst performance at an Olympic Games for two decades, and it's no coincidence that this happened while the team behaviour is so poor. In the coming months, I will make statements to the media about the bullying within the team. About the terrible culture, the poor management and the bad behaviour of some of the team. But what I won't say publicly – what I want to say, but don't – is that I feel the ones who've treated Poort and other junior members of the team worst are Matt Targett, Eamon Sullivan and James Magnussen.

And right now I have Matt in front of me. So I let rip.

'Don't you dare tell me to cheer up! Don't you fucking dare! I've had it up to here with you.' I indicate somewhere in mid-air high above my head. 'For three weeks I've had to put up with your shit. I've had to watch you treat Jarrod like dirt. How dare you think you're better than anyone else!' I swear there is smoke coming out of my ears. But I'm just getting started. 'Who the fuck do you think you are, Targett? Who the fuck? I've been on four of these teams. I've seen it all. But your behaviour over the past few weeks has been something else. How dare you think you can pick on someone else and act like you're better than them?'

Everything I have bottled up for the past three weeks comes pouring out. The whole team is staring at me in horrified silence. The airport security people have stopped work to watch.

'Stop picking on Jarrod Poort!' I shout. 'Just leave him alone! You think he's ever going to want to be on another Olympic team again? Do you? Do you? I wouldn't! Why would you? I'm not going to be around for the next Olympics to stick up for him, so this has to stop now. Now, Targett. You hear me?' Matt stares at me, dumbfounded. 'You need to know that, as my friend, I will not tolerate this from you.'

Matt reaches out to place a hand on my shoulder.

'Don't touch me,' I spit.

I shoulder my bag and head for the gates, then out into the

airport lounge beyond. A handful of our teammates are already ahead of me, so they missed my tirade. They see me approach, red-faced and breathing hard.

'What happened to you? Did you get a cavity search?' someone jokes.

I smile grimly and plonk myself down. 'Don't even ask.' I am breathing so hard. I am seething, shaking and sweating like mad.

I fly home in exile, cut off from my team. It is self-imposed. I have had it. I just want the job done. I sit in silence on the plane, dozing and staring out the window. A fish out of water, 35,000 feet above the Pacific Ocean.

In the end I am glad that I said my piece. I just wish I had said it earlier, when I could have made a difference. Although Matt later apologises, for which I am grateful, our friendship is never the same.

~

When I get home to Brisbane, it's not to my old life. Not how I'd left it. Who knows what life will hold now that swimming is over? It's like Mum said in her text when I made the medley relay team: 'Job done'. My job is done. There is no unfinished business here.

At least not until the day I run into Paul Kent of the *Herald Sun*. It is six months after the London Games, six months since that horrible article, and I am at Fox Sports for a TV interview. A man who I have never seen before approaches me. He sticks out his hand and smiles a wry smile.

'I'm Paul Kent,' he says. 'I believe you know who I am?'

I stare at him, and then at his hand. I make no attempt to shake it. 'I know who you are,' I reply.

I swear at him and shake my head. Then I turn on my heels and walk away.

Now, it's job done.

29

My Way

I announce my retirement on 16 November 2012, at the Valley pool where I used to train with Stephan. It's almost three months to the day since the London Closing Ceremony. My press conference is simple and cruisy: just how I want it.

On the way to the pool, I take Mum out for tea and cupcakes. Nothing fancy. But then, the most expensive restaurant in the world would never be enough to thank Mum for everything she's done for me. In her own quiet way, Mum has been the biggest influence in my life. Always one hundred per cent supportive – but never pushy or opinionated. She let me do my own thing, make my own choices, but without her I couldn't have achieved what I did.

When I arrive at the pool for my press conference I am guided to a ten-foot photograph of my own head. I am to sit in front of it. In the picture, I am mid-stroke, head raised, goggles blazing. I am grimacing with effort, all teeth and flared nostrils. Each nostril alone must be thirty centimetres wide. It's a little off-putting, but then I think about some of the crazy things I've seen during my career, and thirty-centimetre nostrils don't seem so weird.

There must a dozen journos and photographers here today. I

start by telling them that my retirement was a hard decision for me to come to. 'I took my time after London to make sure it was the right decision for me,' I say.

But this isn't exactly true. Deep down I always knew I would retire after London. I always knew London was the end. For me, the only question was whether I could hold on for as long as I did.

I don't prepare a speech. I prefer to just talk off the cuff. Be myself. I know what I want to say without having to write it down. I tell everyone how thankful I am for my career. And for my sport.

'I've ticked every single box in my career and there is nothing else I want to achieve,' I say. 'I'm retiring from swimming, but I still have a very warm place in my heart for swimming.'

I am honest: 'I can't say I've enjoyed every minute of my career,' I say, 'but the highs, when they've come my way, sure have been bloody high.'

'I'm so grateful for the opportunities I've been given, and for the spirit to make the most of them.'

Mum smirks at this. She is always saying she doesn't know where I get my stubbornness from. It's not from her. And it's definitely not from Dad. We've all seen the extent of his stickability. And yet here I am, stubborn as all hell. I am driven and determined and pure bloody-minded. I have never given up, just kept going and going, even when I doubted myself. I've made so many mistakes, done so many things wrong. And I've taken some big risks. Switched coaches, switched states: risked it all so many times. But even though I haven't always made the best choices, I'm proud to say I've always done it my way.

I have an amazing ability to block out everyone else – and everyone else's opinions – and go it on my own.

Then once I do? Well, then I am stubborn and dogged and I see the thing through. If I've dug myself into a hole then I just keep digging! I dig and dig until I finally prove you wrong. This is the reason I made it to the London Games. The reason I got back into my togs after Paul Kent's article. The only reason I ever got up off the floor of that hotel bathroom in Sierra Nevada.

It took me a long time to realise that sport is as much a mental game as anything else. When you step up behind the blocks, when you're on the Olympic stage, if you can't put it together mentally then you're screwed. It took me more than five years of racing at the highest level to figure this out. Racing is seventy per cent mental and only thirty per cent physical, I reckon, and once you master the mental side then you're fine.

I field all the inevitable questions once I've finished speaking: 'Why now?' 'What's next?' 'Have I thought about a comeback?'

I laugh at this last one. I have to retire first before I can come back, I say.

'Career highlight?' someone calls from down the back of the pack. And I pause before answering: 'Winning individual gold at Beijing in 2008.'

It's the obvious answer, but not the only one. I could just as easily have answered: right now. Retiring right now, right here, like this: that's a highlight, for sure. I am lucky to be leaving the sport on my own terms.

By this point in my career, I've done everything I set out to do, I've ticked every box. I'm not walking away feeling dissatisfied at all. I've been to more Olympic Games than any other Australian swimmer. I've won more Olympic medals than any Aussie in any sport (equalled only by Ian Thorpe). I've had a thirteen-year international career. Won nine Olympic medals, ten Commonwealth gold medals. And now I get to retire the way I want, too? Not many athletes get to go out this way. On their own terms. I'm not injured, not sick; I didn't miss out on team. In retirement – as with the rest of my career – I couldn't have asked for more. I am doing it my own way.

There was a poster on the wall of the marshalling area at the London Games. A huge thing, stuck to the wall just by the doorway, so that it was the very last thing you saw before walking out onto the pool deck. It was an old black and white image of the Olympic torch being carried into a stadium crowded with spectators, and there, high above the stadium, were the words of Pierre de Coubertin, the father of the modern Olympics: 'The important thing in the Olympic Games is not winning but taking part. The essential thing in life is not conquering but fighting well.'

I looked at that poster every time I walked out to race at London and each time it affected me deeply. It was a beautiful thing, that poster.

That is what it's all about, I think. For so long – for so much of my career – I had been doing it all wrong. Doing it for all the wrong reasons. Swimming wasn't about me, I finally realised. It wasn't about me at all. It was so much bigger than that. It was about everything. It was about life and taking part and about conquering the human spirit. It took me so long to figure that out.

After all the shit that happened in London, after Stephanie Rice's cruel comments, after the bullying from the boy's relay team, after Paul Kent and fat-gate: after all these things, I finally realised that the Olympics is about more. It's about coming together. About olive branches, not competition. One glance around the stadium, with all its flags, all these countries represented, and it doesn't take a genius to work out it was about so much more than winning a medal.

Yet it took me a long time to realise it. I had made my whole career about winning, but it wasn't the point. It wasn't the point at all.

One of the greatest lessons I took from my career was that my gold medal didn't make me into something I wasn't already. Winning didn't make me a better person, or a more attractive person, and it was never going to. But the *Olympics* might have made me a better person. Meeting people from all over the world; learning to get on with sixty different personalities within a swimming team. Learning how to deal with criticism, learning how to deal with praise. These things might have made me better. I'm a different person to that skinny little kid from Burpengary who first qualified for the team at just fourteen years old. But not because of winning. My medals don't mean much; meeting the people I've met, having the experiences I've had – these are the things that mean something to me.

Next week, I leave on a tour of regional Australia to help host swim clinics in mainly Aboriginal communities. Back to where I came from, back to my roots. There's something circular in that. I may have come full circle, but I've changed along the way.

You may not win everything in life. In fact, you are sure to lose sometimes. But the most important thing is to have a crack. I love that saying. Just give it a go. Just have a crack.

30

Back on Dry Land

The most common question I get asked these days is: do you miss it?

Do I miss it? Let's see. Which bit do you mean? The 4 a.m. starts? Being so tired that I stagger around all day like a zombie, limbs heavy, muscles weary? Never, ever getting enough sleep? Smelling of chlorine all the time? Having wet hair, peeling skin? Do I miss that? Nope. Not on your life.

What I do miss, though, is my friends. I miss being around like-minded people. People who are competitive, who have clear goals and who are as passionate about what they do as I was. Also, as much as the early starts sucked, I miss the routine, the structure. My day used to be organised down to the last minute. I knew when I would eat, when I would sleep and how much time in between I would spend in the pool. I knew exactly what I was doing when – and most important of all, I knew *why*.

That's the biggie. I miss why.

When I was swimming, every single minute of every day was dedicated to getting faster. Swimming is so specific. You always know exactly what time you're aiming for, to the smallest fraction of a second. To two decimal places! Now I find that life's so vague. When I was swimming, I always knew my job. I knew exactly what I was doing and why: when I retired, I lost all that. That was really hard.

A lot about retiring has to do with loss. Lost goals, lost purpose, lost hours of the day. The days seem to vanish. Some days I wonder how I used to fit it all in.

I'm still in the midst of that lost feeling now. It's almost three years since I announced I was retiring, and I still struggle with direction, with knowing what to do. In those first few months especially, I was not clear on why I was doing anything. Why was it I was getting up in the morning? Some days I didn't: I just stayed in bed. I had to find new goals, new directions. I had to learn how to fill my life. All athletes go through this process, and all of them deal with it differently, but I'm in a better place now than I have been in the past. I'm more comfortable in myself. More myself than ever before. I will always be grateful for my swimming, but I am happy that chapter has closed. And as much as retirement wasn't the party I hoped for, I wouldn't change it for anything.

Am I planning a comeback? I know it's quite a popular thing to do. Libby did it, Skippy did it. Even Thorpie had a go. But I've started doing other things now. Commentating, for a start.

My first commentating gig is in Glasgow at the Commonwealth Games in July 2014: the first Commonwealth Games, since 2002, that I attend but don't compete in. I'm doing the late-night program on Network Ten with sports journalist Matt White. It is aired just in time for breakfast back in Australia. We have a great time. Matty is so much fun to work with, so professional. He has been commentating at the Olympics for nearly as long as I was swimming at them, he reminds me. I learn a lot from him, in between all the laughs.

I do a lot of pool-deck interviews, speaking with swimmers straight after their races. I love this; this I can do. It's like chatting with my friends, with my teammates. Most of the time I know just how they feel. Ian Thorpe and Steve Hooker are also on the commentary team with us, and Thorpie and I agree it's nice to be dry, nice not to get in the pool for a change.

The network is happy with my performance at Glasgow and they ask me to do the Pan Pacific World Championships on the Gold Coast straight afterwards in August. The Pan Pacs are more low-key, more relaxed, but it's still a good opportunity to get some commentating experience. Plus, the crew is the same one that we had in Glasgow and we have a ball working together again.

I'm still keen to get more commentating experience, and Network Ten gets in touch with me for a third time. They have a project coming up – something new, something big – and they want to know if I might be interested.

'Definitely,' I say without hesitation.

'This one's different,' warns the network. 'It will be challenging.'

'I don't care. I'm interested,' I say. After all, how challenging could it possibly be?

~

So on 1 February 2015, I am helicoptered into Kruger National Park in South Africa for up to six weeks of gruelling reality television. It's *I'm a Celebrity . . . Get Me Out of Here!*. The premise is simple enough: take ten celebs and torture them with obstacles, challenges and the dreaded 'Tucker Trials' – where they have to eat everything from maggots to ostrich anus – until they cry: 'I'm a celebrity, get me out of here!' and they are evacuated and flown home.

I cannot wait.

Before it goes to air, the show's line-up is top secret, so I can't tell anyone what I'm about to do. Not my family, not my friends. I am sworn to secrecy and I don't tell a soul. But one evening, just days before I fly out for South Africa, my friends and I are at a bar in Surry Hills and the show comes up in conversation. It has been heavily advertised – everyone knows about it.

'Why would anyone do that?' asks one of my friends. 'Why would anyone volunteer to have to survive in the jungle? And on live TV?'

Everyone agrees. 'What's the point?' 'What are they proving?' 'Are these people really at such low points in their careers?' This is the general consensus: that to go on the show you must be desperate. I know a lot of people diss reality television, and that it can seem silly or futile (or just plain gross!). But to me, it's a challenge: an opportunity. And I can't say 'no' to either. I am still the same person I was back in Burpengary all those years ago. The 'Type A' kid. The perfectionist. I need to be better, aim higher, reach further than I did yesterday. And strangely, *I'm A Celebrity* gives me the chance to do that. I mean, how many times in life do you get the chance to be buried in offal? It might sound ridiculous to some people, but I'm always up for a tough challenge – especially a unique one like this.

It doesn't take long for me to discover that reality TV, especially this reality TV, is much harder than it looks. We fly into Kruger National Park and we're immediately required to jump into crocodile- and hippo-infested waters. From here, it's a twenty-kilometre hike into camp, only there are no dry socks for us, so the ten of us go sockless, with damp feet, in our new hiking boots.

This hike is the real deal. It's tough going and uphill all the way. More than once, a cameraperson goes sliding, and a couple of times they really hurt themselves. By the time we reach our campsite, we all have blisters: wet skin and hard boots are not a good mix. Over the course of the next week, our blisters become infected to the point where Maureen McCormick ('Marcia Brady' of *The Brady Bunch*) has pus-filled blisters the size of fifty-cent pieces. My blisters are almost as bad, but it's hard to get medical attention without leaving the show. The best they offer is for us to show our feet to a doctor over CCTV.

We are given seven and a half tablespoons of beans and rice per day, in total. We sleep outdoors, even in the rain. We shower outdoors. We poo in a pit toilet. And we are living this twenty-four hours a day. Viewers only see the highlights, boiled down into seventy-two prime-time minutes. In the jungle, we are pushed to our limits. We are perpetually being tested to see who will break.

It's very boring in camp. Boring and claustrophobic. We can't go anywhere except the campfire or down to the river, so the ten of us bounce around, stepping on one another's heels. We have to ask permission to go anywhere, even to the watering hole, and it can take up to half a day to get it organised and for them to move a camera crew down to where they are needed.

But I never lose sight of why I signed up for this: the challenge. The thrill of pushing myself further than I have before. Back home, I am constantly challenging myself. I do it all the time in the gym. I can't help it; it's just my personality. I am constantly competing against myself. Constantly pushing myself to the limit. Just so I can feel alive.

I am the first person in camp to be voted group captain. I admit, it feels good.

I am gutted when I leave the show after only ten days. I am the first to go, the first one out. And I feel like a failure because of this. In my exit interview, I explain how I had hoped to stay in a lot longer. Not only to raise money for my charity, Headspace (which gives young people a forum to talk about mental health issues such as depression and eating disorders and bullying-related issues), but also because I haven't challenged myself enough yet. I am pissed off about that. It may sound strange, but I'm disappointed that I get off unscathed. I never even get to do a Tucker Trial.

What I did find time to do, though, was unleash my inner bogan. In camp, I become fast friends with the stand-up comedian Joel Creasey. I had never met Joel before the show, never even heard of him, but before long we are joking and mucking around like old mates, like I used to with my flatmate Barnsey. As you'd expect from a comedian, Joel has an awesome sense of humour and together we come up with a host of character roles that we use to amuse and annoy the rest of the camp. There are our anorexic models from Westfield Bondi Junction ('Oh, I love the Junction. Just love the Junny. Have you seen my tiny dog?') and our hipster cafe waiters ('You want a panini? We haven't done paninis since 2005. A panini? More like a pa-no-no.') But my favourites are our bogan mums from the 'burbs: Jeanette and Tracey.

Jeanette (aka me): 'We go out every Friday for Chinese.'

Tracey (aka Joel): 'You and Larry?'

Jeanette: 'Me and Lazza. We love it. Beef and black bean.'

Tracey: 'Oh and sweet and sour pork! And some prawn crackers.'

Jeanette: 'Oh, I love me pork crackles!'

And so it goes. The rest of the camp look at us like we're hilarious, mad and the most dangerous things in the jungle. But Joel and I have a ball. We forget that anyone else – like, the rest of the country! – is watching, and we just have fun. Joel is a world-class comedian (he opened for Joan Rivers), so I don't expect to be able to keep up with him. But apparently my inner bogan is not buried so deep, because it doesn't take long for him to coax Jeanette to the surface.

In my exit interview, Dr Chris Brown asks me, 'How far from Leisel Jones is that character of Jeanette?'

Not far at all, I admit.

And she's really not. Although Jeanette and I differ in many (I like to think fundamental) ways, when I am playing at being this character I am as close to my real self as I have ever been in my career.

When I am mucking around like this, pretending to be Jeanette or a panini waiter or an anorexic model in a Subaru Forester, I am relaxed and silly and looking for laughs. My real self, in other words.

I have never sought the limelight in life. That's not me. I never wanted to be famous. I just happened to be good at my day job. But being on *I'm a Celebrity ... Get Me Out of Here!* was different. I was on TV because I chose to be there. And I was not performing; I was just being me. I could never pretend to be anything other than myself, not for ten days. Nobody could. So the Leisel you saw in camp, the Leisel that's up for a challenge but also up for a laugh: that's the real me.

I have spent so much of my life being something I'm not. Being guarded or self-censored or doing what someone else tells me to do. Swim like this, talk like this, think like this. Win like this. My life has always been so controlled, so structured, from a very young age. There was always an agenda: a media agenda, a sponsorship agenda. I spent so much time giving other people what they wanted. But this meant that no-one saw the real me. No-one saw the Leisel Jones who did bad dancing to amuse her friends. No-one saw the Leisel Jones who stuck food up her nose in the Olympic village to get a laugh. No-one saw Leisel Jones, practical joker, class clown. No-one saw me laughing, but no-one saw me crying or hurting inside either. No-one saw when I cried out for help.

The one regret I have about my career is that people didn't see the real me. I never had much of an opportunity to reveal her, but when I did I kept her stuffed down inside. I kept her shoved under the rug with that moose. I really wish I was more myself. I really wish I had lifted the rug sooner.

Mum says she got my medals out recently and had a look at them. Checked to see they were still ok.

'They're flaking a little,' she tells me over the phone. 'The gold is flaking off some of the older gold medals.'

'Really?' I say, half-listening. I am cooking dinner and checking my emails at the same time I am talking to her.

'You could get them re-dipped, you know,' Mum suggests.

We talk for a while longer. Then we wind up the conversation. 'Think about it,' Mum says, at the same time as something begins boiling over on my stove.

'About what?' I say, as I rush to take the lid off.

'About re-dipping,' Mum says.

I will, I promise her silently. *I will consider re-dipping.*

But for now – for possibly the first time in my life – I am content with the way things are.

Acknowledgements

Thank you:
To Mum for never limiting my belief that I could achieve anything in this life. You have always allowed me to think anything was possible and for that I thank you.

To Damo for coming into my life and just being you. You have been by my side when I have been feeling lost, and you have listened to me complain while I'm still finding my way. I can never thank you enough for making me laugh. Here's to many more years of supporting each other to achieve our dreams and, more importantly, laughing our way through life. Bunghole.

To Mum and Brian for always providing a level-headed answer to most of my problems. You have always supported my decisions and I'm lucky to have parents like you.

To my family: Poppa always said 'Count your blessings'. I'm so lucky to love every single member of my family. We're pretty lucky to sit down to Christmas lunch with fifty people and all enjoy each other's company. I count you all twice! Love ya, Mikey.

To my girlfriends Sam, Lola, Angie, Alice, Schlangs, Lana, Kristy, Vanessa, Tay, Marieke, Gierke, Faustina, Telena, Kirsty, Loz and KP:

thank you for just all being you. You've all been there when things were great, but you have also all had my back when I needed you. Thanks for your support and I'm so glad you were all a part of this story at some point.

To Rohan: I still believe someone sent you to save me in Sierra Nevada. You were the greatest coach and I was so lucky to work with you. We had our differences but it was basically me being stubborn. You got me to where I needed to be and taught me some of the greatest life lessons. I'm forever grateful that I met you for coffee in Moonee Ponds that day.

To Barnesy and Brock: we've had some fun times living together. Thanks for putting up with me on a daily basis!

To Dan: thanks for keeping me fit. I told you I would put you in here! You not only push me in the gym but I also feel like I can call you a friend.

To Jeanne and Kelly: your never-ending support throughout this whole process has been cherished. Jeanne, from the moment I mentioned that I would like to write a book you never doubted it would be amazing. It has been a wonderful ride and I don't want it to end.

To Felicity: we have had the most incredible time writing this story and I'm so glad we chose you to tell it. You have captured my voice perfectly, and you have told my story just the way I wanted it. This could have been labour-intensive: instead, it was a joy to catch up. We still need to write our restaurant reviews!

Leisel Jones

www.ingramcontent.com/pod-product-compliance
Lightning Source LLC
Chambersburg PA
CBHW070736170426
43200CB00007B/538